NEVER SEE
THEM AGAIN

Also By M. William Phelps

Perfect Poison
Lethal Guardian
Every Move You Make
Sleep in Heavenly Peace
Murder in the Heartland
Because You Loved Me
If Looks Could Kill
I'll Be Watching You
Deadly Secrets
Cruel Death
Death Trap
Kill For Me
Failures of the Presidents (coauthor)
Nathan Hale: The Life and Death of America's First Spy
*The Devil's Rooming House: The True Story of
America's Deadliest Female Serial Killer*
Love Her to Death
Too Young to Kill

NEVER SEE THEM AGAIN

M. WILLIAM PHELPS

KENSINGTON BOOKS
Kensington Publishing Corp.
http://www.kensingtonbooks.com

Some names have been changed to protect the privacy of individual connected to this story.

KENSINGTON BOOKS are published by

Kensington Publishing Corp.
119 West 40th Street
New York, NY 10018

All Kensington Titles, Imprints, and Distributed Lines are available at special quantity discounts for bulk purchases for sales promotions, premiums, fund-raising, and educational or institutional use. Special book excerpts or customized printings can also be created to fit specific needs. For details, write or phone the office of the Kensington special sales manager: Kensington Publishing Corp., 119 West 40th Street, New York, NY 10018, attn: Special Sales Department, Phone 1-800-221-2647.

Kensington and the K logo Reg. U.S. Pat. & TM Off.

Library of Congress Card Catalogue Number: 2011943217

ISBN-13: 978-0-7582-7338-3
ISBN-10: 0-7582-7338-X

First Printing: March 2012

10 9 8 7 6 5 4 3 2 1

Printed in the United States of America

This book is dedicated to Bill W.

Truth means more than knowledge: knowing the truth leads us to discover the good. Truth speaks to the individual in his or her entirety, inviting us to respond with our whole being.

—Joseph Ratzinger

AUTHOR'S NOTE

THE TOTALITY OF this crime is deplorable: four victims attacked in a blizzard of gunfire, two of them also beaten to death. A mass murder that took place inside a suburban home in an upper-middle-class neighborhood: Clear Lake City, Texas. Two teenagers. Two others in their early twenties. All of them murdered before their lives had a chance to begin. In the scope of the work I do, this crime spoke particularly to the culture of death we live in today; and provides an important glimpse into how some of us place so little value on human life.

There is a component of drug addiction to this story. For that reason, I chose to change several names connected to this case. My wish in doing so was to protect confidential informants and others who spoke to police (and me). It needs to be said that not every person's name I changed was a confidential informant. Some asked for a name change; while with others, I did it on my own. I want to point out that this—the changing of a person's name—does not take *any-thing* away from the integrity of the story. I have heard that if a person is not willing to come forward and put himself or herself out there for the sake of justice, how can his or her information be trusted? That's simply unfair and untrue.

Part of this judgment stems from the Wikileaks war documents scandal, which makes an important point for me here within the context of my argument. As a journalist, you need to take into account a source's credibility, reliability, his or her relation to the players in the story, whether he or she testified during the legal portion of the case, and if this person *benefits* or is put in danger from being exposed publicly. We (journalists) cannot just name everyone involved in a criminal case based on the fact that *some* people think a person who chooses not to identify himself or herself cannot add anything to a nonfiction story.

It is unfair to the source. Unfair to the victims (who cannot obviously speak on the matter). And unfair to justice and its future. After all, every rape victim is a Jane Doe until she decides to come forward and reveal herself. Does this mean every Jane Doe has a hidden agenda in telling her story?

The journalist is always aware of the person's real name. I never use a source, for example, who would call and claim anonymity without him or her providing proof of identity. I am old school, I guess you could say, where it pertains to the use of sources. The late Jack Olsen, a true-crime author I respect more than just about anybody in the business, spoke in his no-holds-barred way about defending the use of pseudonyms in his true-crime stories. I will paraphrase what he once said: *If there are not a few name changes, I do not feel I am getting the entire story.*

Think about it—Jack's statement makes a lot of sense.

JUST WHEN YOU THINK you've seen a case that has been well documented—and I have commented on those in previous books—along comes an investigation with more documentation than you think you'll be able to manage. This was one of those: there were thousands of pages of reports and additional documentation, on top of a large trial transcript, and close to one hundred hours of interviews I conducted with scores of sources. I should also mention that for the ease of reading some of the conversations and dialogue in this book have been trimmed and edited for clarity and cohesiveness. Nothing that impacts the meaning or the intent was changed, however; conversations were, like in any nonfiction book, reduced at times for editorial purposes.

This book truly needs no more of an introduction. I think you, the reader, will agree that this "nonfiction thriller" is one of the most comprehensive murder mysteries in quite some time.

PART ONE

RABBIT TRAIL

CHAPTER 1

IT WAS JUST after six o'clock on the evening of July 18, 2003. For the past ninety minutes, eighteen-year-old Brittney Vikko (pseudonym) had been calling Tiffany Rowell, one of her BFFs since middle school. Something was wrong, Brittney felt. She kept dialing Tiffany's number, but there was no response.

Brittney had spoken to Tiffany's boyfriend of several years, Marcus Precella, earlier that day, after Marcus had answered Tiffany's cell phone.

"She's in the bathroom," Marcus said. It was close to three o'clock then.

"I'll call back," Brittney told him.

Thirty minutes later, Brittney started phoning her friend again.

But no one—not even Marcus—picked up.

"I was in the area, so I drove over to Tiffany's house," Brittney recalled later. Brittney's boyfriend, her nephew, and her boyfriend's cousin went with her.

Brittney drove. They stopped at a McDonald's after leaving an appointment Brittney had downtown at 4:10 P.M. A few minutes after six, Brittney pulled into Tiffany Rowell's driveway in the stylish suburban neighborhood of Millbridge Drive, Clear Lake City, Texas, and noticed immediately that Marcus's and Tiffany's vehicles were there. Tiffany's truck was parked in front of the house; its back wheel up on top of the curb. Marcus's car was positioned next to the garage.

Why aren't they answering their phones?

Brittney pulled in behind Marcus's car.

Odd, she thought, looking at both vehicles. *They must be here. . . .*

Brittney got out and rang the doorbell.

No answer.

She rang it again.

Not a peep from inside the house.

She knocked. Then she tried to look through a nearby window, cupping both hands over the sides of her eyes to block the light.

But again, no movement or sound from anyone inside.

Brittney kept banging, harder and louder, eventually forcing the unlocked door to creak open.

Brittney's boyfriend and the others watched from inside Brittney's vehicle as she slowly walked into the house.

"Tiff? Y'here?"

Something seemed peculiar about the situation. It was eerily quiet inside the house. There was a steely, metallic smell in the air.

The door left unlocked and open? Both cars in the driveway and no one around? It was so unlike Tiffany.

Where was everyone?

Brittney walked through a short foyer before entering the sunken living room.

She took five steps. Then found herself standing and staring at a scene that, at first, didn't register.

As Brittney's boyfriend got out of her vehicle, he watched Brittney run like hell back out the same doorway she had just walked through.

Brittney Vikko was screaming, with a look of terror on her face.

"Call the cops!"

Out of breath, approaching her boyfriend, who was now looking toward the house, Brittney yelled again. "Call . . . the . . . cops!" She was hysterical.

Her boyfriend walked up to the doorway and approached the inside of the house.

Then *he* came barreling out of the same doorway, screaming.

Brittney was on the ground by then, crying, smashing her fists into the grass. Her boyfriend noticed a neighbor across the street talking on his cell phone. So he ran toward the guy, yelling, "Call the police! Call the police!"

The man dialed 911.

"There was blood everywhere," Brittney's boyfriend later said, describing what he had seen inside Tiffany Rowell's house.

CHAPTER 2

IT HAPPENS WHEN life seems arrested by adolescence. Just out of high school, you're still running on a full tank of teen angst. To think about college seems, well, overwhelming—so far in the future. Your parents are getting on you. Adulthood is not something you want to think about. You want to go with the flow. Take the summer and, as they say, discern. Yet that's when a good dose of reality, in all of its matured ugliness, grabs hold and shakes the childhood right out of you.

When you're least expecting it.

Within the second largest city in the southern central portion of the United States, the atmosphere was volatile on July 18, 2003, those familiar three *H*'s annoyingly present: hazy, hot, humid, a fourth counting the city of Houston, the largest in Texas, right there in the top five of the country. The dew point was a balmy seventy-five. "Oppressive," they call stickiness in those numbers, about as high as it can get without rain falling. In addition to the stuffy air, it was almost ninety degrees; the kind of day when a "severe storm," the kind those talking heads on the Weather Channel get excited about, can roll in at any time, darken the skies as if it were night, turn on the torrential downpours, kick up damaging winds, and drop hail the size of Ping-Pong balls.

Ah, yes, summertime in the Bay Area of Greater Houston. Sunny out one minute, and the next you're running for the nearest storm shelter.

As the skies decided what to do, yellow POLICE LINE DO NOT CROSS tape fenced off Tiffany Rowell's modest house from the road and the swelling crowd. Strands of the familiar crime-scene ribbon fluttered in mild gusts of wind, slapping and whipping, making the noise of a playing card flapping in a child's bicycle spokes. Lights of blue and red flashed against the sides of the Rowell house, pulsating a warning to the residents of this exclusive community just outside Houston, where, some say, "the city's wealthiest and best educated" live, that something horrific had happened inside this one-story contemporary. Brittney Vikko running out the door, screaming, and neighbors heading outdoors, just to have a look, added to the talk circulating the block: Word had spread that evil had reared its nasty face in this otherwise quiet residential neighborhood. Something so horrendous had taken place inside that house, no one, it seemed, could come to terms this early on with just how bad the scene truly was beyond the front door.

All the cops roaming around didn't help matters. The coroners' vans—emphasis on the plural—were parked along the street. The detectives huddled together, talking things over: pointing, measuring, comparing notes. Flash bulbs inside the house made lightning strikes in the setting sun and the otherwise cozy and comforting dusk light. Whatever was beyond that slightly ajar door into Tiffany Rowell's house was going to be big news in the coming hours and days. Anybody standing, staring, wandering about the scene, was well aware of this.

Ironically, Clear Lake City, Texas, "a pretty peaceful area," according to many residents, was used to the sort of high-profile crime, especially murder, the discovery inside the Rowell house was going to reveal. After all, who could forget about that homely-looking woman with those large-framed glasses, a dazed look of emptiness in her eyes, Andrea Yates? While her husband was at his NASA engineering job nearby one afternoon in June 2001, Andrea chased their five kids through the house and, one by one, held each underwater in the family's bathtub. Then she calmly called police and reported how she'd just killed them. And what about the infamous astronaut, Lisa Nowak, who would (in February 2007), while wearing an adult diaper, drive from Clear Lake City to Florida—some nine hundred miles—to confront her romantic rival at the airport, the tools of a sinister plot to do her opponent harm inside Nowak's vehicle. And lest we forget about the orthodontist's wife Clara Harris, a well-regarded dentist in her own right, who would run her cheating husband down with her Mercedes-Benz after catching him with his receptionist, with whom Harris had gotten into a hair-pulling catfight only moments before.

Those notorious crimes, on top of all the murder and rape and violence that *doesn't* make headlines and "breaking news" reports, happened here, within the city limits of this plush Houston suburb, just around the corner from this quiet neighborhood where all the attention was being thrust on this night. In fact, inside the Rowell house, some were already saying, was a tragedy of proportions dwarfing anything Nowak or Harris had done: if not for the severity and violence connected to the crime, then for the fact that among the four dead bodies cops were stepping over, taking photos of, studying closely, not one of the victims had reached the age of twenty-two—and sadly, three of them were teenagers.

NEIGHBORS, REPORTERS, AND bystanders gathered on the opposite side of the crime scene tape as cops did their best to hold back the crowd.

Some cried openly, their hands over their mouths.

Oh, my God . . .

Others asked questions, shook their heads, wondered what in the world was going on. This was Brook Forest, for crying out loud: a "master-planned community." Panning 180 degrees, street level, you'd find well-groomed lawns (green as Play-Doh), edged sidewalks, expensive cars, boats on trailers propped up by cinder blocks waiting for the weekend, kids playing in the streets, dogs barking. Brook Forest certainly isn't the place where violence is a recurring theme. Not to mention, it was just after seven o'clock on a Friday evening, the scent of barbeque still wafting in the air, and the murders had occurred, by the best guesstimates available (Brittney Vikko's initial timeline, that is), somewhere between quarter past three and three-thirty in the afternoon.

The middle of the day.

People were saying, *Wait a minute. A mass murder had occurred in* this *neighborhood, at a time of day when soap operas are on television, and no one had* seen or heard *anything?*

It seemed unimaginable.

Investigators were talking to Brittney Vikko, getting her version. But she had walked in *after* the fact. As far as neighbors standing around could see, nobody had noticed anything outwardly suspicious in the neighborhood, or at the Rowell house all day long. The Rowell place was located on Millbridge Drive, a cul-de-sac in a cookie-cutter farm full of them, a neighborhood sandwiched between the Lyndon B. Johnson Space Center and Ellington Air Force Base. Galveston Bay is a ten-minute drive east; Clear Lake is just to the south, ultimately spilling into the Gulf of Mexico. This is suburban bliss, likely created in an infrastructure lab somewhere, maybe by a former NASA engineer (the region is full of them), or by some city planner driven to construct middle-class perfection. Certainly, this was not a haven for a crime on the scale of what was being rumored: young kids murdered in the middle of the day, home-invasion style, for no apparent reason.

"I walked inside and saw Tiffany and a guy on the couch," Brittney Vikko told police, "and another girl on the floor in front of the television. At first, I thought they had been partying too much—and then I saw all the blood on the floor."

With the sight of such carnage in front of her, Brittney Vikko bolted out the door and screamed for her boyfriend to call the police. Neighbors, cops, fire trucks, and emergency medical technicians (EMTs) arrived shortly thereafter.

Consoling the community best he could, Houston Police Department (HPD) Homicide Division officer Phil Yochum released a statement, hoping to calm things: *"I think it happened very quickly,"* he said in the release, *"but it was very, very violent. It looks like some type of confrontation happened at the front door, then moved into the living room."*

There had been no sign of forced entry—that familiar set of words cops use when they don't have a damn clue as to what the hell happened. A news release gave the concerned and worried community a bit more detail, but was still evasive and vague, though not by design:

> *The bodies of four people were discovered . . . two males, two females . . . shot multiple times, and two of the victims had sustained blunt trauma to the head.*

The last part was an understatement. Two of the victims had been beaten badly. And the blood. My goodness. From one end of the living room to the other: the carpet, the walls, the couch, even the fireplace. Two of the victims were found sitting on the couch, facing the television, as though sleeping. Looked like neither had moved in reaction to what had happened. One of them had a bullet hole—execution style—through the center of his forehead. There looked to be powder burns on the side of his head, ringed around another hole, which meant someone had carefully and deliberately placed the barrel of a hand-held weapon up to his skin and pulled the trigger. Police call it "tattooing," an imprint of the weapon on the skin.

As patrol officers did their best to hold back the swelling mob outside, a woman pulled up, parked sharply with a shriek of rubber, jumped out, and limboed underneath the crime scene tape.

Police stopped her before she could get close to the front door.

"Tell me that it's *not* the Rowell house," she said. "Tell me . . . please tell me it's not the Rowell house. *Please!*" The anguish in her voice was undeniable.

Police officers looked at each other.

The woman doubled over and fell to the ground; then sobbed in loud bursts of guttural pain. An officer went over and helped her up, eventually walking her off toward a private area of the yard, out of eyesight and earshot of the crowd.

Maybe within all that grief and pain was some important information.

EARLIER THAT DAY George Koloroutis had taken off on his Harley from his home in Clear Lake City, the Pine Brook section, just a few miles away from Brook Forest. Although his alibi would soon be checked by police, George said he was in a meeting at work at the time of the murders. It was around 3:30 P.M. when George said he got this "sinking feeling" that . . . *something's wrong.*

Something happened.

George wasn't a believer in Karma, ESP, or any of that see-into-the-future nonsense. But this sudden heavy feeling pulled at him.

"Something was out of order," George recalled. "My perfect little family unit was in a funky state. My girl is somewhere where I don't want her to be." He was talking about Rachael Koloroutis; she had been staying at the Rowell house with her best friend, Tiffany. George wanted Rachael back home with his wife and Rachael's sisters. But what could he do: Rachael had her own life, she was old enough now to make her own choices, whether Dad and Mom agreed.

With George's oldest daughter, Rachael's sister, off at college (but home for the summer on this July 18, 2003, evening), the disunity in the Koloroutis family unit got to George and he scooted out of work early, around four-thirty. When he walked in the door at home, George asked his oldest daughter, Lelah (pseudonym), if she wanted to head out for a ride with him on his bike and grab a bite to eat. George wanted to talk to Lelah about Rachael, who had been out of the house for a little over a month, ever since graduating high school. George thought Lelah could offer some insight. He didn't like the path Rachael was heading down; it felt thorny and already beaten down by others who had ended up lost. He figured talking to Lelah, whom Rachael looked up to, and with whom she had been as close as sisters could be for most of their lives, would help.

The ride, the food, and the conversation turned out to be overly emotional for George. He dropped Lelah back at home and took off alone on his Harley—"I was not feeling good . . . this whole Rachael thing"—and decided to go out and find Rachael and talk to her. He ended up not being able to locate Tiffany Rowell's house (he'd been there only a few times, and the neighborhood, if you don't know it, is akin to a labyrinth), but instead found a neighborhood bar, where he ordered a few beers, sat and listened to a band play loud music in front of him.

Consequently George couldn't hear his cell phone going off as details of what had happened at Tiffany Rowell's house hit the airwaves and people started calling.

"I'm glad I didn't hear it," George later said, looking back, "because the messages on my cell phone were horrifying."

George finished his little cooling-off period at the bar and headed home. As he pulled into his driveway, he noticed that his wife's car was gone.

Strange. Where has she run off to?

His oldest daughter came running out of the house before George could get the kickstand out and the bike turned off. Lelah had a look of absolute fear; the color drained from her face.

"What's wrong?" George said, dismounting.

"Dad! Dad," Lelah screamed. "There're four teenagers dead at Tiffany Rowell's house! They know that two of them are Tiffany and this guy Marcus."

George's stomach tightened. His heart raced.

Rachael!

George went into the house, grabbed his youngest daughter, just nine years old, told Lelah to get into the car. They were dropping the youngest off at a neighbor's and heading over to Tiffany's house.

After dropping off her little sister, Lelah explained what she'd heard as George drove toward Tiffany's, under Lelah's direction.

Lelah said many things, but all George could hear was: *Four teens found dead*.

Four.

Not two. Or three.

But four.

In a panic George pulled up. Saw all the vehicles. The police tape. That large group of people milling about in the street, in front of the house. Police officers roaming all over. He told Lelah to sit tight inside the car behind the yellow police tape. Wait until her mother arrived.

"I'll be right back."

George crossed the police line and started for the door heading into Tiffany's house.

"A big old cop" stopped him before he could walk in.

"My name is George Koloroutis," he said. "You can't stop me, man, please. I think my little girl might be in there."

Tears.

George was a big dude, with some serious bulk, and perhaps out of his mind by this point. All he could think about was Rachael inside that house needing his help. George had always been the protector in the family; the man who took care of everything. Suddenly he felt helpless and weak as gum.

"Mr. Koloroutis, please," the cop said calmly. "Please don't make me have to stop you from going into that house. I don't want to have to do that." There was something in the cop's voice telling George he wasn't kidding; he would do whatever he had to do to stop him. "If I have to do this, Mr. Koloroutis, other cops are going to run over here. We're going to have to hold you down. Cuff you. And it's going to be a miserable experience. Please just *don't* go in there."

There were several reasons—all of them worthy—why police did not want George Koloroutis to go inside the house.

George looked at him. "I understand. I just need to know if that's my daughter."

By now there were close to fifty people gathered. George fell back into the crowd, understanding that getting into trouble was not going to help the situation. His wife, Ann, arrived.

George, Lelah and Ann stood, waiting, their hearts thumping.

CHAPTER 3

TO **THE RIGHT** of the front door heading into the Rowell house (the same area where Brittney Vikko had entered) was a spacious two-car garage. A formal dining room, attached to a half bath and a large kitchen, just beyond that. Walking into the house from the front door, the sunken living room greeted you just beyond the foyer. Tiffany Rowell lived in the house with her boyfriend, Marcus Precella. Tiffany's mother had died years back from that dreaded middle-age serial killer, cancer. Sally and Chester Rowell had adopted Tiffany as a young child. Sally's death crushed Tiffany. Sally had never smoked a cigarette in her life, yet had developed lung cancer. (Go figure.) The diagnosis was the strangest thing. There was such a connection between mother and daughter that a few days before Sally died, Tiffany felt peculiar all morning in school. She had what she later described as "a feeling." It was so profound that Tiffany went to the nurse's office and asked to go home. "I knew she was going to die," Tiffany later said of that moment. "I could feel it." Sally couldn't even move by that point; the cancer spreading like spilled liquid throughout her body, stripping all her senses and emotion. But on that day, to Tiffany's great comfort and surprise, Sally rolled over in bed and smiled at her daughter.

She died two days later.

Chester Rowell owned the Clear Lake house. Chester was a musician. He had remarried and lived with his new wife on a farm in Manvel, a forty-minute ride from Clear Lake.

Eighteen-year-old Rachael Koloroutis was Tiffany's best friend.

Rachael had been staying at the house with Tiffany and Marcus since Rachael had left home weeks earlier after she and her parents had a blowup over a cell phone bill. The problems at home had started for Rachael almost a year earlier, when Rachael had a major blowout with her mother over a few personal issues.

"She turned eighteen," George Koloroutis later said, "and we got the feeling that she was saying, 'Screw it, I am going to go and do what I want.' "

Kids . . . when you're eighteen, nineteen, even into your early twenties, life is about the moment—you think you have all the answers. What can a parent do but allow his or her child to go out into the world and learn for himself or herself.

Technically, you couldn't say Rachael had run away from her Noble Oak Trail home, slightly more than a two-mile, six-minute ride on the Clear Lake/Friendswood town line. Legally, Rachael was an adult. Still, to her family, Rachael had left abruptly and maybe even bitterly. She might have felt she couldn't cope and decided to run. Yet, on July 16, 2003, two days before she was found dead, Rachael had been in the mood to reconcile things. She had left her mother a voice message: "Mom, I really just want to talk to you. I want to talk to [my little sister]. I've got to go, but I'll call you again later. Love ya!"

Earlier that same day Rachael had sent George an e-mail, expressing how happy it made her that they were all going to sit down and talk, make amends:

> I'm looking forward to getting together . . . and all that good stuff. . . . I will consider everything you said. I can see the truth in it. I will try to call you. . . . It is hard. I am afraid to see [Lelah] or even Mom. . . . I feel bad. . . . I do not know when I can face y'all. I don't know exactly what to do. There are many times I want to pick up the phone but just am not able to. I love you all and will try to get up the courage to call.

She signed the e-mail as she generally did:

> Always your little girl, Rach.

After George received the e-mail, he was driving down Clear Lake City Boulevard, heading home on his Harley from a day's work. He happened to look to his left and spied Rachael, who was sitting in the passenger seat of Tiffany Rowell's pickup. Seeing George, Tiffany drove up next to him in the left lane. George looked over. He was wearing dark shades and, in his words, "trying to be cool by giving them a head nod and slight smile." Inside, he later admitted, he was screaming: *"Honey, please come home!"* Rachael smiled and waved. Tiffany blew George an exaggerated kiss with her right hand. They sped away from each other.

"I watched my little girl drive off," George said later. "I felt sad, but I knew she needed me and her Mom and sisters back in her life. I knew we would be reunited soon."

George never saw his daughter alive again.

Ann and George had raised a smart child, loving and caring. Both Tiffany and Rachael had graduated—not two months before—from Clear Lake High School.

They were kids.

Both had their entire lives ahead of them.

THE TWO OTHER victims found inside the house were Adelbert Nicholas Sánchez and Marcus Ray Precella, Tiffany's boyfriend. "D," as they called Adelbert, was Marcus's cousin. According to the medical examiner (ME), he had been killed by "multiple gunshot wounds," one of which pierced the middle of his forehead. Another round entered Adelbert's neck. A third hit his left arm. Two rounds had been pumped into his torso, another into his left shoulder. Adelbert was sitting on the couch opposite his cousin's girlfriend, Tiffany. He wore blue shorts, a T-shirt, and white sweat socks. Lying there, his head leaning slightly on the soft contoured headrest of the couch to his right, D looked as though he was sleeping. With the exception of a large bloodstain halo in the back cushion of the couch outlining his upper body, and D's eyes closed, a person would expect the boy to wake any minute. He looked so peaceful. Yet, as the forensic evidence would soon prove, a hail of gunfire had killed this twenty-one-year-old, who had recently gotten his high-school diploma from W. T. Hall night school.

Nineteen-year-old Marcus Precella, dressed in plaid boxer shorts, a white cotton undershirt, white sweat socks, had been shot in the head, stomach, right forearm, and right shoulder. There was also a graze wound running across his chest. It appeared that Marcus had been beaten, too. He ended up with what the coroner referred to as "blunt-force head injuries." There was a cluster of patterned abrasions on his right temple and five lacerations found on the back of Marcus's head. There was also a star-shaped pattern of blowback, the remnants of gunpowder from Marcus's killer walking up to him, holding the barrel of the weapon on his head, and firing, likely to make certain he was dead. Marcus was lying on the carpet on his side, almost directly in back of Adelbert, his chest and stomach up against the side of the couch.

This was significant to police as they went through and studied this incredible crime scene. It was an indication, maybe, that they were looking at four execution-style slayings.

Rachael had been beaten the worst, considering how many lacerations, abrasions, and blows her skull had endured; but she had also been shot in the lower abdomen, directly in the vagina (could this be a clue?), five rounds into her right thigh, three to her left shin, one to her right foot. There was even a gunshot wound in Rachael's left buttock, no doubt fired as she tried desperately to run away from her assailant. Rachael was found facedown on the floor at the foot of the television. She had bruises police believed had likely been sustained from a fall to the ground. Rachael wore a pink top, part of which had been pulled up her back, blue jeans, and white (with gray stripes) Adidas sneakers. Bruises on the back of her left hand were consistent with a person trying to protect herself from a beating—which meant Rachael Koloroutis was possibly alive at the point of which she was beaten to death. Rachael also had a clump of what would turn out to be her own hair in her right hand, a second indication that she had put her hands over her head, trying to protect herself from a violent pistol-whipping.

"To me," said a detective who would later step into the investigation and put some of the pieces together, "it seemed that Rachael had put up her hands to protect herself, perhaps saying, 'Why are you doing this to me?' This, mind you, *after* being shot multiple times."

Considering all of these wounds, many of which would have been ultimately fatal if she didn't get immediate help, it appeared Rachael's murderer had a tremendous amount of anger directed specifically toward her.

Not an indication of an execution-style murder.

Tiffany was on the couch, one foot leisurely on the chair in front of her as though she had been using it as a leg rest. She wore a white sleeveless top and faded blue jeans. Her curly, dark brown hair had flowed naturally down her back and over her shoulders to the top of her breasts. There was a pink blanket to her right, a cup holder armrest in the middle, between her and Adelbert, who sat on the opposite side of the couch. A Sprite can sat in one of the armrest cup holders. Eerily, it appeared Tiffany and Adelbert were watching TV one minute, drinking Sprite, maybe laughing and joking; and the next, dead. No warning. This indicated that they were not afraid of their attacker and perhaps knew him or her, simply because they had not moved. Of course, playing devil's advocate, one could say that their killer held them there, on the couch, with his or her weapon. ("Don't move!") Nonetheless, Tiffany's white top was now dark red from all the blood, which had run down her head and soaked through her blouse and jeans. She had a bullet wound straight through her forehead, nearly in the middle; she had also been hit in the chin, left cheek, left shoulder, lower left abdomen (an injury that probably produced most of the blood soaking her jeans and lower body), just to the left of her vagina, right leg, right knee, and right shin.

Make no mistake, this was a bloodbath. Or as the prosecutor who would eventually get the case observed, "It's unfair to the word 'crime scene'. . . because . . . it was outright carnage. . . ."

Whoever murdered these kids had walked into the house and unleashed a barrage of gunfire. At least that's what appeared to be the case from a first look. Any police officer could come to this theory straight away. The kids still had plenty of bling on. Some even had cash. There was lots of valuable merchandise spread throughout the house. From a quick look it seemed as though Adelbert and Tiffany were taken out immediately so as not to be a threat. More than that, with so many gunshots—close to forty—from two different-caliber weapons (twenty shell casings left behind telling that story; bullet fragments lodged in the walls and even outside in the fence), it meant one killer had brought two weapons, which told cops that he or she knew there was going to be a large gathering at the house. Or there had been two shooters, which also alluded to the idea that the killer(s) knew what they were walking into.

Papers, magazines, soda cans, and other household items were scattered all about the living-room carpet in front of Tiffany and Adelbert. This indicated a struggle. Rachael, found in front of the television facedown on the floor, had one leg crossed over the other. There were large patches (smudges) of blood all over the carpeting, a trail of smeared blood leading up to the fireplace. In front of the fireplace, crime scene techs located blood droplets, which led to Marcus's body, found to the right of the fireplace in between the wall and the side/back of the couch, where Adelbert and Tiffany sat. The way Marcus's body was positioned—his back facing the direction of the shooting—it looked as though he was walking (not running) away from the shooter, another indication he didn't feel the shooter was a threat.

There was a small foyer leading down the hallway, where the bedrooms are located in the house. There were nine shell casings on the tile and edge of the carpet in the foyer near a dozen or more pairs of shoes. In the corner, by an electrical socket, police found a small pink cell phone that looked as if it had been tossed there or flung out of someone's hand as he or she fell to the ground.

Between the dining-room and the living-room was a wall cutout with decorative spiral spindles separating the kitchen and a formal dining area. Above that cutout, heading toward the ceiling, was a small air-conditioning/heating vent. There were small blood droplets—spatter—in an arced pattern heading skyward, giving rise to the belief that someone had repeatedly hammered the weapon into the back of Rachael's head and, while doing so, spattered blood on the wall as though shaking the excess paint off a brush.

North of Rachael's head was her cell phone, sitting on the ground underneath the leg rest of a lounge chair. Her hand was stretched out heading for the cell phone as though she had been reaching for it when she died.

The photographer snapped a photo of the cell phone, as he did the remainder of the house, inside and out. So many rounds had been fired that several had even gone through the window in the back of the house and found a place in the wooden fence.

One cop walked into the kitchen. There on the counter was a plate of spaghetti, a fork poked into a mound of pasta. Next to it was an opened Tupperware container, pieces of garlic bread inside, crumbs on the counter next to it. Someone had been eating—likely Rachael—when whoever walked into the house, or some time before, unloaded.

Inside the living room, the ME reached inside Rachael's back pocket and found her driver's license and a business card. Rachael's license had a bullet hole through her date of birth.

As they stood and looked over the scene, blood all around them, police realized that the most they could do now was shake their heads and begin to consider what a scene of this magnitude told them. There certainly was going to be many secrets within the context of it all. All they could do now was search for any trace evidence left behind by the killer; maybe a cigarette butt or a hair, a fiber of some sort. Anything that could help point in a direction. Anywhere, essentially. Because the way it looked at this moment, the evidence spoke to someone who had beamed down out of thin air and fired at these kids until the clips and chambers of the weapons they had come in with, and had taken with them, were empty. Then the shooter quickly disappeared back into whatever dimension he or she had emerged from.

Middle of the day and no one saw a thing?

Didn't make sense.

Then again, four dead kids, for no obvious reason, wasn't computing well, either.

Houston is home to approximately 2.3 million. The suburb of Clear Lake City had never seen a mass murder of this nature. Nor had any other region of the city and its surrounding counties. Four kids mowed down in cold blood with enough firepower to stage a small war. Who could have done such a thing? Maybe more important to solving the crime at this point, why?

What George Koloroutis, or anybody else—including detectives showing up, patrol officers minding the scene, and crime scene techs searching room by room—knew then was that the answers to this mystery would take years of old-fashioned gumshoe police work; some of it done by George Koloroutis himself. Little did any-one know at this point it was going to be three years—almost to the day—before a suspect worth considering was brought in. Or that it would turn into a case that would take investigators through nearly a dozen states, halfway across the country, and involve one of the most intense and puzzling murder investigations the HPD had ever probed. And when all was said and done, wouldn't you know it, the murderer had been right under everyone's nose the entire time, there, within reach. The least likely suspect imaginable.

CHAPTER 4

THE EXISTENTIAL QUESTION every police officer inevitably faces at the beginning of a murder investigation comes down to this: Is one piece of evidence any more significant than the other? Sure, DNA uncovered at the scene might be a bit more exciting than a witness who thinks she saw something, or, rather, *might* have seen something.

That's not what we're talking about here.

What a murder victim has done throughout his or her life, which is pertinent to any investigation of the magnitude HPD encountered on Millbridge Drive, became the focal point immediately. The fact that HPD found out the kids were into drugs turned out to be extremely relevant. Yet, a crime victim's life is not something that should blemish an investigator's sense of where to go with a case. You don't solve murders with blinders on, in other words. You don't track down killers by denying the obvious or looking the other way, either. You simply check your judgment at the door and follow the trail.

No matter *where* it leads.

It was no secret that the four murder victims found in Clear Lake City had been dabbling in an active and highly energized Houston drug culture—some more than others. Tiffany and Rachael had just started working at Club Exotica, a topless strip joint on the Gulf Freeway. And on the surface, if that's all you looked at, you'd be inclined to draw some conclusions about these girls. Strippers and blow (cocaine) went together like bulimia and runway modeling. Indeed, you could probably scrape up a few residue lines of coke on the back counter of any stripper's dressing room. But digging deeper into Tiffany and Rachael's lives, you'd see that neither danced, although they had been asked to do so more than once. They waitressed and bartended; two gorgeous teenagers who fought the guys off with clubs, and could have made a bundle exposing what they had been born with. However, they chose to keep their clothes *on*. That said something about Rachael and Tiffany; it spoke to the kind of people they were at heart. And let's face it: the difference in the tips waitressing at a strip joint as compared to the local Chili's or T.G.I. Friday's is tenfold.

"People might get the wrong impression of my daughter," George Koloroutis later said. "But she was involved in church activities and taught vacation Bible school. She was a *good* kid. There are parts of her life that bear no relevance to her murder."

Still, what if some whacko strip club patron developed an obsession with one of the girls and decided to take out Marcus and Adelbert after following the girls home from the club and knocking on the door?

Collateral damage: Marcus and Adelbert.

Investigators had to consider this.

Or what if Rachael and Tiffany had been mistaken for someone else? Maybe one of the two boys at the house had been a target?

Those scenarios had to be looked into.

In fact, there were so many different avenues the investigation could take in its initial stage, HPD realized, to start developing theories now would be absurd and purely inconsiderate to the memories of these kids. It would stifle progress. Slow the natural evolution of the investigation and what the evidence was about to bear out.

The job of juggling all of these questions was given to Detective Tom Ladd, a seasoned cop nearing the end of nearly three decades of work in HPD's Homicide Division. Ladd spoke like a character out of *The Last Picture Show* or *Lonesome Dove,* Larry McMurtry's Texas masterpieces. Ladd had an unshakable Western accent, a slight lisp, and a scratchy throttle from too many cigarettes.

It was 1969 when Tom arrived at the police academy in Texas, where he spent four months. Then, as Tom later put it, he "was put there on patrol in one of the black areas, here in Houston, called the Third Ward."

Ladd spent three years patrolling one of the highest-crime districts in the city at the time. He was moved down by the docks, the Harrisburg Canal region, and made a decision while there that would ultimately change the person he became.

"I decided to study for detective," Tom recalled. "And I scored high enough to qualify, and they put me into Homicide."

It was 1975.

Ladd never left.

This Clear Lake City case, the massacre of the four out on Millbridge, was Detective Tom Ladd and his partner Phil Yochum's case. Not because Ladd had some sort of long-lost wish to solve a case of this magnitude, but because of the time of day that the murders had been discovered. Ladd was one of the night men on HPD's Homicide Division, the "skeleton crew" chief, as he put it, working the three-to-eleven or four-to-midnight watch. When this Clear Lake case came in, Ladd was busy finishing work up on a serial killer case. The problem, he said, with taking cases on the evening shift: "We didn't have the luxury, because there was so few of us on the evening shift, to work just *one* case. A lot of times we would get assigned another case and it forced us to decide, 'Okay, do we work *this* case, or do we work *that* case?' It made us selective in the cases we followed through on."

Tom was born in the Midwest, a little town in Missouri. When he was seven, his family moved to Houston. He played college football for Barry Switzer's University of Oklahoma Sooners, and took that Johnny Unitas brush cut of his youth into adulthood. The days that Tom spent at the University of Oklahoma playing for the Sooners schooled him in humility, you could say. Tom stood about six feet four inches, had some bulk on him, at just over two hundred pounds, but he was by no means heavy. He was perfect for the football field of his day. But not once did Tom ever kid himself into thinking that he had the potential to play professionally. He suffered an injury then that he still feels to this day. Or, as he liked to put it, "I got my knee ripped up." Tom also realized as he looked around at the other kids coming into training camp as he was heading into his final years of college, he just wasn't big enough to make a play for the NFL. "My playing weight at OU was two hundred seven. I was what they call a 'weak guard.' While I was there, guys were coming in who were two hundred seventy-five to two hundred eighty pounds—but who moved just as quickly as I could!"

His days on the HPD Homicide Squad began on October 25, 1975, and Tom's weathered eyes told a familiar story, showing the wear that the years of being a witness to the sickness of society can take on a human being. Surely, Tom had seen things that the public thought happened only in movies. He'd been inside places most people didn't think existed. Ladd was a cop who thought long and hard about what he said before opening his mouth, an attribute he learned from his years behind the badge. It was those times—and Tom admitted to plenty of them—when he didn't keep his tongue tied, that he got in trouble. There was no middle ground with Tom Ladd. He was polarizing; people liked him or hated him (many more coming on the side of the latter). He'd been called a "bigot" and a "racist," as if the two were different somehow by saying both words in the same breath. But Tom himself would tell you, he spoke his mind. Period. If you didn't like that, there's not much he could do. Moreover, Ladd had investigated some high-profile cases throughout his career. The "Railroad Killer" was part of Tom's past. Angel Maturino Reséndiz was a vicious psychopath (executed in 2006 for his crimes) who murdered fifteen people along the railroad tracks of Texas.

"My partner and I," Tom said humbly, "were the ones who led to the identification of him [Reséndiz], and the Texas Rangers got involved and developed him as a serial murderer."

Tom and his brother, Jim Ladd, a former HPD detective himself, were involved with the Carl Eugene Watts case. Watts was the notorious serial killer known as the "Sunday Morning Slasher," a man who had confessed to, by some gross guesstimates, taking the lives of eighty females during a twenty-plus-year killing spree.

"I think he's probably done *more* than that," Tom said of the man he called "Coral." "His memory was amazing." Coral showed Tom and Jim where he buried his victims, sometimes three to a single grave; but there was one day during a two-week period when Tom and his team interviewed Coral on a daily basis and Coral shocked Tom. The serial killer looked at the detective and, as calm as a Texas wave before a hurricane, said, "If I ever get out, I'll do it again."

* * *

THE HOMICIDE DIVISION lieutenant called Ladd on the night of July 18, 2003, and let him know what they had on Millbridge. Of course, the Patrol Division was the first to respond. Then HPD's Crime Scene Unit (CSU).

"We walked into that mess," Ladd said of the night shift detective squad, "and they were all there, going through the scene."

Word of a quadruple homicide got around quick.

Ladd found a patrol sergeant outside the Rowell house as soon as he arrived on the scene. The guy gave him the details they had at the time. Four bodies. Multiple gunshot wounds. Several people who had walked into the house but had run out (Brittney Vikko and several neighbors). No one in the neighborhood they had spoken to so far had seen or heard a thing.

"Looks like a drug deal gone bad," someone at the scene said.

Sure did, Ladd thought.

But what were these kids dealing in—pounds of dope?

The tall, soft-spoken detective found a CSU officer and asked what, exactly, they had inside the house. The layout. The gruesome reality beyond the front door.

The investigator explained.

Shell casings were everywhere. Blood was all over the place. Shots fired at close range and from a distance. Even looked like several of the victims had been pistol-whipped or beaten with a blunt object, something small and hard.

Tom Ladd and Phil Yochum had this in mind as they walked into the house.

First thing that hit Ladd was the shell casings right there as you crossed over the threshold of the front doorway.

Did the shooter start firing the moment one of the victims opened the door?

Yochum and Ladd remained quiet for a time and "gingerly," as Ladd explained, walked around the bodies, looking things over.

What a mess, indeed. Such a damn tragedy. Four kids cut down like this—and for what?

Homicide had developed a system for murder investigations. They worked by what's called a "homicide card." One side was responsible for the scene; the other locked onto witnesses.

"Phil," Ladd said, "take the inside here, the scene."

Yochum understood. He was young. He could take it. Yochum was not as experienced, Tom knew, but having the CSU there to help him was what Phil Yochum needed.

Ladd set out to develop witnesses. Talk to people. Run the periphery of the scene, which, experience told him, was where a cop could find his best perspective this early.

What were people in the neighborhood talking about?

Before walking out of the house, taking a look around, Ladd considered the drug-deal-gone-bad theory: *A drug killing?* He'd seen plenty of them. *Four kids. All shot.*

Not a hard sell.

"It wasn't *concrete* in my mind," Ladd was quick to point out, "but it just *looked* like a drug killing."

The telltale marks could not be ignored.

Thinking further, studying all the shots the CSU had identified on the victims thus far, Ladd came to a second conclusion, one that told him maybe they were looking at something else entirely.

Good shots.

Whoever had fired the rounds had hit his or her intended targets accurately.

It wasn't like there was a lot of misses.

"I used to be on an officer-involved shooting team," Ladd recalled. "It was amazing how many times I showed up to a crime scene where officers had fired and not hit *anything.* Then I walk into that [Millbridge Drive] scene that night and everybody's got rounds in them! Yeah, that told me somethin', all right."

Before finally leaving the house, Ladd walked over to the fireplace and bent down on one knee. He looked square into the rabbit cage sitting on the base of the hearth. The rabbit was jumpy. Wired and fired up. Little guy seemed to be anxious, as maybe all rabbits are.

Ladd looked at the furry creature for a few moments. Then he stood: *If only that rabbit could talk*, the detective told himself, shaking his head as he walked out the door.

CHAPTER 5

BY **11:14 P.M.** a canvass of the neighborhood had turned up a few witnesses. There was a couple, Craig and Michelle Lackner, who lived next door and reported seeing two people near the Rowell house earlier that afternoon. But what did that mean? Without names or recognizing who these people were, what could this tell police?

A detective was assigned to interview the couple, to see what they knew.

The Lackners had been living in the Millbridge development since January 2003, or about six months. They both recalled the day quite well. They had just gotten back from an extended, fourteen-day vacation in Mexico and were taking some time to relax before going back to work on that Monday. Craig was watching television in the living room, lying comfortably on the couch, when he was approached by his wife, Michelle, who had just gotten out of the shower. It was 3:15 P.M., Michelle later remembered. She knew the time because she had checked.

"Come here, come here," Michelle said. "I want to show you something."

Craig begrudgingly got up from the couch. Michelle was trying to be sly and get Craig into the bedroom.

At that moment the Lackners' dog started "going nuts," Michelle later explained.

Odd, the dog had never barked like that, Michelle noticed. "Go get him," she told Craig.

Craig went outside and let the dog in.

He returned to the bedroom. Their kitten was over by the window. When Craig looked over at the cat, he noticed two people outside the bedroom window, which looked out over toward the Rowell house, directly next door.

"Hey, honey," Craig said jokingly, "you're going to give these two kids a show!" Michelle was half dressed, just out of the shower, standing there in a towel. Craig stood in the doorway between his bedroom and the living room. Michelle was over by the window.

Michelle said something to Craig.

He responded, "Okay . . . but you just flashed two people walking down the street." He laughed.

There were two people outside the Lackners' window, both dressed in black. This was strange, considering it was hotter than hell outside, with humidity making temps appallingly uncomfortable.

Craig walked toward the window to get a closer look. He was about "thirty feet," he later estimated, away from where the two in black stood outside his window. He could see them fairly clearly, same as Michelle.

They stopped at Tiffany's truck and looked in the side window at the back of her vehicle. Craig continued watching them because they looked sketchy, like maybe they were going to burgle the vehicle. Michelle went and got dressed.

When Michelle returned, she stared at the girl. She "stood out to me, because she was a white female, sandy blond straight hair, fair skin, and clear complexion. She was cute. Maybe eighteen to twenty, five feet seven or so, one hundred fifteen to one hundred twenty pounds."

Women notice other women. Those were numbers police could work with.

Upon a closer look, Michelle noticed the girl was wearing a black top, white shorts, black platform sandals, and a black bandana around the top of her head. She also had a black purse slung around her right shoulder. It appeared to be weighty on her bony build.

"She was carrying the purse as if it was heavy. And she had her hand in her mouth looking around."

The boy with her, Michelle and Craig agreed, was a white male, fair complexion, sandy blond hair. He was actually shorter, they recalled, than the female. They guessed his age to be about eighteen to twenty, same as the girl. He was thin.

Michelle and Craig Lackner had never seen these people before. After they headed toward Tiffany Rowell's house from the truck, up the driveway, and disappeared out of view, the Lackners didn't think anything about them. That would come later, they explained to the detective, when they returned home near seven that night to find utter chaos outside Tiffany's house.

The Lackners ultimately went downtown and sat with a sketch artist, who made two drawings of the male and female. Those composites, along with the Lackners' interview reports, would be put into a growing file. Tom Ladd and Phil Yochum were gathering so much material as the first twenty-four hours after the murders passed, they would be unable to keep up with it all.

Just how important would these statements by the Lackners and subsequent drawings turn out to be in the years to come?

"[Those kids] were walking toward this house," the prosecutor who would get the case would later say, "as if they didn't have a care in the world. Had [Michelle Lackner] not gotten out of the shower [when she did] . . . this case would have *never* been solved."

A YOUNG WOMAN, scared but willing and courageous enough to talk, walked into HPD late that same night and informed the desk sergeant that she might have information relevant to the Millbridge Drive murders. Turned out the twenty-four-year-old, Nicola Baldwin (pseudonym), was a friend of Tiffany Rowell's.

Nicola sat down in an interview room and started talking. She was the first of what was going to be an ambush of people to talk to, Tom Ladd and his team knew.

Nicola explained that she worked as a waitress for an Italian restaurant downtown. It was around two forty-five on the morning of the murders when Nicola showed up at Tiffany's Millbridge Drive house. Marcus Precella was there, too. So was Adelbert Sánchez and Nicola's brother. They were hanging out, partying. Marcus received a call from Tiffany at some point.

"I gave my keys to a stripper who works here," Tiffany said. Apparently, she had been drinking and didn't want to drive.

Nicola could not recall the stripper's name, but "Tiffany wanted us to come to the club and get her." She had no other way home.

Marcus and Nicola got into Nicola's vehicle and headed out to Club Exotica. Adelbert and Nicola's brother stayed behind.

Tiffany stood by the front door into the club with a blond dancer. A bouncer from the club kept an eye on them. Nicola and Marcus got out and hugged Tiffany.

"What's up?" Nicola offered.

"She needs a ride, too," Tiffany explained, nodding at her dancer friend. "She lives near Jersey Village."

A bedroom community, Jersey Village is north of Houston, heading toward Weiser Airpark on Highway 290, or about an hour's drive one way from Clear Lake City.

"No problem," Marcus said. He took out a set of keys he had brought from Tiffany's house so he and Tiffany could take her truck. They could drop off Tiffany's friend first and then head back to Clear Lake. The others could return to the house in Nicola's car.

Nicola drove straight to Tiffany's. When she arrived, Adelbert and her brother were still up partying. Now, though, there were two strippers at the house, who had shown up while Nicola and the others were out picking up Tiffany. They were all sitting around, laughing, smoking some weed, getting their drunk on.

According to Nicola, it was another typical night at Tiffany's house.

Nothing seemed to be out of whack, Nicola explained. Things seemed to be going all right throughout the early-morning hours.

"Is there anything else you can tell us?" the interviewing officer asked Nicola. She seemed scared, frightened to think that a good friend had been murdered in such a choreographed, concerted way, and she had been at the same house hours before. As far as the public knew then, someone had walked into the house and mowed them all down. No warning. No explanation. It wasn't hard to tell that perhaps someone the kids knew had been invited into the house and decided, for some reason, to open fire on everyone.

Later on that night (after the murders), Nicola told police, she was at a friend's house when her manager called and asked if she knew how to get ahold of Tiffany Rowell's father. This was a strange request. Nicola could not ever recall her boss phoning for this reason.

"Why?" Nicola asked him.

"I think Tiffany was shot and killed inside her house."

"I don't know . . . ," Nicola said.

"Try to get ahold of Tiffany, okay?" her manager said before hanging up.

Nicola said she would.

And that was about all Nicola knew. Yet through that interview, Nicola had given cops her brother's contact information. He might know a bit more, she said. He had been at the house partying with Adelbert while Nicola was out. Nicola said her brother had stayed behind, too, after she left to go home as the sun came up.

Detectives caught up with Nicola's brother.

"I left about nine-fifteen A.M.," he said, adding that he had been at Tiffany's house since two forty-five in the morning, and arrived with Nicola, as she had claimed. One of the strippers whom he and Adelbert had partied with gave him a ride to his grandparents' house later that morning because Nicola had left. "We had a good time, and there were no problems. Marcus and Tiffany went to bed [at some point] and we [the stripper and I] just sat there in the living room smoking and drinking. . . . During my time there, I did not hear or see anything out of the ordinary."

The officer pressed for more information. Was there anything he thought might have contributed to the murders? Strange phone calls? Maybe someone lurking about the yard? An unexpected visitor?

There had to be something.

Nicola's brother said he did not know Marcus, Tiffany, or Adelbert that well. In fact, it was the first time he had ever been over to the house.

CHAPTER 6

IF SOMEONE WOULD have taken time-lapse video of the scene outside the front of Tiffany Rowell's house, a subtle, yet awfully sad picture would have emerged on the morning following the murders. As the midnight hour approached, then one, two, and three in the morning, that time-lapse photography would have shown the crowd growing increasingly sparse. People were disappearing, walking away like at the end of a rally, as the morning came to pass—that is, all but three individuals: George, Ann and Lelah Koloroutis. The three of them had stayed all night, waiting, praying, hoping against their better (gut) judgment and that sinking feeling that at some point a detective would come out and tell them it *wasn't* Rachael inside, after all. There had been a terrible mistake. She wasn't there. It was another girl. Some other family would have to suffer the loss.

At certain points throughout the night, a cop would come out and speak to George, dancing around the reality that Rachael was one of the victims.

"Does your daughter have long reddish hair?"

George would drop his head in his hands. "Yes, sir, she does."

"Okay. We're just not sure yet it's her, sorry."

They stood outside, "being eaten alive by the mosquitoes," George recalled. "We knew. But we just kept praying and praying and praying."

A kindhearted couple, as George described them, who lived nearby, invited George, Ann and Lelah into their home at some point so they could get out of the humid, oppressive weather and sit down for a moment with a glass of water. The three of them were dehydrated, running on adrenaline. They had no idea what time it was or how long they had been waiting.

It was near three o'clock in the morning when two investigators came out of the house, carrying something in a bag. George, Ann, and Lelah looked on as they approached; both men had serious looks on their faces.

George knew.

"We have something here," one of them said. "Yes, it is your daughter."

Rachael's wallet.

Ann fell backward to the ground and screamed so loud, George remembered, it hurt his ears. George caved in and began whimpering. Lelah kept slowly repeating, "No . . . no . . . no," almost in a whisper.

Confirmation. The worst result ever. Rachael's driver's license.

Ann and Lelah walked off after a time and got into the car; both women were shells of themselves, overcome with emotion, curled up, crying, now locked inside all that pain.

George stood and stared at the house.

I don't know what to do.

One of the investigators asked George if he was okay. George looked out of it, staggered and dazed. "A blubbering fool," he called himself later.

A statue.

"What do I do now?" George whispered to the investigator. He was crying.

"Mr. Koloroutis, you have to go home and take care of your family." The cop looked over toward the car where Ann and Lelah sat, waiting.

There was nothing more George and his family could do at the crime scene.

George and Ann both had cars there. George got into his, as Ann was able to pull herself together enough to drive her vehicle.

"I got to the end of the street," George recalled. He was leading the way home. "And I didn't know what to do—which way to turn. Here's the big leader . . . the big man of the house, and I have no idea what I'm doing, where I'm going."

Ann pulled in front of her husband and took off toward the house.

George followed.

The sun was coming up as they arrived home. Not knowing what to do, having no playbook to follow, George got out of his car and walked into the house.

"Here it is," George remembered, "my little girl is dead. *Dead!* Not hit by a car or struck by lightning. But another human being *murdered* her."

Ann went for the couch, where she lay down and wailed. Lelah walked straight for the bathroom, vomited, then sank against the wall, crumbling to the floor, crying until it seemed there were no more tears left.

George had a hard time processing what happened. He walked up the stairs, went into Rachael's room, and looked around. Then he walked into Lelah's room. Did the same. After that, he found himself in his and Ann's room. Finally he realized he was wandering the hallways of the house, head in his hands, unable to come to terms with the night's events. George was the provider; he was the man of the house who was supposed to make everything better. But this—how in the hell was he going to manage?

How do I fix this? If I could only fix this. . . . Something's broken. . . . If I could find out what it is, I could put it back together.

SEVENTEEN-YEAR-OLD Nichole Sánchez saw her brother, Adelbert, on Wednesday afternoon, July 16, 2003. Being cousins, Adelbert Sánchez and Marcus Precella hung out together. Marcus had been living with Tiffany Rowell. They were in love and planning a life together. On this day Marcus had called Adelbert, who was at his older sister's house with Nichole, often called "Nona." Marcus said something about a party at Tiffany's that night. Did Adelbert want to go?

"Yeah," Adelbert said. "Come and pick me up."

When Marcus arrived, Adelbert looked at his little sister and said, "Nona, I'm leaving now. See you later."

"Well," Nichole said, "you need to be careful." Nichole had no idea why she said it. It was just a *feeling* she had on that day; and Nichole was someone who went with her feelings. She and Adelbert were not prone to wish each other safety or hug and make good-byes into sentimental displays of affection. But something told Nichole on this day to reach out and say something to the brother she idolized and adored.

D, who was also sometimes called "AD," gave one of his signature smiles to his little sis, saying, "I'm always careful, Nona."

Marcus piped in, "Hey, don't worry. I'll take care of him."

Adelbert sensed that Nichole was acting a bit strange. He walked over, gave her a big hug, and then kissed her on the cheek. "Don't worry, Nona. I'll be fine."

"We really weren't ever touchy-feely with each other," Nichole recalled. "If I got a hug from him, it was usually followed by a slap in the head." You know, a big-brother thing.

Looking at his sister, Adelbert said, "Hey, I love you. . . . *Don't* worry. I'll be careful. We'll talk soon."

One memory of her brother that Nichole took comfort in was the family's annual camping trips when they were young. "We were always given whatever we wanted," Nichole said. "My parents spoiled us. Clothes. Electronics. The finer things in life kids want."

As they were packing for a camping trip, Nichole looked at D and said, "What are you doing?"

He had a garbage bag filled with sneakers: brand-new, unscuffed, a pair to match any outfit. D had this big suitcase with a change of clothes for what Nichole joked later seemed like "two weeks."

She told him, "We're going only for the weekend—two nights! What are you *doing*?" But that was D: he would change outfits two or three times a day. He had to have clean clothes, spotless, all the time.

"You'd think," Nichole said, laughing sadly at the memory, "he thought that he might be giving a fashion show in the woods, instead of camping."

That year they went camping, D jumped in the river. "Come on in, Nona. . . . It's shallow. Look, I can touch the bottom. See! Come on, it's warm."

Nichole was hesitant. She did not know the first thing about swimming. But what the heck? She trusted her brother.

She took the leap and went straight to the bottom.

"I was just kidding with you," D said. "It's deep. It's deep."

Their father had to jump in and drag Nichole out.

That was D: the jokester. The consummate chameleon who could adapt to, and have fun in, any situation.

Not long after waking the following morning after seeing Adelbert off with that strange embrace, Nichole recognized that she was mad at her brother. He had promised to call her, but never did. Nichole figured he was having fun with Marcus and some other friends. D had a penchant for the girls. The ladies adored him and he had no trouble keeping a string of them. Perhaps he had hooked up with someone new and took off.

"He had girls chasing him, left and right," Nichole recalled. "We never really saw him with one girlfriend." There was one particular girl that Adelbert was interested in, Nichole added, "and she came around often, but they were really never a couple."

Adelbert was more focused on his music, according to Nichole and other friends. D had dreams of being a rapper, and some said he had the chops to fulfill that dream. For the most part his mind was set on the Houston music scene. He was getting his demo together, before heading off to Los Angeles or New York. New Orleans-based Untouchable Records, Nichole said, was showing some interest in D's music.

D and Marcus grew up together in the same Houston neighborhood: the Northeast end of the city, which is mostly Hispanic.

"Where Adelbert grew up and lived," said a law enforcement source, "the neighborhood is the type that you would see Christmas Lights on the parked cars left on the front lawn. Whereas, where the kids were killed in Clear Lake, the lights would be hung on the house."

Clear Lake was a forty-five-minute drive on a good day, usually fifty to sixty. Marcus and his family moved out to that area at some point when the kids were young, but Adelbert and Marcus stayed tight. As cousins nearly the same age, they gravitated toward each other. Marcus was always coming back to the neighborhood to hook up with Adelbert and buzz around town, even after Marcus met Tiffany Rowell and moved in with her.

Nichole believed Adelbert was going to be back at the house on Thursday or Friday, or at least she'd see him at some point throughout the weekend. By Monday, things would be back to normal. Adelbert might even be sleeping late waiting for his mother to cook him breakfast—"He had to have fresh tortillas with *every* meal," Nichole remembered—and then he'd get dressed and head out to work on his music. There was even some talk lately from D about going to college.

On the evening news that Friday, July 18, Nichole and her parents saw that there had been a quadruple murder in the Millbridge Drive neighborhood. They had no idea what Tiffany's house looked like, so the news wasn't alarming in that respect. There was no way they could have planned for the horror that was about to be delivered to them because they didn't know where Adelbert had run off to. However, Nichole and Adelbert's grandmother, watching the report, both said, "I pray for whoever's family that is." They knew that the families were going to be dealing with more pain than anyone should be forced to endure. It was such an immense tragedy—the loss of young people always is—but on a scale of this nature, simply unheard of.

Looking closer at the report, Nichole's grandmother said, "That looks like Marcus's car." She pointed to a portion of the report that showed Tiffany Rowell's taped-off driveway; a reporter stood in the street, her back to the house.

The following morning, July 19, Nichole was at home by herself. Her parents had left early on a fishing trip so they could drive down to a family member's house and stay the rest of the weekend. Nichole was supposed to go, too, but she stayed home. It was that nagging feeling about Adelbert, still weighing on her; she had not heard from him and had no idea where her big brother—"my protector"—had gone off to. Adelbert hadn't come home the night before, nor had he called. He was having a few issues with his father and mother, but it wasn't something, Nichole said, that would keep him away from home. Nichole didn't know it, but D was sleeping at the Rowell house these days. To her it wasn't such a shock or big deal when D didn't come home—he was twenty-one. Nichole felt a pang of *something's wrong* as she woke up. There was a reason, she knew, why she had stayed home. Maybe it was just a sense of something heavy holding her back, even though she didn't quite know what. Close siblings experience this phenomenon: they have a Karmic sense about them, a way of knowing without actually understanding the feelings, almost like twins.

Sure enough, near nine in the morning, Nichole's parents' telephone rang. There were two lines in the house.

"Hello?" Nichole said, still a bit groggy from just having woken up.

It was her aunt. She was asking for Nichole's mother's cell phone number, or a number for the house they were staying at.

"Let me look it up for you. . . ."

"I'll call back."

Nichole started cooking herself some breakfast. She didn't figure it was that urgent for her to find the number, but the telephone rang again.

This time it was Marcus's sister.

"Is this Melissa (Nichole and Adelbert's older sister)?"

"No."

"Is this Nona?"

"Yes." Nichole's radar went up. She could sense the urgency in Marcus's sister's voice, a definite panic. It woke Nichole right up. This heightened sense of anxiety on the other end of the line even scared her.

"Where's Melissa?"

"She's out of town fishing right now."

"Where's your mom?"

"She's there . . . too. What's going on?"

"I need to speak to them."

"Why? What's happening? What's going on?" Nichole was getting nervous, more concerned by each word; that thumping in the chest when you know—you just *know*—bad news is forthcoming.

"You need to have them call me."

"Why? . . ." She paused. "Where's my brother?"

Holding it together best she could, Nichole's cousin lost it. She started crying. Then she handed the phone off to Nichole's aunt.

"What is going on?" Nichole demanded.

"Marcus and Adelbert were shot last night."

"Okay . . . okay. Well, *where* is he? I need to see him *right* now. Where's he at?" She thought D was in the hospital somewhere, fighting, needing his family by his side.

"You need to have your mother call me right away."

"Why? *Where* is my brother?"

Worry. Dread. Fear. All there. It was beginning to consume Nichole.

There was a brief silence, just the buzz of the static on the telephone line between them.

"Marcus and Adelbert were . . . shot . . . and *killed* last night," the aunt finally said.

They hung up.

Nichole had just turned seventeen. She was home alone. This news, this horrible pain, which would change her family for the rest of their lives, was all on her. She didn't know what to do with it, how to immediately react, or if what she had just heard was real.

She found her mom's number and called. As she did this, Nichole remembered that at some point between the calls she had started breakfast. She went back into the kitchen to find that the stove was on fire. The smoke alarm was going off—same as her insides. There was chaos in the house, and she was all alone.

Getting the fire under control, Nichole phoned her mother. Before she even spoke, Adelbert's mother knew something was wrong.

"Nichole, what's going on there?"

Not long after she got the words out of her mouth, Nichole could hear her father and mother screaming and wailing in the background. The worst news a parent could be given had ripped their hearts open.

Life was never going to be the same for the Sánchez family.

CHAPTER 7

LATER **THAT MORNING,** the Seabrook Police Department (SPD) responded to a burglary call. Seabrook is a workingman's waterfront community comprised of shrimpers and oil rig workers. It's located on the northeast corner of Clear Lake, about a ten-minute ride from the murder scene. The woman claimed she'd been robbed while she was out the previous day.

"What time?" the responding officer asked.

"Oh, between six P.M. and three A.M.," she said.

"What's missing?"

"A rifle and a pistol."

The red flag here was that there was no sign of damage to the back door of the single-family dwelling. The front door faced a busy street, so the woman and the police believed the thief must have entered the house through the back. But there was no indication of a break-in.

Strange.

The cop asked the woman if she could describe what type of weapons had been stolen. A teletype had gone out the previous night to all the local police departments, spelling out the murders in Clear Lake City, asking for any information. If two weapons had been lifted from a home shortly before the murders, and they knew the caliber, HPD could figure out relatively quickly if it was a possible match. Cases are sometimes solved by these random acts of crime. Could the HPD be that lucky?

"They were my father's rifle and pistol," the woman said. "Taken right from his bedroom. My dad is out of town."

"Why do you think the intruder came in through the back door?"

"The last time I went to take the dog out," the woman explained, "the chain on the back door was not on, and I always put the chain on the back door when I lock it."

The officer asked, "Do you usually lock the back door *and* the screen door?"

"I do."

"Does anyone else have access to the house, ma'am?"

She thought about it. "Yeah. . . ." She gave the cops the girl's name, then mentioned a little bit about the girl's checkered history with law enforcement.

"Do you still associate with these 'friends' who engage in criminal activity?" the officer asked.

It was clear to the cop that the woman who had been robbed had a past herself. She'd been friends with people who had been in trouble.

"I don't hang around with them anymore," she said. "I hang with people at my work."

"Show me where the items were taken from."

They walked into a room she described as her "father's bedroom." She pointed to a gun rack. There was a weapon missing. Then she opened the nightstand next to her father's bed.

"There was a pistol in here, too." She closed the drawer. "It's gone."

There were plenty of other guns in the closet, the cop noticed. But it did not appear that anything was disturbed throughout the room. Nor did it look like a thief had rummaged through the bedroom searching for other things—besides the guns—to steal. It was as if the thief knew what to search for and where the weapons were.

The woman said she had no idea what type of weapons had been lifted.

The officer handed the woman his business card. "Listen," he said, pointing to the telephone number on the card. "When your father returns, have him call us . . . so that I can get the rest of the information from him."

CHAPTER 8

BRITTNEY VIKKO WAS still talking, only now she was ruminating on the lives of her friend Tiffany and Tiff's boyfriend, Marcus Precella.

HPD ran Tiffany's name through the system and it came back clean. She had a few vehicular violations and accidents, but nothing that raised any concerns. Same with Rachael Koloroutis. Marcus and Adelbert had no criminal records whatsoever. Neither had been arrested. HPD had no background on either of them. If one or both was a big-time dealer, as some witnesses were saying, there was no history of it anywhere HPD could find.

"I knew Tiffany and her boyfriend, Marcus, used to go to the Club Exotica on Forty-five and Fuqua and party a lot," Brittney told HPD. It was late, near midnight, when they interviewed Brittney. It was Saturday, July 19. She said it had been a long day and a half. Her friend was dead. Her friend's boyfriend was dead. Two others she really didn't know all that well were dead. Where was the sense in any of it?

"They had asked me to go with them [to the strip club] two or three times," she continued, "but I told them no. I knew that they had occasionally done cocaine together because I had seen them doing it at their house before."

This piqued Tom Ladd's interest when he heard about it later. Ladd was one of those investigators who liked to sit back and listen to witnesses talk. He'd ask questions, but one of Ladd's strengths was pulling out of a witness exactly what he or she knew, without coming across as pushy. There would be a time for that good cop/bad cop nonsense, but not now. Not in the midst of what was looking to be an investigation that was going to include interviews with scores of people these kids knew.

"Anything else you can recall?" Detective Phil Yochum asked Brittney.

She thought about it. Now was not the time to hold back information, thinking you were protecting a friend.

"Yeah . . . about a week or so ago, my boyfriend and I were going to Clear Lake and we passed by the [strip] club. I saw Tiffany's car parked there and I remembered her saying that she might go to work there. I called Marcus right after that. He told me she was working there as a waitress. I knew she had been working at the Flying Dutchman in Kemah as a hostess, so I guess she must have quit. . . ."

Yochum and Ladd looked at each other. This was great background information, but in the scope of the murders, it meant squat.

"What else, miss?"

Brittney shuffled in her seat. She seemed uncomfortable. She continued to speak, however. "I was already aware that Marcus was dealing Ecstasy and cocaine, because he had called me and offered to sell me some," she said, quickly following up by adding, "Which I declined! My boyfriend and I were at Tiffany's . . . about two weeks ago. While I was at the house, I asked [Marcus] if he had gotten rid of the cocaine, and he told me that they had done a lot of it themselves and sold some of it. About a week or so ago, I called Tiffany's cell phone and Marcus answered. He told me he was in Northeast Houston, in the 'Four-Four' with his cousin, and they were about to pick up some cocaine."

This neighborhood, often dubbed the "fo-fo," is an urban inner-city community northwest of Houston. It got the name "Four-Four" or "Forty-Four" supposedly because of the metro bus line #44 running through the district; yet others claim the name originates from the .44 Magnum. The low-income apartments in the area are hangouts for denizens of crime. What makes the neighborhood different is that within the district there is a largely wooded area intermingled within the projects. If you were looking for cocaine, and/or any other hardcore drug, for that matter, the fo-fo is a good place to begin that search, or so claimed a few who were familiar with this particular 'hood.

Brittney Vikko explained how she and Tiffany had met and where they had gone to school. She said they had lost touch for a time, then hooked back up again over the past few years.

Other than that, she didn't know anything else. But if something came up, she'd be sure to call.

Tom Ladd and Phil Yochum had Brittney sign her statement. Told her she was free to leave. Thanked her for coming in.

TOM LADD CARRIED a Smith & Wesson .45-caliber automatic weapon on his hip: a big gun for a big guy. Yet this case, at least from where Ladd stood with all those years of police work behind him, nagged at the detective. He sensed something bigger going on here. Something out of the norm. Good homicide cops never pigeonhole themselves, or lock into a theory this early on in an investigation. That would be detrimental to the case and any potential progress. Still, when he sat back and thought about it more thoroughly, Ladd considered a few things that the crime scene screamed at him.

"Well, I guess probably the fact that, look, there's four bodies in there. We got a little girl that's apparently injured or shot dead right there in the living room in front of the TV. And then the thing that stuck out most to me was the one boy and the one girl just sitting there on the couch. Marcus was between the couch and the wall. And you had to move around to see him. But you go in and you see two people just sitting there, like they're watching TV, but dead from gunshot, that made me think it was real quick. Whoever came in there was really deadly and did everything real quick."

It was as if professionals were involved—which fed more into the theory of a drug deal gone badly, or maybe a drug cartel sending a message. HPD had seen those types of brazen homicides. The same pockmarks were there in Clear Lake. And yet, if one of the boys had reneged on a deal, a better business model for a doper would be to pull him out of the house and shoot him in the head in front of the other dealers and users. That would send more of a direct message to the drug community. The other problem, in looking at the murders being drug related, became the idea that if Marcus was dealing, he was dealing without the security of owning a weapon himself.

When Ladd looked closer, he figured the body in front of the television (Rachael Koloroutis) was the person who answered the door; and the way she had been found pointed to a theory:

NEVER SEE THEM AGAIN   45

A knock or the doorbell . . . Rachael walks over and
opens the door. She lets the person in. Turns, begins
walking back to the part of the house where she had
come from—the hallway leading to the bedrooms, or the
kitchen, where she could have been preparing a meal—
and is shot as she passes by the television set just as
Tiffany and Marcus, on the couch, are shot.

This indicated two shooters instead of one; and it also told police (if the theory was somewhat accurate) that someone in the house knew the shooter(s). Or that Rachael was comfortable with opening the door and letting the shooters in.

Ladd and Yochum didn't need Brittney Vikko, or anyone else, to convince them that they were dealing with a drug-related killing. To them, this seemed obvious "right away," Ladd said. It could not be overlooked.

"Through [Brittney] and everyone we began talking to, all they could tell us," Ladd recalled, "was how Marcus was selling drugs. So we had to *assume* it was because of that, that the murders occurred."

The other factor became the idea that not a lot of drugs had been found in the house. This could mean two things: they were barking up the wrong tree entirely; or the shooter cleaned the house out before he left. Yet, both Marcus and Adelbert had money on them.

So . . . the goal was murder all along?

The one thing Ladd saw as interesting was the fact that everyone they talked to thus far had provided names, as if passing the buck. It didn't take shining a light in anybody's face to reveal names and drug dealers and people they believed might have been involved.

"We'd end up with close to four hundred names," Ladd recalled, "when all of it was said and done."

On Sunday, July 20, a tipster—one of soon-to-be dozens—called in. She said her son had been "running his mouth" and talking about how awful it was that the four kids had been "killed execution style, beaten and shot."

"I'm concerned," the boy's mother reported to a hotline operator, "that my son knows too much information, more than the media was putting out on the news, so I asked him how he knew so much."

"What did he say, ma'am?"

"He said a girl came into the Starbucks and told [some people] working on Friday. . . . She couldn't even talk. She was so hysterical. . . ." The
girl apparently knew what had happened at Tiffany Rowell's house
and talked about details different from what any news organization
had been reporting. She had gone to school with Rachael and
Tiffany. "She said her boyfriend"—who also knew both girls—"was
dealing heavy into drugs."

There was that drug connection bell ringing again.

The woman had called from a pay phone. She wouldn't give
names, only the Starbucks location. This was enough, of course, to
send a few investigators to check it out.

Meanwhile, another woman telephoned. She was younger. She
said her friend, whom she named, was riding a bus and heard two
men talking about the murders. One of the men said he had been
with Marcus earlier on the day he was murdered. Marcus had even
asked the guy to go with him over to Tiffany's, but the guy turned
him down—a decision that likely saved his life.

The conversation was overheard on a shuttle bus running employees to the Kemah Boardwalk. The Boardwalk is sandwiched between Clear Lake, with State Highway 146 running between Kemah
and Seabrook (where those guns had been supposedly stolen from a
private residence), and the Gulf of Mexico (Galveston Bay), and is directly on the ocean.

The man got off the bus and walked in the direction of a restaurant. The caller gave investigators the name of the establishment.

And this—all the phone calls coming in—Tom Ladd began to see
was going to become a problem. The case was on the night shift's
shoulders. Ladd had a skeleton crew to work with, as it was. Houston
was a major metropolitan area. HPD had other homicides to deal
with, more coming in; the Brook Forest murders couldn't take priority over cases they had been working on for months and even years,
or new cases coming in.

"If we had the help," Ladd said, "we could have put eight guys,
full-time, on the [Clear Lake] investigation."

Investigators, as several names turned into several *dozen* names,
ran thin. Ladd could only do so much with Phil Yochum, who was
looking to get out of the Homicide Division altogether. Ladd's shift
didn't start until three or four in the afternoon. Because he was ded-

icated, and had no tolerance for upper management, and hated the idea that crimes went unsolved because of lack of resources, Ladd got up in the morning and started his shift before noon, heading out to interview witnesses and run down leads. Tom didn't want a pat on the back for going the extra mile—this guy was not about being rewarded for his work. He wanted to solve the case so he could move on to the next one.

The following day, July 21, Ladd and Yochum caught up with a dancer who worked with Tiffany at Club Exotica. Candy Apple (pseudonym) lived in Houston. She wrote her occupation on the witness statement as "entertainer."

Interesting.

Frank Sinatra: entertainer.

Chris Rock: entertainer.

Candy Apple: stripper.

Candy told detectives she had left high school during her junior year and started dancing shortly after.

"I'd known Tiffany and Rachael about a week," Candy said between drags of a cigarette. Both girls had just started working at Club Exotica. They were nice. Friendly. Willing to help the other girls. That much was clear within a few days of Tiffany and Rachael working at the club. Yet, there was something about Rachael, Candy mentioned, that she liked more than her run-of-the-mill friends. She saw something special in Rachael.

Ladd and Yochum explained to Candy that she had been sworn under oath to tell the truth about what she knew. If there was something she had been holding back, it was going to come back and bite her in that ass she used to make money.

Candy understood. She had nothing to hide. She wanted to help any way she could. All the dancers did. Everyone at the club was devastated by Tiffany and Rachael's deaths.

Last time she saw Tiffany, Candy explained, was on the Thursday night before the murders. On that night, Candy danced; Tiffany waitressed. Rachael had not been scheduled to work, but she was hanging out at the club. She was helping. (And that was the type of person Rachael was, Candy added.)

Candy soon brought up something interesting, explaining that, as she understood it, "I knew Tiffany and Rachael and Tiffany's boyfriend Marcus and Marcus's friend were staying together at the house on Millbridge."

The indication from Candy was that Adelbert was living there. But no one in Adelbert's family could agree with this. Adelbert, although he had left his house and would be gone for days sometimes, always came back home, where he had a bedroom. True, he and his father were at an impasse about what Adelbert was doing with his life, but Adelbert certainly had a bed at home to slip into every night, according to his family.

"On Thursday, the club closed at two A.M.," Candy continued, "and I think Rachael and I left about two-thirty. Tiffany was still inside the club, working. Rachael and I went to the house on Millbridge and got there about three or three-fifteen. When we got there, a Hispanic dude, Marcus, and Frankie (pseudonym) were there."

Candy described how Marcus took off to pick up Tiffany because someone else had her keys. This verified, of course, a part of the night HPD had gotten from another witness, which told them that it was likely true.

Good sign.

"[Frankie's] sister stopped by at about three forty-five. The Hispanic guy and [Frankie's sister] went outside on the patio to smoke some weed. . . . Rachael was inside the house on the phone."

Frankie's sister left. Candy told the others she'd drop Frankie off on her way home in the early morning. Candy said something about Frankie and Adelbert—"the Hispanic dude"—doing X (Ecstasy) and cocaine, which made them "fidgety." Because she was hungry, Candy said, she cooked a meal for everyone: "Fettuccini noodles and marinara sauce," adding, "Everyone helped themselves."

And there was the answer to that meal left out on the counter; it wasn't Rachael, after all, who'd fixed the meal. It was Candy Apple.

As they ate, Candy said, they watched a "Girls Gone Wild" DVD. Soon, just about everyone fell asleep or passed out on the couch, floor, and the easy chair in the living room.

Candy woke around 7:30 A.M. Everyone else got up soon after. Then they all went outside and smoked some weed. Candy left about eight-thirty in the morning. She dropped Frankie off at his house; then she took off to the gym to meet her personal trainer for an appointment.

Pot. Pasta. Nap. More weed. Then a workout. The battle cry of the young!

Candy wanted to party some more after the gym, so she tried to find the Millbridge Drive house again, but she had trouble locating it. She ultimately got into work on Friday about 4:30 P.M. and her boss was already "tripping," she said.

"Why?" Ladd asked.

Candy blew a puff of smoke, stared at the tip of her cigarette, and looked up. "Because [Rachael and Tiffany] were not showing up for work."

They had called in sick, apparently.

"Anything else you can recall?" Ladd said.

Candy took a breath. Stubbed out her cigarette. There *was* something, in fact. Getting back to how she felt about Rachael, something she had touched upon when she first sat down, Candy said that she wanted to begin dating Rachael—something Rachael would have wanted no part of.

CHAPTER 9

NICHOLE SÁNCHEZ AND her family were devastated by the deaths of Adelbert and his cousin Marcus. They had no idea what could have happened, what could have brought on the murders, or who might have been responsible. It was all they could do to wrap their minds around the idea that they had to bury a son, a brother, a cousin, a pair of boys who seemed to have so much life ahead of them. So much potential. So much love to give to the world.

"We had no idea what happened," Nichole said. "All we really knew was what was on the news. We didn't know why. We didn't know anything."

Any information Adelbert's family was getting early on, at best, was sporadic and fragmented. The implicit nature behind the murders, which all the news organizations were running with, was, of course, a drug deal gone badly; whereas Nichole and her family felt different.

"My brother didn't even own a cell phone," Nichole said. "I mean, my brother didn't really know anybody from *that* side of town. He was at the house with Marcus. He was unfamiliar with a lot of Marcus's friends."

There was never any talk within the family that drugs could have played a role in the murders. They were not naïve people, however; or ignorant to the reality of a kid in this day and age out in the world. Any parent or sibling knew that wherever a teenage or twentysomething party loomed—be it downtown Houston, Texas; Ogden, Utah; New York City; Bethlehem, Pennsylvania; Greenwich, Connecticut;

the sticks; the burbs; the hood; anywhere—there was likely going to be a buffet of drugs.

This savage crime had the earmarks of emotion behind it. The killer (or killers) was angry. He or she had made it personal. It was clear the killer(s) had known one, two, or perhaps all of these kids; after all, revenge is one of the top three motivators for murder, right there behind love and money.

Regardless of why they were killed, there was the overwhelming task ahead of dealing with it. Nichole's mother called family members to the house.

The police, according to Nichole, were not giving them much information. In fact, she added, one investigator was trying to say it was, in not so many words, likely that the murders were "Adelbert's fault." This made matters worse for a family coping with the death of two children. At one time, Adelbert's dad was asked to take a polygraph, which he declined to do after speaking with his lawyer.

"It made us feel horrible," Nichole remembered. "Just horrible!"

So there was some disunion between HPD and the Sánchez family as the investigation continued and the Sánchezes went about making plans to bury Adelbert.

Because such an outpouring of grief and show of support was expected, the funeral home staging Adelbert's wake and funeral had set back a few funerals. And the turnout didn't disappoint. Hundreds came (same as with the other three victims' funerals). When a young person dies, a community stares into the face of its own mortality. You're dying, essentially, the moment you arrive on the planet. Sometimes that process is sped up by cancer or heart disease or any number of ailments; other times it's just in the nature of God calling you home early, if you're a believer, or your ticket being pulled. But the sudden death of a child—no one can prepare for that. It is debilitating, numbing, and shakes you to the core.

Adelbert's family wanted to bury him with class. Adelbert had always wanted this one specific type of Houston Astros baseball team jersey, a white-, orange-, and yellow-colored shirt, with a big star off center. It was something Adelbert had talked about but never got around to buying. So the family agreed he needed to be buried in that jersey.

"He had been begging my mom to buy him one," Nichole said.

"He wasn't into suits, ties, dress shirts, and the like. So my mom didn't want to bury him in clothing that wasn't him."

So Adelbert was buried in his Astros jersey, a Houston Astros ball cap placed next to him, and his pallbearers all wore the black Astros jerseys with stars.

With all four victims in the ground, the reality of life without them began to settle on family and friends. Nichole probably spoke for all the families when she said life would never be the same again. Birthdays. Christmases. Fourth of July celebrations. Three Kings Day. Family gatherings. Births. And even deaths, too. There, invisible and obvious, weighing everyone down, the memory of a loved one not being able to take part in the affair. It's like having a piece of your soul stolen; you just don't know what part. It's hard to figure out what, exactly, hurts more: the loss itself, how the person was taken, or the simple fact that he was here one day—talking, joking, loving, laughing—and the next . . . gone. Vanished like dust. There's no filling that void. There's no scratching an itch you cannot find. It will *always* be there. And you'll never quite understand or entirely accept it. Time doesn't heal this wound—it only stops the pain from completely destroying you.

AN INVESTIGATION SUCH as the one HPD's Homicide Division was looking at postmurder could get out of control quickly. It took a delicate hand to keep things under control. Dead people—especially victims of murder—reveal a story; their lives, told from the grave, paint a picture. Working example: On July 22, 2003, four days after the murders, HPD got word of a man, Jason Uolla, who had been beaten with a baseball bat and left for dead in the parking lot of the apartment complex where he lived. Uolla had attended Marcus's funeral. He hung around with Marcus. He knew Adelbert through Marcus.

He was known as "JU"; and he was someone HPD had been looking at, without telling the families, as a potential suspect.

"He was on the radar screen . . . for the killing," one detective said.

Ladd was focused on JU. In talking to many of the people inside a local group of dope dealers, HPD learned that Marcus was looking to become what one detective described as a "big-time dealer," according to JU. The supplier JU used, whom JU viewed as one of the biggest connections in the Houston area, turned out to be nothing more than a mule for the *Los Zetas* in Mexico and had been, HPD confirmed, skimming off the top of whatever load he transported for the *Los Zetas*. The *Zetas,* as they are known, according to government sources, is "the most technologically advanced, sophisticated and dangerous cartel operating in Mexico" today. This is a gang, it should be noted, that does not negotiate. They do not tolerate theft. They do not take kindly to punk kids trying to rip them off, or skimming from the top. They don't ask questions. They kill you. Period.

JU's connection was ultimately whacked himself, along with his girlfriend inside a Clear Lake City hotel. The HPD knew that JU, Marcus "and even Adelbert" were naïve to the fact that they were messing with big-time players in the drug world.

Now JU lay in a hospital bed, his skull beaten so badly with a baseball bat that he had been transferred to a second hospital, where a neurosurgeon was waiting to operate and relieve pressure accumulating on the young man's brain.

It was always tough for a cop to get information out of friends and family gathering at a hospital, milling about the waiting area, wondering whether to plan a celebration or funeral, trying to come to terms with the idea that a loved one, no matter what he's done throughout his life, was inside an operating room, fighting. Nonetheless, a quadruple homicide had taken place—and the trail led to JU.

Ladd did some digging and found out that JU had gone over to a friend's house (a girl who had dated Adelbert at one time and had been with him recently). As the first story of what happened went, JU was there with his girlfriend (a dancer at the Club Atlantis, another Houston area strip joint). They fell asleep. At one point during the night, JU went out to his car to get some clothes. Someone—or a group of people—must have been waiting for him. Because, one source claimed, "unknown suspects" came up and "struck [JU] with a baseball bat." The attack took place, HPD was certain, inside the parking lot of the Bayridge Apartments, in League City, just south of Clear Lake.

A League City patrol officer had interviewed JU's sister at the hospital.

"He's in critical condition," she said. The girl was a mess. Crying.

Shaking. Unsure of whether her brother was going to pull through. The brain can only take so many shots without sustaining irreversible damage. If JU made it through, was he going to be in a vegetative state?

"Any idea what happened?" the officer asked.

"None . . . but I'm concerned about a possible tie to what happened in Clear Lake because Jason was a friend of . . . Marcus's."

"They knew each other well?"

"Jason had seen Marcus two hours before the murders!" she said, impassioned by this piece of information. The girl also mentioned how she was under the impression that the cases were related because she had heard that one of the victims in Clear Lake had received similar injuries.

This was true, Ladd knew.

JU's friend had taken him to the hospital. An officer contacted the friend and interviewed him in another section of the hospital, where he sat with JU's brother. Word had since come down that there was a good chance JU would pull through the operation, but there was no telling how he would be afterward, or how long it would be before he was alert enough to speak.

"We just don't know," the doctor said.

JU's buddy explained what happened at Bayridge that night. He knew because he was there and had seen it. The story HPD had gotten earlier (JU heading out to his car to get some clothes) was wrong.

There was a party, the kid explained. He had also passed out, same as JU and JU's girlfriend, who had woken the friend up at about four in the morning and told him that JU was hurt badly, bleeding all over the place, out in the parking lot.

"I walked out," he explained, "and saw that Jason was bleeding from lacerations to the left side of the head."

"Was Jason awake then?"

"Yeah . . . yeah . . . he was conscious and aware of his surroundings."

"Did you two talk?"

"I offered to take him to the hospital, but he declined."

But then came a different story from what JU's girlfriend had given police. As JU's friend explained, JU didn't head outside to his car to grab a change of clothes. He and another guy at the party, Brad Carroll (pseudonym), asked JU to go out into the parking lot at about 3:00 or 3:30 A.M. "to look at a new 'system' in his car," a stereo with subwoofers and enough power to shake the windows of the car next to it at a stoplight.

"What happened when they got out there?"

The friend had asked JU that very question before JU passed out and was taken away to the hospital. "[JU] told me that when he went to go look inside the car, he was attacked from behind with a metal tube or baseball bat."

"Did he see any of his attackers?"

"Yeah, yeah. . . . He said he turned around to block the attack and saw that it was Taz Herald (pseudonym) striking him. He also said he believed it was Brad who lured him outside to facilitate the attack and that Taz was waiting for him outside in the bushes. He saw them both running away from the scene after the attack. They left in Taz's vehicle, because Brad left his car there."

"What type of car was it they left in?"

"Ah . . . um, a green Plymouth or Dodge. Brad's car is a blue Cadillac with paper plates."

Names, car models, times. This was the type of information investigators wanted.

It wasn't until an hour after the attack, when JU began to sweat and vomit, that they decided to take him to the hospital. JU didn't want to go. In the car on the way, though, he passed out. By the time they got to the emergency room (ER), JU was going into convulsions.

What was the connection between JU, Brad, and Taz? the investigator wondered.

Turned out that Brad and Taz were best friends and "had a long-standing feud" with JU and JU's brothers. Taz had even "jumped" JU a few months before the attack and had sent JU to the hospital. It all stemmed from a beating JU had put on Taz in Seabrook some months ago, and had been ultimately arrested for. It appeared this was retaliation for that beat-down, not something that was in the least bit related to the Clear Lake case. Both Taz and Brad, however, were at Marcus Precella's candlelight vigil a few nights before the baseball bat/metal pipe attack on JU and had "mad dogged" JU when they ran into him. Mad dogging is a term often associated with gay men staring at each other and locking eyes, but can also be used as an urban way to describe giving someone you are feuding with the "evil eye," if you will, letting him or her know that their "time" is coming.

Arrest warrants were issued for Brad and Taz.

Meanwhile, the following morning, JU was "able to talk," surprisingly, and had even requested a sit-down with police.

JU admitted to the ongoing feud with Taz and his brother. He said he had, in fact, jumped him. Taz had called JU, he said, on the day of Marcus's candlelight vigil and said, "I don't like you, but on this day, we should squash it for the event." *It* being the feud between them. They should act civil, in other words, for the sake of the vigil and respect to the families. "Just stay away from me," Taz said.

Ladd and his team, however, were still unconvinced that the attack on JU wasn't connected in some way to the Clear Lake homicides. The other problem investigators faced was the idea that capital murder in the state of Texas, if one was convicted and sentenced to death, truly turned into a death sentence. And murdering four people in the aggravated way that the Clear Lake case exhibited was a crime that was going to be tried under the death penalty. Everyone knew it.

CHAPTER 10

SEABROOK POLICE WERE back at the woman's house who had called in that burglary (the rifle and the pistol stolen from her father's bedroom) days before. She had heard about the attack on JU and claimed to have information.

"I spoke to [a friend] who was present when JU was assaulted in League City," she told the responding officer. "He said he saw Brad Carroll holding a handgun that night that matched the one stolen from my father's bedroom. I also heard that Brad and Taz were on their way to Florida in a Cadillac."

"That it?"

"I'll try to get the name of the city where they're heading."

WITH ALL OF THESE names—dozens coming in every day—crossing HPD Homicide Division detective Tom Ladd's desk, it was enough to drive the seasoned lawman crazy with frustration. How was he ever going to check out every single person's story? And everybody seemed to have one to tell.

"Some of [the stories]," Ladd said respectfully, "were just total BS from the beginning, and we didn't deal with them—but we *still* had to check these people out. And, of course, everything we did, everything we learned, just went right back to Marcus dealing drugs."

Ladd and his brother, between them, had spent fifty-seven years of their lives in the Homicide Division. Almost six decades searching for murderers.

"We went from kids to old men working murder cases," Ladd said with the fatigue of those years texturing his voice.

Envision the life of a Homicide Unit cop: Every day you wake up and you're looking at another dead person, and the life he or she led. You step into someone's world, begin ripping it apart, and you learn things not even their closest friends, spouses, or family members know. You get jaded after that many years wading through so much darkness. Nothing surprises you. Then you try to turn around and question family and friends about what you've learned, and sometimes the tables turn. You become the bad guy.

"Everybody we talked to kept giving us name after name after name after name," Ladd said. "We started out with four Homicide investigators on this case." (Which turned into Phil Yochum and Tom Ladd after a week or so.) "The [others] had their own cases to work," he added. "We were just overwhelmed."

"There were some idiots," Ladd said bluntly, "that led us down rabbit trails, and two or three days later, you realized that this dummy just wanted to be involved with this big, high-profile case. He doesn't know anything. He just wants to be a part of the investigation."

MILLBRIDGE DRIVE WAS designed as part of a development. When looking down on the neighborhood from a bird's-eye view, you'd see how the infrastructure of the community was laid out conducive to the profit-inspired idea of fitting the most houses into one space, while at the same time giving each piece of property its due for raising a couple of kids and maybe a dog. Millbridge is a cul-de-sac, as are several other streets in the immediate vicinity. This was one of the reasons why it had been so difficult to find Tiffany's house if you only had been over there once or twice. By the same token, if you were someone who spotted a vehicle in the neighborhood on the day of the murders, there was a good chance you'd remember— simply because most vehicles heading into a cul-de-sac are not lost drivers, kids out for joyrides, or part of the normal cycle of everyday traffic; most vehicles heading down Millbridge were driven by people who lived on the street. So a vehicle that didn't belong stood out rather sharply to the eyes and ears of the neighborhood watch.

Tips filed into HPD in a barrage of phone calls. Callers reported every type of vehicle imaginable: black truck, light blue four-door, maroon four-door, blue-green Volvo, silver two-door, brownish gray car, with patches of maroon, and so on. Dozens of concerned citizens called in any car that was seen in the neighborhood directly following the murders, some even on the day of the murders. Several reports gave descriptions where drivers and passengers were specifically mentioned: black male with white woman, white male with black female, black males, white and black males. White, black, and every ethnic race in between was reported. One caller, who refused to give his name, rattled off a list of people entering and exiting Tiffany Rowell's house during the days leading up to the murders.

Where to go from there?

George Koloroutis was a strong guy, no doubt about it. Big. Husky. He rode a Harley. At one time in his life, George was all about working out, lifting weights, and even managed a few gyms. These days George felt a little softer, but he was still, as anyone around him knew, tough as weathered leather.

"There's still muscle," George said of himself, trying to lighten the mood, "but it's underneath a layer of fat."

George had lived through the big-hair days of the 1980s and came out the other end with a few war stories of his own. He understood that kids getting out of high school liked to go wild a little bit. Yet, this full-bodied man, who had prided himself in being able to take care of his family financially, emotionally, and certainly physically, had been brought to his knees by the savage murder of his daughter Rachael. Her death was, of course, devastating to the Koloroutis family. As the one-week anniversary of Rachael's murder came to pass, George and his family were beside themselves with grief. They didn't know what to do. George had been in management his entire professional life; he had run small and large companies. He knew how to get things done. George had people working under him. He could delegate. He could ask someone to step it up when he wasn't satisfied. In that respect George would be the first to admit that he was a bit of a control freak. The way he dealt with things was to jump in headfirst, take a look around, and find out where he was going to be most useful; then he would get busy making things happen. With his daughter's murder, about the only thing George Koloroutis could do at this stage was pray that those responsible were soon caught and brought to justice—and justice, at least in this type of case, meant a last meal, a T-shaped, padded table, maybe a priest or cleric, if you believed, and then a cocktail of Sodium Pentothal, pancuronium bromide, and potassium chloride—the one chemical that ultimately stops the heart and shuts out the lights for good. Texas courts do not mess around when it comes to carrying out death sentences, George understood. Texas was on the top of the executions-by-state list, beating out its closest competitor by hundreds of executions; Harris County alone had put more criminals on death row than any other *state.* By the end of the year 2003, Texas would execute twenty-four males, from all walks of life. And by George's estimate, nothing less would suffice for those responsible. And if the state didn't get to them, George was considering (although not telling anyone) a plan to take care of his daughter's killer or killers himself.

George liked Tom Ladd's style: that old-school investigator type who didn't take crap from anyone. Ladd was a guy who went about his business the way he thought was best for the case, told people exactly how he felt about them, and didn't give a damn what the brass said.

Bust the door down first, ask questions later.

George could relate.

"Tom is a tough old guy," George observed. "We developed the kind of relationship that was respectful. . . . I would cry—literally—on his shoulder. A tear from Tom is like a hand over your shoulder to console. The guy has seen more stuff than we'll *ever* imagine."

Ladd could sense George's pain. He knew how badly a family that lost a child suffered, with no end seemingly in sight. Not to mention, as journalist Lisa Miller writes in her book *Heaven*, how that overwhelming grief and numbing pain of losing a child "obliterates everything else." You feel like you'll never laugh again. That you have no more tears left to cry. That pang of numbness is always there. You're angry and on edge. And all these feelings, wherever they're stored in the emotional psyche, can come up for no reason. Ladd had dealt with plenty of families in similar situations; he knew George was volatile and apprehensive, ready to burst.

As George made himself more available to Ladd as the days went on, Ladd realized something else. It was obvious that George was going to be involved in this case on an inherent level, placing him in the faces of the Homicide Division, likely, on a weekly, if not daily, basis. It was clear George was not going to let this go until his daughter's killer was behind bars. As deeply hurt and beaten up by his daughter's death as he was, George Koloroutis knew that keeping focused on catching Rachael's killer was going to help him through that endless well of anguish and pain. The man saw a light. He needed to find its source.

"How are things going, Tom?" George called and asked one afternoon. George had phoned the detectives on call and/or Tom Ladd just about every day since Rachael's funeral. Here it was July 29, now eleven days after the murders, and it seemed HPD didn't have a clue as to what had happened inside Tiffany Rowell's house. News reporting of the murders had dropped off considerably. Homicide hadn't mentioned it was onto something, per se. Thus, any armchair investigator, or anyone who has watched his share of *CSI, Forensic Files,* or any other crime show, knew that each day past the date of the crime—those prized forty-eight hours postmurder—was a mile further from catching the perpatrator(s).

"Not too bad, George," Ladd said. He didn't know what to tell the guy. "We're working on some things."

Things: such a relative, shallow term.

"Let me know if I can help," George offered. There, between both men, was an unspoken commitment that these two strong personalities respected. George was saying, without coming out with it, that he was *not* going to let this go for too much longer. Ladd knew it had been George at the crime scene on the night of the murders, and cops nearly had to restrain him.

Guys like that, Ladd thought, you had to take it easy with them; the pain was dictating George's actions, especially this early.

GEORGE KOLOROUTIS WAS born in Washington, grew up an army brat while traveling the world with his parents—Germany, Boston, New Jersey, Texas—and then he settled back in Washington as a married man with three kids. As the children grew, George was offered a job at a company that had an office opening in Houston, and he was asked if he wanted to move south and run it.

"We had a wonderful life," George said of his days with Ann and the kids in Olympia, Washington, and even later, when they first moved to Texas.

George went south first, before his wife and kids, making the move to the nation's second largest state (area and populationwise). There was quite a bit of difference between Washington and Texas. But that was okay. George and Ann were up for the move. George traveled down before the rest of them and lived in corporate housing for 120 days to check things out and look for a home. The Clear Lake area, for no apparent reason, drew George in. He soon found a nice house with a yard in Clear Lake City.

Then something strange happened—at least it seemed so when George looked back on it later.

As George was looking around at different houses, a very high-profile abduction case hit the news. The abduction had taken place right there in the Clear Lake region. George couldn't believe it. The crime terrified and shocked him. Here he was moving his family to a foreign place, and this ghastly crime involving a young child was in his face.

"It made a lot of press. . . . She was taken and murdered."

George asked his Realtor about the case, which was all anybody talked about as he prepared to sign a contract for a house that he had found.

"I remember having the thought as the Realtor and I spoke," George recalled, " 'God, I hope nothing ever happens to my little girls.' "

The middle child, Rachael, and her sisters acclimated themselves well to their new surroundings and the new curriculum, which was somewhat different in Texas than it had been in Washington. As she grew, it was clear to George and Ann that Rachael was mama's girl, as opposed to her older sister, Lelah, who was daddy's girl. As a small child, Rachael was quiet and docile, laid-back, like her mother. In a sense, George said, when she got into her late teens, Rachael developed into "a rare combination of her mom and me—easy to get along with and kindhearted (her mother), but stubborn as hell (me). . . . Like me, too, Rachael liked [what life had to offer]. She loved a good movie, a good meal, and just loved the things that I did."

Rachael was all about the color purple. She adored drawing, coloring, doodling. She was a Barbie girl, in the sense that she loved playing with the dolls. She and Lelah, her older sister by a year and change, were inseparable when growing up. Together every day, they were close enough in age that they got along instead of competing. So close, in fact, they had made up their own language.

The family attended church and became involved with many of the programs revolving around the church. They donated a lot of their time, believing that giving back was something anyone blessed with prosperity, such as they were, should do. The girls and their mom joined the theater group at church. They loved it: playing different roles, entertaining churchgoers with big productions. Lelah wrote many of the plays. Rachael acted and directed, but soon became involved with the youth groups, helping the younger girls, serving as church counselor with Lelah, going to summer camp and helping out.

Life was on a fast track—and much of it was flawless bliss. The Koloroutises were the quintessential American family, enjoying the fruits of their work in the community and from George's success in his professional life. They gave back. They enjoyed life together.

Then another side of Rachael emerged, George explained, as she grew from her junior high years into a teenager and entered high school.

"She liked to party—and that's how she ended up with that group of friends in Clear Lake she was involved with."

Despite a proclivity to go out partying with friends once in a while, Rachael picked up a fondness for, George noted, "police work." Rachael was from the *Law & Order, NCIS,* and *CSI* era of television. She simply *had* to watch those types of shows every week. It was one of her vices: a dose of crime television. And through that, one would imagine, she developed a fevered passion for going into law enforcement, dreaming of one day becoming a female FBI agent.

"Whenever I'd go to D.C. on business," George remembered, "I'd bring her back something with the FBI symbol on it, a shirt, jacket, or something. She loved that."

Everyone agreed on one thing where it pertained to Rachael: She was a "very soft-spoken, kindhearted girl." When she was younger, Rachael was the kid who stood beside her dad, grasping his leg, twisting a lock of her hair, not speaking a word. Yet, at the same time, she was watching your every move, sizing you up. "Shy" was what girls like Rachael were sometimes called. But that was a simple explanation for a complicated girl, who was not necessarily cautious or nervous around others more than she was curious and wanting to know you before she allowed you access into her world.

Then Rachael went through a period where her hair was all over the place, bushy and plain-looking, and her teeth were big and crooked. But George and his wife got their girl braces, and Lelah taught her little sister how to fix her hair, and everything changed. Rachael came out the other end "stunningly beautiful," George said proudly. She was five feet four inches, and very thin. She was a petite girl, now with a smile that could grace the cover of any magazine. She had the looks and body of a supermodel, a sweet and genteel personality to go with it. Rachael was on her way. She had even met and started to date a popular boy (who had gone off to college the year before she was murdered, according to George) at Clear Lake High School.

Rachael seemed happy.

Like most teenagers, Rachael led two lives—the one at home (the churchgoer, family person, responsible young adult getting ready to go off to college) and the one out in the social world of high school and "Teen Land," where you were judged on everything you did. Not that Rachael was two different people, consciously splitting her personality to satisfy both sides. George pointed out that that was "not at all what" he meant by agreeing his daughter led two separate lives. Rachael was like any other teen who acted one way around friends, another way around family. It's part of growing up. A rite of passage into the adult world through that sieve of teen intercession. Maybe even a survival mechanism for kids in a tough world today of bullying and being constantly judged by what you wear, the music you listen to, and the people with whom you hang around.

This problematic period of her life began when Rachael entered those final years of high school. Part of it had to do with a bad acne problem Rachael developed during those years, George was convinced, and the fact that Rachael began taking a popular prescription drug for that skin problem. Her "behavioral problems" and going on that drug coincided with each other. George was certain of the connection.

"We had at first attributed the problems to me and Rachael's mother being overprotective of our girls. We didn't let them go out and do a bunch of stuff, and you could have called us 'very strict.' "

So when Rachael began to get into things, especially after high school, when she expressed a desire to move in with Tiffany in Clear Lake City, George believed part of it was due to Rachael wanting to "go wild a little bit and enjoy some freedom" from her overbearing parents. Many kids do this. That first year out of high school, if the kid doesn't head directly off to college, becomes a transitional year; it's a time to think about the road ahead, and what life was going to offer.

When Rachael went on that acne drug, she was prescribed forty-five milligrams a day. It was early in the life of the drug.

"Today," George said, "you can't get over twenty milligrams, and only one out of every ten dermatologists will put a kid on the stuff because of all the class-action lawsuits related to [it]."

The side effects most associated with this particular drug include mood swings, an increased rate of suicide, colitis, Crohn's disease, inflammatory bowel disease, severe depression, liver damage, and so on.

"We wonder when we look back over that last two years of her life, if *some* of her acting out was related to taking that drug."

George wasn't blaming the drug for his daughter's risky behavior. But as many of the witnesses coming forward had explained to Tom Ladd and Phil Yochum, Tiffany and Rachael were exceptionally naïve to their surroundings and the people they hung around with in Houston. Casual drug use—picking up some cocaine on a Friday night and having a party with friends at the house, snorting a couple lines, having some beers, talking all that gibberish about saving the world people high on coke often do—was certainly one thing. Dealing grams and "eight balls" (an eighth of an ounce) was quite another.

CHAPTER 11

Rachael Koloroutis met Tiffany Rowell at Clear Lake High School in 1999. They became best friends almost immediately. If Clear Lake High sounds familiar in the realm of crime circles, it is probably because during a period between September and October 1984 the school was thrust into the national spotlight when six students supposedly made what some claimed was a "suicide pact" and killed themselves. The story drew the *New York Times* and other major media outlets.

This idea that students had all agreed to commit suicide together, however, turned out to be something of an urban legend.

"Rumors of a pact in which 20 to 30 students swore to commit suicide within six weeks," a *Times* article written in late 1984 noted, "were generated by a student who, according to the students and counseling staff, circulated the story 'as a lark.'"

Prank or not, the school had quite the reputation before it was tarnished by this dark cloud. If not for that one instance of gossip getting out of control, Clear Lake High was celebrated for producing some of the more engaging star athletes in professional sports: Major League Baseball relief pitcher Jon Switzer, National Football League players Craig Veasey, Jeff Novak, and Seth and Steve McKinney, and even Ultimate Fighting Championship tough man Mike Swick. Besides, could you ask for anything more American than having your school colors as red, white, and blue? In addition, Clear Lake High School catered to a majority of kids whose parents were oil company execs and NASA employees, and so the hierarchy had a bar set fairly high for a good portion of the students. Many came from money.

And according to one news report, within that social pyramid: "Rachael Koloroutis and Tiffany Rowell stood on top."

Like any high school, Clear Lake was no different when it came to cliques and various groups of kids chastising one another for reasons we know all too well. Tiffany and Rachael, though, were never like that. They were more of the celebrity type: the pretty girls walking through the halls whom every boy wanted to date, but wouldn't dream of asking for fear of being rejected. And even that would be a misconception, a judgment; because Tiffany and Rachael were, by far, more approachable, according to former students and friends, than most other girls in the school. They were well liked, and kind to everyone, regardless of his or her status. Didn't matter who you were, where you were from, how much money your parents had. They were in total accord with helping out whomever they could.

Tiffany had dreams of going into social work. Some said she was a very "talented actress."

Rachael and her sister Lelah, a senior when Rachael and Tiffany were juniors, met Tiffany together, but it was Rachael who became closer to Tiffany Rowell. Tiffany's mother had died not long after Rachael and Lelah had befriended her. Tiffany had hit a rough patch in her young life, having just lost the only woman she had ever known as a mother (Tiffany was adopted at a young age). Her life had been overwhelmed with grief at a time when it should have been filled with wonder and anticipation of what was around the corner. In this respect Rachael filled an important role in Tiffany's life, and Tiffany understood and appreciated it greatly.

Rachael and George had talked about Rachael joining the Reserve Officers' Training Corps (ROTC). Undecided on which branch of the military she wanted to go into, the ROTC could fill that desire Rachael had expressed for law enforcement. Every division of the military had a criminal investigation unit of some sort. The ROTC was a good place to begin that career path. Rachael would learn discipline and routine and possibly earn a scholarship. She'd be taught leadership skills, something her father had already given her in genes. She could step into military life as an officer, essentially. Nothing would make George and Ann Koloroutis happier than to see Rachael get involved with the ROTC program.

Rachael was supposed to join her sister at college after what her father described as Rachael's one "wild and crazy summer," which now included Rachael moving into Tiffany's house. Rachael had a plan—she just wasn't following it immediately after graduation, and this greatly frustrated her mother and father.

Lelah had been enrolled at the University of North Texas in Denton, and Rachael was planning on doing the same. UNT was where Rachael could enter into that ROTC program. From there she could do whatever she wanted.

"Because there were some behavioral issues there during that last year or so of her life," George said later, "I thought the structure of the air force (which Rachael had finally decided on) would be good for her. She did, too. She agreed with the plan."

George was all about helping his kids organize and plan their lives. He had sat down with Rachael more than once and talked about what she was going to do. Yet Rachael, George pointed out with a laugh, "had become a staunch liberal by the time she was a junior in high school." Being a GOP man himself, George admitted this caused some friction; and they butted heads over those differences more than once.

"When she got an idea in her mind," George said, "there was no changing it. That was it."

That stubbornness on Rachael's part, however, would help her in life, George knew. When she put her mind to something, Rachael generally did it.

Ann Koloroutis saw this side of Rachael, too—more so during Rachael's senior year at Clear Lake High School. Rachael and her mother were not on good terms when Rachael left the house to go live with Tiffany. There had been an issue between her mother and father, and Rachael had no choice but to side with her dad. Still, Rachael had confided in her mother about a girl in school who had been picked on and laughed at by many of her classmates. Rachael said she and Tiffany had stepped in and befriended the girl, who was a year behind them. They both felt sorry for her.

Her name was Christine Paolilla. Christine was a short, somewhat cheery, not too overly confident transplant to suburban Houston (the town of Friendswood, just over the Clear Lake city limit). Christine suffered from a rare condition that made her hair fall out: alopecia (defined simply as "loss of hair"). It's a debilitating disease for women—the pain being more cosmetic than necessarily physical. Because it is such an obvious condition when a breakout occurs, it can turn quickly into psychological trauma because of the stigma attached.

Christine lost her father when she was two years old (he died in a tragic construction accident, she said, but would add later that "he was also a heroin addict"). She'd had alopecia for as long as she could recall. She wore wigs and painted on her eyebrows, always trying to do the best she could with what she had.

"But it made her look like a clown at times," remarked one source.

And this only added to the peer punishment she endured at school.

There was also the pockmark Christine had of having a mother who, at one time, had some rather well-known problems with drugs herself.

Rachael and her mom pulled up to the school one morning and there was Christine waiting by the door.

"That's her, Mom," Rachael said, pointing.

Ann looked. It wasn't hard to tell who her daughter was referring to. Christine looked homely and out of place.

"People make fun of her," Rachael said.

Rachael and Tiffany didn't much like the idea that students razzed Christine. It wasn't Christine's fault she was born with the affliction. Rachael and Tiffany had reached out to Christine not long after Christine had moved into town. They helped her pick out better wigs, more trendy and modern. They consulted with her on makeup.

From the time she showed up on the Clear Lake scene, until she met Tiffany and Rachael, Christine was unattractive and shabby. You could tell by looking at her that there was something not right about her appearance. That clown reference was also made by more than one person—and it wasn't always meant in a bad way. It was mainly the best description of how she wore her eyebrows, the way she overdid the rouge and makeup, and wore gaudy wigs seemingly to make up for and take the focus off the hair loss.

But not long after hooking up with Tiffany and Rachael, things changed for Christine. She started to look better. You really had to look closely to figure out there was something different about her—

something missing. In fact, Christine was so grateful and became such good friends with Rachael, especially, that Rachael kept a photo Christine had given her in one of her pocketbooks. Christine was open about how she felt. On one side of the standard class photo was a smiling Christine, wearing a long-haired reddish wig, a bright and boastful smile, maybe too much lipstick, a garish, bulky chain around her neck, and a white blouse. Still, she looked good. Even happy. She wore that broad smile proudly, it appeared. *Damn,* Christine wrote on the back of the photo, *we've had some crazy memories.* She mentioned how she and Rachael had always been there for one another. There was even some illusion to a romantic tryst they might have been involved in together; both girls were obviously experimenting—if only jokingly—with their sexuality. Christine mentioned how she would never forget their " 'special' friendship." Christine even wrote *I love you* with text symbols before signing her name.

And what a year 2003 turned out to be for Christine Paolilla at Clear Lake High—after Rachael and Tiffany had taken her under their wing and mentored her. Because of all the work Rachael and Tiffany had put into helping Christine's appearance, the homely-looking girl who wore the bulky Halloween-like wigs had "transformed herself," ABC News later reported, "from an awkward misfit into a high-school Cinderella."

Yes, indeed. Christine was even voted "Miss Irresistible" at Clear Lake High that same year.

"They did it because they felt that she was the person who they just loved," Christine's mother, Lori Paolilla, told ABC's *20/20,* "because of the way she was, the person she was."

After Tiffany and Rachael graduated, they somewhat lost touch with Christine, who still had a year of school left, and was rumored to have taken off somewhere with a boy. No one had really seen Christine around much. The girls knew that Christine, who had turned seventeen on March 31, 2003, was going to come into a truckload of money on her eighteenth birthday, a year away. On the day she turned eighteen, Christine could draw on a trust established for her after her father's accidental-death insurance paid off.

Christine was slated to receive what one report claimed was a whopping $360,000, a lot of money for anyone, but especially for an eighteen-year-old kid.

Yet, that friendship that Rachael had had with Christine, and the way she reached out to her and helped the girl through a tough time, proved to family members that Rachael's life at Tiffany's house was an ample reflection of the person she had *never* been. Rachael was a giver, not a taker. It was now the beginning of August 2003 and HPD could not tell the Koloroutis family, or any of the other families, that they were closer to solving the case.

On balance, justice was about all the families had left. Mercy, too, would come later, when the perpetrator was behind bars and true healing could begin. But right now it was about HPD catching a break.

Just one solid lead.

CHAPTER 12

TOM LADD SAT down and looked at this case on some days and became frustrated for the lack of manpower helping him. Ladd would stomp his feet, say a few words to his captain, then hit the brick, find a witness who brightened his spirits a little, and remind himself that the case *was* solvable. With enough luck, on top of some shoe-leather police work, the case could be closed.

A friend of JU's came forward one afternoon with a theory that seemed credible. If for nothing else, this new information put Ladd and the HPD deeper into the ominous drug culture that Marcus was getting himself more deeply involved in as each day of the 2003 summer came to pass.

Talking to the kid, Ladd felt right away he was onto something. For one, the kid had no trouble saying that JU, who was still recuperating from that violent thrashing he took to the head with a bat/pipe, was into selling all sorts of drugs: cocaine, Ecstasy (X), marijuana, Xanax (he called them Z-Bars), you name it. But JU also sold codeine syrup and something called "wet" and "hydro," embalming fluid–dipped marijuana joints, which gave the user an entirely different angel dust–like high. You could even dip a cigarette in the fluid and get off. Embalming fluid used in this manner is powerful stuff, toxic and highly dangerous to the nervous system. You start smoking wet joints/cigarettes and you might as well pack it in, because you're now on a treacherous path. There is no turning back. The side effects from this stuff alone range from convulsions to muscular rigidity to coma and, of course, death.

By the time the kid finished naming off all the drugs JU sold, Ladd wondered if there was a drug JU *hadn't* pushed. Add to that the idea that Marcus had reportedly owed JU $10,000, something the HPD was beginning to hear from several witnesses, and Ladd could not, with any seriousness, scratch JU off what was a short list of suspects. If anything, it was time to put JU on the top of the list.

Listening to the kid talk, essentially dropping a dime on someone he described as a "good friend," Ladd could almost hear George Koloroutis in his ear on the day he explained the Marcus-JU connection: *"It's got to be Jason U. It's got to be."*

A DAY LATER things became even more interesting. Tom Ladd's sergeant, G. J. Novak, handed the detective a fax he had received earlier that day. It was from Ladd's new best friend, George Koloroutis.

Ladd took the fax pages, walked back to his desk, sat down, then flipped the cover page over and read.

George had done some online sleuthing. He had discovered what he felt might be useful information. While surfing on a few Internet comment chat boards—those public forum spaces on news sites underneath an article, where anyone who has a PC or, nowadays, a cell phone can pop in and comment about anything—George noticed some chatter about the case.

In the fax cover letter, George spelled out the access codes and website addresses for Ladd, so the detective could go to the source himself. He also included several pages of posts within the body of the fax.

The ones that concerned George most had been posted by someone online calling him- or herself "Faith1581."

Each post was signed as "Someone Who Knows."

George was firm in his instructions to the Homicide Division: *Don't know if this person really "knows" or not—but this has to be looked at.*

The first comment George pointed to was rather cryptic and unhelpful in and of itself. Back on July 21, at 10:42 P.M., Someone Who Knows said too many people who didn't know a damn thing were talking "smack" about the case and what actually happened inside the house. There was some mention of "the MEDIA," which, by all rights, is almost always wrong where some of its early reporting comes into play on any high-profile murder case.

Someone Who Knows wrote to a previous commenter on the news article in question: **All you know are what people are telling you. . . .**

Then Someone Who Knows went on to say how the truth hurts: **So does it hurt much?**

Within ten minutes of the first comment, Someone Who Knows had posted two additional comments. The second was as mysterious as the first, but George was convinced the "poster," as he called the commenter, "more than subtly" suggested that "he/she 'knows' things." It was the final sentence in the comment that George was most interested in. Someone Who Knows seemed to be angered by the fact that people were taking what the media had to say as gospel, concluding: **You will never know the things I know.**

Three minutes later, Someone Who Knows was talking about the four victims having been at the wrong place, at the wrong time, telling the comment board how "far" away "from knowing the truth" they all were.

Ladd thought about this. To say that two people who lived in a house "were at the wrong place" was ignorant and a shot in the dark, at best. George believed it would all have to be checked into further. Yet, in the scope of what had been written, it appeared Someone Who Knows knew about as much as anybody else.

Which was, at this point, just about nothing.

CHAPTER 13

THE CONVERSATION TOOK place a few days after the Clear Lake murders. Tom Ladd and Phil Yochum were just learning about it, though, on August 4, 2003, when a tip to go interview a known Houston drug dealer spending some time in Montgomery County Jail for failure to appear on an aggravated robbery charge came in. It seemed to be the first concrete lead to a potential suspect—someone they had on radar already—HPD had gotten thus far.

There had been a vigil held by victims' friends and family on Millbridge Drive in front of the house a few days after the murders. People were beside themselves, not knowing what to do. You could only put so many Blessed Virgin Mary and Jesus candles, flowers, photos, roadside crosses, and other trinkets in front of the house as memorial remembrances. In light of how many people were struggling to cope, candles in hand, some words of inspiration and grace could go an awfully long way toward finding a road that would lead them toward the process of understanding and mending. One didn't heal from a loss of this nature; one simply accepted it and moved forward with life.

The Montgomery County Jail confidential informant (CI) told Ladd that a friend of his girlfriend's had seen someone she knew on television walking with the vigil group. So the CI called the kid to see what he knew about the murders. The CI gave Ladd and Yochum the kid's name, Billy (pseudonym).

"I specifically asked him if he had sent his brother to do the killings," the CI explained to Ladd.

"Nope," Billy responded during that phone call with the CI. "I sent my *homeboy*. . . . He did the job!"

"Who's that?"

Billy wouldn't say.

"But I know," the CI told Ladd, "who he is. . . ." He gave the name to the detective, referring to the "homeboy" as "a Mexican dude."

DETECTIVE SERGEANT TOM Ladd had been thinking about retiring. On some days the thought was a peaceful one. Now would be the best time to squeak out a good twenty years of life without having to spend his days looking for thugs. On the other hand, detectives do not like to walk away from the job with cases left unsolved. But what could Ladd do? He had several unsolved murder cases and not enough manpower to work them. This Clear Lake case had turned into one witness after the next coming in to give up a new name. It took lots of man-hours to track down witnesses and potential suspects and interview each one.

As August passed and September settled in, Ladd realized that, as much information as they had been collecting, none of it was bringing him closer to an end result. Everyone was willing to come in and drop a name, but each time HPD checked it out, it led to a "maybe" or a "possibly." Nothing definitive. JU's name kept coming up in conversation. On paper JU was a prime suspect. George Koloroutis believed JU was their man, as did other family members. And George and the others were not waning when it came to keeping the Clear Lake case in front of the media and their faces in front of HPD.

"George was the spark," Ladd said later. "Basically, it was George who kept the interest up in the newspapers and in the department. Koloroutis is a good guy. He always wanted to know this and know that. I spent more time talking to George than I did my own lieutenant on this case!"

Still, there comes a time in a person's life, Ladd said, when "you just have to stop. You cannot keep going on, investigating murders until you're ninety years old."

With that, Ladd knew that by the end of spring, the following year, 2004, he was going to be spending his days with his grandkids and his family. Watching television all day, or whatever the heck he wanted to do with his time. But no more murder. No more bureau-cratic PC nonsense. No more BS.

There was a young detective in the squad room who had been with HPD for eight years. He poked his nose around the Clear Lake case every so often, adding two cents where he could, making his theories known to Ladd and Yochum, even helping out once in a while.

Ladd understood this case needed to be solved and, more impor-tant, it was a solvable case. Some aren't. Some murders you take a look at after they run cold and you know that without a suspect com-ing forward, or an admission somewhere, they'll never be resolved. But the Clear Lake case didn't have that feel.

As September met October, Ladd became involved in a major homicide case within the department, a cop-involved shooting. The lieutenant wanted Ladd to handle the case because he had some ex-perience with these types of delicate investigations. It was going to cause some trouble for everyone involved and had to be handled with care. The right person was Tom Ladd—that is, if you ask brass. To Ladd, a cop-involved shooting was not the type of case he wanted to go out on. But he had no choice, essentially.

Detective Brian Harris was that young, fiery investigator, passion-ate about his work, a certified expert in interrogation, who could take over the Clear Lake case and look at it with a fresh set of eyes. Harris was the man Ladd looked to when it appeared Ladd could not devote the time and attention he wanted to it anymore.

"I got Harris involved because I needed help. He was young, full of piss and vinegar, and just a good, *good* kid."

Lots of mutual respect there between these men.

The Clear Lake case and the days ahead were going to take a tough, tenacious cop—someone who could overlook all the non-sense and move forward in spite of the obvious obstacles.

Harris had the desire; Ladd knew this from speaking to him and watching him work on other cases.

"I knew Harris would *work* this case."

Important word there: *work*. Harris would put in the effort—and more.

"Hey, Brian," Ladd said one day. "You want this?"

Harris was already working it. He had been helping Ladd out when he could spare the time. Harris knew the case well already.

"He's kind of a cocky little [thing]," Ladd explained. "But a good guy. The perfect cop for this case. A lot of people think *I'm* a cocky big [thing], but, hey, it is what it is."

Harris worked the day shift, the only reason why the Clear Lake case wasn't his to begin with. Harris had spent years on nights and paid his dues.

From the first moment, Harris saw the Clear Lake murders as a major investigation. It struck him as peculiar right away, actually, when he didn't see an entire task force formed to solve it.

"There were initially six to eight people working on it," Harris recalled. "But after about a week, they had their own cases to work on and it came down to Tom and Phil."

Every time Harris ran into Ladd and asked about it, Ladd brought up JU, mentioning how JU was likely their guy. They just didn't have enough for an arrest warrant.

Harris was with Ladd and the lieutenant one afternoon when he overheard them talking about Ladd and his retirement.

"Look, Tom, you cannot have a quadruple and retire," the lieutenant said respectfully, perhaps hoping to get a few more years out of Ladd. "You're not going to be able to retire until you solve that case. We cannot have a case like that unsolved and the lead detective retiring."

"Well, you know . . . ," Ladd said. He talked about the controversial police shooting he was now responsible for investigating. He was swamped with work. Ladd knew the district attorney's office and HPD brass would be, in his words, "up his ass," with the DA and the review boards wondering and waiting on word about the police shooting. Those cases have a tendency to take up a lot of time, be it PR or interviewing witnesses and piecing together what happened.

Standing there, explaining himself to his boss, Ladd had bags under his eyes that he'd had forever, it seemed. He smelled of cigarettes, the nicotine and tar radiating from his pores. His skin was yellowed. He looked fifteen years older than his years and felt it.

"How the hell am I going to be able to do it?" Ladd said, responding to the lieutenant.

"We'll help you out," the lieutenant offered.

Ladd stopped in his tracks. *Help?* It seemed like a foreign word.

"Yeah?" Ladd said.

"We'll put a couple of guys on it."

Brian Harris was standing there. Harris had already been helping.

"Great," Ladd said. He didn't believe it.

"Whatever you need, Tom. I'll give you Brian. He can field some calls during the day. Help you out where he can."

Harris lighted up. So did Ladd.

"Yes," Ladd said. "We'll have a meeting today, two o'clock." He walked away. If they were serious, they'd be at the meeting.

Ladd went and printed what he had. He gave the reports and copies of some of his notes to Harris.

As Harris read through it all, he knew he was stepping into a career case. He wanted to dive right in.

That same afternoon Ladd came to the table—that meeting—and said, "Look, we need to look at each victim. Basically do a psychological autopsy on each victim. Brian, your job is now looking at Adelbert Sánchez and tearing his life apart. Relationships. Family. Anything at all that could have led to his murder."

Harris liked Ladd's style. Sounded like a decent plan.

CHAPTER 14

ONE OF THE first things Brian Harris did was familiarize himself with the case on an intrinsic level. He sat and read through the reports, closely taking in everything he could, paying mind to the notion that he needed to develop a strategy—of course, all under Tom Ladd's direction. Ladd was still running the show.

Two names popped out to Harris immediately: Michelle and Craig Lackner. The Lackners were the couple who lived next door to Tiffany Rowell and had reportedly seen two people walking toward the Rowell house on the afternoon of the murders. As Harris read through their statements, it was clear that they had likely seen what Harris now believed to have been the two murderers, or certainly two witnesses who could help move the investigation forward. Michelle Lackner had gotten out of the shower, and not long after she and her husband saw two "kids," as she and her spouse had described them, both dressed in black, walking sketchily toward Tiffany's house from the walkway out front.

Why hadn't anyone made anything more of this connection? Harris wondered.

Next door to the Lackners', two houses away from the Rowells', on the same side of the street, on that same day, July 18, Nancy Vernau was inside her living room, feeling tired and sleepy. Nancy had been a Millbridge Drive resident for twenty-seven years. She knew the ins and outs of the community, maybe better than most, and had viewed the area as a safe haven. She had retired from her kindergarten teaching job and was enjoying the golden years of her life in a place she believed, like mostly everyone else around her, to be a wonderfully—and certainly securely—suburban neighborhood, where nothing much of anything happened.

"The neighbors all get along well," Nancy said later. "We visit with each other and take care of each other."

Harris settled himself at his desk and read the interviews with these witnesses carefully. After finishing with what the Lackners had to say, Harris was interested in what Nancy Vernau had reported. In fact, he couldn't believe it.

On July 18, Nancy was waiting for someone to visit her at her Millbridge Drive home. The person had called Nancy at exactly 2:55 P.M. and said she was on her way. Nancy thought, *Heck, I have about forty-five minutes to kill. Might as well lie down on the couch and catch a little nap.* She had been working around the house and outside in the yard that day. She was bushed. It was about three o'clock when Nancy plopped down on the couch and fell asleep almost as quickly as her head hit the pillow.

Minutes later, Nancy remembered distinctively, she was startled "awake . . . [and immediately made] aware of a noise I heard coming from the general direction of, well, what I thought was Craig and Michelle's house."

The Lackners lived next door.

"I was thinking the noise was coming from [there] because I knew that Craig had been out working with tools in his yard or . . . garage."

Harris was excited about this. It was as close to eyewitness testimony of the actual time of the murders as they'd had.

To Nancy, the noise, as she stood up from the couch, sounded "like a metallic pinging sound. . . . There were two pings at regular intervals with a slight pause in between, and then a light pause, and then five *very* fast pings."

She even referred to the noises as fireworks.

Pop . . . pop.

Then . . . *pop, pop, pop, pop, pop.*

Nancy looked at the VCR on top of her television as she got up from the couch, thinking about her visitor coming over and an appointment she had later that day. The LCD clock said 3:17 P.M. on the nose as those "pings" went off.

Those *pings,* Harris knew, were Adelbert, Marcus, Tiffany, and Rachael being shot to death.

It was about three and a half hours later when Nancy Vernau and Craig and Michelle Lackner realized that what they had heard and seen, in their own separate ways, was something more than what they had originally thought: which was, at the time, nothing but the sights and sounds of life going on around them.

It was 6:45 P.M. when Nancy walked outside and considered that what she had heard earlier wasn't Craig working with his tools in the garage—it was gunfire. Looking at the Rowell house, with all the cops pacing about, all of the people around the front on the street not knowing what to do with themselves, Nancy first thought maybe someone inside Tiffany's house had had a heart attack. Then someone at the scene, a neighbor, came up to her and said, "You heard what's going on, right?"

"No. What?"

"There's been a shooting inside."

Nancy put her hand over her mouth—*Oh, my goodness.* ("I realized then that's what I had heard—and *only* at that point.")

At nearly the same moment, Craig and Michelle had been driving down Millbridge. They spotted the commotion going on next door to their house. Craig parked. They got out and walked to where Nancy stood. Craig later recalled how Nancy looked flustered.

Nancy explained what she knew.

The Lackners told Nancy what they had seen earlier: those two kids dressed in black.

"Oh my," Nancy said, "you've *got* to tell the detectives."

The Lackners found a detective, gave their statements, and eventually sat with a sketch artist. And that's where those leads had stayed, Harris recognized—with the sketch and reports inside one of many boxes marked "Clear Lake homicide."

As Harris took a look at it all with fresh eyes, he could not get over how crucial this information seemed to be to the investigation. Yet nothing had been done about any of it. Not only did it give Harris an all-important time frame for the murders, but the possibility that *two* suspects, not one, became a significant part of the focus for the first time. Two shooters might lend itself even more systematically to the drug execution-style slaying theory.

Harris immediately thought, Homicide would have to get Craig and Michelle Lackner into the station house for a sit-down and have

them take a look at a spread of photos and perhaps pick out a suspect via a photo lineup. The Lackners could be the key to identifying
the murderers and solving the case. Or at least point investigators toward additional witnesses. More than that, Harris knew while looking at the Lackners' backgrounds, they—and Nancy Vernau—were
upstanding people in the community. They had good jobs. Had
never been in any trouble. The type of untouchable witnesses a prosecutor dreamt of. The Lackners, unlike a lot of the kids lining up to
throw their friends under the first bus speeding by, could be trusted.
On the other hand, Harris needed "quality" suspects before he could
play the identification card. So, as promising as the Lackners' descriptions seemed, Harris was going to have to wait.

Harris then found out (from telephone records that had just came
in) that Rachael Koloroutis's cell phone had dialed 911 at 3:14 P.M.
and put that up against the information from the Lackners and Nancy
Vernau. Now a direct timeline came into focus. There was no one on
the other end of Rachael's phone when it called 911. Rachael—if she
was the one using the phone at the time—must have realized danger, dialed 911, but was killed before she could complete the call; or
the killers noticed what she was doing and hung the phone up. It
was still helpful information: very solid circumstantial evidence coming together to tell a story.

Then something worried Harris: *Why hadn't Tom and Phil done
anything with the sketch or any of this?*

"Tom did not release the sketch because he and Phil thought the
Lackners were possibly describing an event from the previous day,"
Harris explained later.

This comment, in all of its simplicity and perhaps assumption,
puts into play the question of how important it is for law enforcement to synchronize information as it comes in, and to work as a co-
hesive unit.

"They [Tom and Phil] also considered that those two people the
Lackners saw were drug dealers and did not want to tip them off,"
Harris added, "which would be the reason why *I* would not release
the sketches. Some said Tom and Phil simply overlooked it. But I
never thought so. Tom was a man who *always* had a strategy."

Harris wasn't going to judge. He was going to use the information, now that he knew about it, to help him solve the case.

Tom Ladd had shown the sketches to George and Ann Koloroutis weeks after the murders. Ladd arrived one day at the Koloroutis house with two photographs: one of a female, the other of a male.

"Do you recognize these people?" Ladd asked George and Ann, who said they had never seen them. Putting the photographs aside, Ladd then pulled out the sketches. "The reason I showed you those photographs [first] was because here is something that a witness reported."

George and Ann looked at the sketches, but nothing rang familiar. Weeks went by. George called Ladd and asked about the photographs and the sketches. Was anything happening with either of them?

"How come we haven't gone public with those sketches?" George pressed. It seemed like the logical next step.

Ladd said that after carefully examining the lead, the Homicide Division believed the sketches were of two people wandering through the neighborhood that day and were likely heading toward someone else's house, not the Rowell residence.

"Tom Ladd believed it was JU and some sort of a revenge killing gone wrong," one source later said. "He had good reason to make that determination. The evidence pointed in that direction."

So it was easy, in other words, for the Homicide Division to write off those sketches early on. They didn't mean much in the scope of JU and his girlfriend—the two people in the photographs Ladd had shown to George and Ann before revealing the sketches.

CHAPTER 15

THERE WAS A day some weeks later when Ann Koloroutis was reading through Rachael's autopsy report. George could not bring himself to read the report in the same manner as his wife. Ann was studying it: looking for anything HPD might have missed, or some clue the murderers might have left behind. This was their life now—George and Ann—focused on catching their daughter's killer. It was the only fuel in the tank keeping them from going insane at the thought of losing their daughter—that and the secret desire George had to find these killers before anyone else so he could execute the death penalty without a trial or verdict.

"I was fixated on the drawings accompanying the autopsy reports," George recalled. "I could not get over how many holes were in my little girl, and I am wondering, 'Who would do this?' It's driving me crazy."

And filling him with revenge and anger.

As Ann read through the report, she noticed there had been a hat found near Rachael's body. It was black.

"Wasn't the girl in those sketches Tom showed us wearing something on her head that was black?" Ann asked George.

"Yeah, you're right."

They wondered if maybe the killer had left a hat behind at the murder scene.

George got Brian Harris on the phone.

Harris told them to come down to the station.

Ann and George explained the scenario, telling Harris about Ladd and how he had shown them the photographs and then the sketches.

According to George, Harris said, "What drawings? What sketches?" It was as if Harris had not heard about them and had no idea they existed.

But Harris had never been told that the Koloroutises—or anyone, for that matter—had seen the sketches. So he really didn't know how to respond to George and Ann.

Regardless of why, or the politics involved in the reasoning, the sketches and the information surrounding them were buried under what had been, incredibly, about two hundred witness statements and one hundred additional interviews with various people involved in the case on so many different levels it was hard to keep track of anymore. Add to that the idea that up until this point there had been, at any given time, fifty-seven law enforcement personnel involved in the investigation on different levels, and you can see how easy it would be to overlook *one* item, suffice it to say when—full-time—all you had were two investigators working the case, both of whom had additional murder cases to contend with. Sifting through reports made by all those cops, along with hundreds of new leads and additional pieces of evidence being continually collected and processed, was not easy for two investigators to handle. It was a blessing, truthfully, that more had not been overlooked.

"And remember," George Koloroutis said, "there's a sense of entitlement that comes with being a victim's relative. You are not patting detectives on the back. You are constantly badgering them about the case. They do not get *any* credit whatsoever."

Whipping posts, indeed.

So there is a tremendous amount of pressure on them: from their bosses, the department, the family members of the victims, the public, the media. Everyone is looking at them to solve the cases posthaste.

Detective Brian Harris was on it now. And that's what ultimately mattered most to the families. Here was a new investigator: someone without all the baggage of the past few months trailing behind him. The only problem Harris had at this juncture was that it wasn't his case—Tom Ladd had logistical jurisdiction over everything until he retired. Harris had been brought in, yes; but he had been *assigned* to look into Adelbert Sánchez's life and background. He'd have to wait if he wanted to take things further on his own.

Harris thought about it. The Lackners and the Nancy Vernau info was too important to push aside and "get to later." He found Phil Yochum one day and asked him why the sketches had not been released. Not in a way where Harris was trying to one-up Yochum and Ladd, make them feel or look bad, but maybe they had a bigger purpose in mind: something about the sketches Harris wasn't being brought in on.

"I don't know why we didn't release them," Yochum said. "We just had so much info. Plus, the pictures resemble so many of the kids we interviewed, we just didn't do it."

Maybe the Lackners had confused the day and the people—perhaps those two kids dressed in black were friends of Tiffany and Marcus's? Michelle Lackner had said herself in her statement that people were coming and going up to the Rowell house at all hours of the night. There was also a report that Marcus and Adelbert had started hanging out in front of the house, smoking and talking, constantly looking in all directions, as if they were expecting someone, or afraid someone might sneak up on them. At a time when they had been using the backyard as a place to hang out and smoke.

Whatever the case might be, the Homicide Division had to decide what to do with the information now that it seemed important.

George Koloroutis said he wanted to gather up some funds, donations and the like, and get a reward started. Some of the other families pledged to help out. George even said he'd start a website with information about the crime and the victims, and maybe put the composite sketches on there at the right time. He planned to set up a memorial fund and offer what he hoped to be a Crime Stoppers $100,000 reward "for information leading to the arrest and charges filed in the case." George was determined. He told Brian Harris and Tom Ladd that if he couldn't come up with the money through donations, he was going to fund the reward himself.

This was huge, in Harris's view. Taken into account what the Lackners had witnessed, what Nancy Vernau had heard, a report of the Lackners' dog going uncharacteristically wild during that same time period (3:17 P.M.), and Rachael's 911 call, the case was moving forward.

Meanwhile, Harris was onto another lead regarding a relative (by marriage) of Adelbert's that Harris had traced to Jacksonville. So he contacted the Feds and made plans to head east to Florida.

For the first time in the investigation there was a sense of urgency and a feeling of the case moving. Little did anyone know then, though, that it would be an additional two and a half years, several more red herrings, and scores of interviews before detectives had those two young people dressed in black—who were, in fact, the murderers—in their direct sights.

Suspects, everyone would learn, who were in the midst of the case the entire time.

PART TWO

A FATHER'S PAIN

CHAPTER 16

GEORGE KOLOROUTIS WAS fraught. Part of the desperation and anxiety George felt was for selfish reasons, which he wasn't sharing with anyone. There was a deeper need, other than the obvious, for George to find his daughter's killer. If he could get to Rachael's murderer before police, George hoped, he could kill the perpetrator himself. The absolute terror his daughter had experienced in her final moments—her head being bashed in while she tried reaching for her cell phone to call for help—was too much for the guy to think about. He had to do something about all of the pent-up emotion and anger.

In recent days George and Ann had purchased a dog.

Sally, the boxer.

When George began to hear there was a good chance the Clear Lake murders were drug-related retaliation, or maybe even gang related, he thought it prudent to get a dog that he had been told was "as fierce as any guard dog." Boxers, which are generally stocky and squarely built, are known to be protective and can be vicious if trained properly.

"I anticipated retaliation," George said later. "In the early days we were all but sure it was [over] revenge . . . or gang related. I thought that because I was making so much noise—in the news, the papers, the community—that the killers would come to shut me up. It was weird because I was actually hopeful *and* scared. Hopeful they would come when I was there—the house was wired well and no one could get in or out without me knowing. Scared because I thought they would come when I was *not* there and kill my family."

Even Lelah was terrified, later saying, "I remember those times. I remember driving home from school every day [and] expecting to walk in and see the whole family slaughtered. I'd be panicking. In tears. Driving as fast as I could, feeling that everyone down to the dog and bird was going to be lying there [dead] when I got home. It was horrible times."

This was the sort of testimony, George added, that brought him to tears when he heard about it. "Just knowing 'her pain' related to the loss is hard to handle. When you lose a child, you suffer from your own pain. But even worse is when you think of the pain felt by the others you love, who are suffering from the same loss. It hurts like nothing else. And you are helpless and can do nothing."

Through that emotional roller coaster, George wanted to face the people who had taken his daughter's life. He welcomed the day. Ten years in prison might be worth a bullet to the head of the person who had killed Rachael and her friends. George was staying up most nights, weapon in hand, heading out to investigate every strange noise, walking the grounds of his home with a police flashlight, circling the perimeter like a burglar. I was "hoping," George put it, "those [people] would come so I could blow their . . . heads off."

Sally stayed in the house, watching over things there. George walked around the yard two or three times each night, paying special attention to a spot behind the detached garage, which was the perfect hiding place for a killer looking to silence a family.

"Sally was meant to be a guard dog—but was really a softhearted chicken," George remembered.

Through this period, every creak or noise George and Ann heard was thought to be "them," George said, "coming to get us.

"We were sort of 'out of our minds' through this period. After all, someone had slaughtered our daughter and we had no idea why."

In a weird way, George said, the unhealthy behavior (lack of sleep, festering on revenge and hate) was an imperative for this tortured father, helping him to keep his mind off the overwhelming pain. By filling his imagination with what he would do to Rachael's killers, it was almost like he was bringing Rachael back to life.

There was one day when George, Lelah, and her boyfriend went out driving through the town of Seabrook, the urban section of town

George referred to as "the bastard child of Clear Lake and Houston." Rumor was that Seabrook, or at least a small ghettoized portion of it, held a connection to the murders.

As George drove through town, he and Lelah spotted a guy who looked vaguely familiar. He had short hair to match his short stature. Looked to be about twenty. He was skinny. He also had a wiry, shifty look to him, as if he'd done his share of dope over the years.

George drove past him, then made a U-turn and doubled back.

Pulling up, rolling down his window, George said, "Hey!"

Lelah and her boyfriend looked on.

The guy turned, startled. "Yeah?"

"You know who Rachael Koloroutis and Tiffany Rowell are? Marcus Precella and Adelbert Sánchez?"

The kid thought about it. "Ah . . . yeah, as a matter of fact, I do."

"Well, then, you understand they were murdered. We're trying to find what everyone knows." George explained who he was and how they were hoping to track down information.

"I'm on my way over to a dude named Fazz's (pseudonym) house right now," the skinny kid said. "I know Rachael was over there a few nights before the murders." He pointed to the house Fazz lived in with his mother. It was right up the road.

George pulled into the driveway.

Fazz's mother walked out of the house. She and George talked. Fazz's mother said she'd had Rachael's cell phone at one time; Rachael had left it at her house. "Rachael said she was going to live at Tiffany's."

This was nothing new, of course.

Fazz soon came out of the house. "Hey," he said.

George asked him if he knew anything about the murders. They were doing a little investigation of their own. George was hoping to uncover some things.

Fazz found a spot on the ground and stared at it, hands in his pockets.

"What is it?" George pressed, walking closer toward him. Then George looked at Lelah and her boyfriend. He didn't have to say it: *This kid knows something.*

"I know a guy who knows what happened," Fazz admitted, although the statement didn't come out as sincere as they might have hoped.

Maybe he was scared?

"You'll show us where he lives?" George asked, exalted and excited, more of a demand, not so much a question.

Fazz jumped into George's car and told him where to drive. "I'll go with you."

There was a Kroger grocery store up the street. Fazz said the guy worked there. He told George to pull up in front. They could go in and talk to him.

George parked. Fazz popped out of the car quickly, and then ran into the store. As George walked in, twenty or so paces behind him, Fazz had the guy by the shirt. He was saying something to him that George couldn't hear. Fazz kept looking back at George while he was talking to the guy. It seemed to George as though the two men were almost agreeing on something.

As George later retold it, "We then pulled this guy out of the store."

Dragged him out by the shirt was more like it.

"Look, my girlfriend drove up to that house," the Kroger guy said when they got him outside and George asked what he knew. "She saw this guy run out of the house. He started chasing her. . . ."

"You saw someone running out of Tiffany Rowell's house on the day of the murders?" George asked, fairly shocked by this disclosure, wondering why in the hell this punk had never taken the information to the police.

"Yeah . . . yeah," the guy said, most of the time with his eyes locked on Fazz.

George grabbed the Kroger kid and held him down. Then he told Lelah to take his cell phone and dial up Tom Ladd.

"I've basically taken this employee out of Kroger's and I am holding him in custody," George recalled. Looking back at the situation, he realized how crazy it all was; but truly, George Koloroutis believed at that moment he had stumbled onto something big—something that was about to solve his daughter's murder.

George got Tom Ladd on the phone and explained the situation.

Ladd laid into George, yelling, "Damn it all, Koloroutis! You have to stop doing this! What the hell! You're not a damn cop."

By the end of the conversation, the guy agreed to go downtown with his girlfriend the following day and submit to an interview.

"It turned out," George later said, "that it was all just one massive lie."

The Kroger kid had made it up for some strange reason. HPD checked it out and confronted the kid, and he admitted to lying about the entire story.

But he never said why.

Sometime later, George and Ann were driving through Seabrook on George's Harley. They pulled up to Kroger. George saw the punk who had initiated the entire debacle with his ginormous lie. He stood in front of the store, on the sidewalk, with two old ladies. They smoked cigarettes.

George pulled right up on the kid, the front tire of his bike nearly brushing his leg. Without dismounting from his bike, George stared at him. There was that trademark George Koloroutis look: the sadness and intensity of a man who was looking only to find out who had taken his little girl away from him. He had the look of someone you didn't want to be messing with.

The Kroger guy's hand trembled. George could see how nervous he was as he brought the cigarette up to his mouth for a drag.

After a short time George asked, "Why did you lie to the police?"

That was all George wanted to know. Like many, George believed there were a few things you didn't meddle with in life: one of those was a father whose daughter had been murdered. George was looking into this kid's eyes for an answer. He needed something, or he was going to step off the bike and beat the snot out of him.

"Hey, man, they put that [stuff] on me," the kid said. "They put that [stuff] on me."

They? Why they *and not* he *or* she? George wondered.

"Who did?" George asked.

"They did, man. It was *them!*" The kid looked at the head of his cigarette and flicked the butt into the road and then walked back into the store as quickly as he could. He was finished talking.

George turned to Ann. "What in the hell is he talking about?"

They.

Then it hit him: *Fazz!*

When Fazz had gone into that store on the day George grabbed the kid and pulled him out, had Fazz told him to manufacture a story about the night of the murders?

HPD told George they'd look into it.

THAT WEBSITE GEORGE had promised to create with the announcement of the reward money was written and designed by him, but put together and created for the Internet by a good friend in information technology (IT), Shane Merz. MRE Consulting, in Houston, the company Merz cofounded in 1994, also gave George a substantial sum of money to put toward the reward.

"Shane is a really great guy," George said. "He put one of his key guys on building the website."

Merz was smart, too. Not every IT guy you meet has a master's degree from MIT.

The website received lots of hits almost immediately—loads upon loads of unique visitors from all over Texas and the rest of the country. People were certainly interested in looking at the info on the site (those sketches would be put up, front and center, on the home page in the coming months), on top of reading about how to get the reward money.

HPD and George decided to have someone (from George's end) monitor the site to see if a particular Internet protocol (IP) address frequented the URL; if so, there was a good chance, George knew, they had their killer out there fixated on his or her work. Many law enforcement agencies today do this to entice suspects into visiting the e-scene of the crime.

All they could do now, however, was wait to see what happened, maybe hope for a suspect to walk into the trap.

CHAPTER 17

BRIAN HARRIS WAS confident that following the evidence would lead to an arrest in the Clear Lake case. A seasoned investigator, Harris knew most cases were solved by putting together that puzzle without a picture. Websites were great tools; they could ultimately help. Interviews were supportive. Ballistics and trace evidence collection was central. Yet, catching killers was a science that hadn't changed in a century: you beat a path until a suspect emerged.

Still, tracking killers was not always what Brian Harris had in mind when he saw himself as a working adult in the real world. Quite incredibly, Harris had followed a rare, albeit interesting—and quite unbelievable—track into police work. His vocational story didn't involve some sort of a torch being passed down from one generation to the next, a proud grandpa and papa standing, clapping at Brian's graduation from the police academy, their boy following in "blue gene" footsteps.

No. In Harris's past there was nothing of the sort. Brian Harris, instead, took the *scared straight* route: some time in jail actually opened up a doorway into HPD.

Harris was born in Westchester County, New York, located near the Connecticut border; he was the youngest of five children. The television shows *T.J. Hooker* and *CHiPs* influenced young Brian, he said, about as much as playing cops and robbers had when he was a tyke running around the neighborhood. Harris thought of being a cop, but there was nothing there early on to guide him in a specific direction. It was simply a dream: *That's what I want to be when I grow up.*

After high school Brian moved to Huntsville, Texas, and attended Sam Houston State University, under the pretenses of making criminal justice his major.

"I was going to go to college in Buffalo, New York," Harris recalled. "My parents were spilt up. My dad lived down in Houston. School was a lot cheaper down there."

Brian's Texas welcome was not all that, well, welcoming. Here was an East Coast Yank, with red hair, freckles, and a small frame, trying to make a way for himself down in good ol' boy country.

Mistake number one: He went to a pool hall the second night he was in town. Hurricane Alicia had hit the Houston and Galveston region, a spinning hell of fury that had blown in and blew just about everything in its path to bits. Most notable was how the hurricane had shattered thousands of windows in downtown Houston, which made a terrific mess of the streets. The cleanup was going on when Brian arrived. He and his dad, along with a brother, were driving around, surveying the damage, checking things out. His dad pointed out the touristy spots in town, hoping to get young Brian acclimated to city life in southeast America, his new home.

Life would be different in Texas for a kid from suburban New York.

They found a local pool hall, located off a busy, bustling strip of clubs and restaurants. Brian walked over and placed some money on the side of the table so he, his bother and their dad could play the next game. This was standard practice in any bar back home. You put your coins on the table to say you wanted some action.

A group of cops happened to be inside the bar, playing pool next to the table where Brian had just put down his money.

"And we were arrested for gambling," Harris said, laughing, "by none other than the Houston Police Department."

Holy crap, Harris thought, *here I am heading to a Texas jail!*

He was just a little thing. Definitely about as un-Texan as one could be.

"I looked like I was fourteen."

Inside the jail, Harris said, he saw some things that would later shape him as a police officer; teaching him how he wanted to treat people—suspects, "turds" (Houston slang for perps), and people in general—with dignity and compassion.

They were lined up outside the jail: Brian, his dad, and several other prisoners. This short officer, a little bit of a Southern *y'all* chip on his shoulder, walked over to a tough-looking dude with some serious street battle scars.

"Were you in 'Nam?" the little cop asked.

"Yup," the guy responded.

"What division, son?"

The guy told him, or made something up that he thought the cop wanted to hear.

"Well, boy," the cop said gruffly, "did ya kill y'self any gooks?"

Sitting in the jail cell later, Brian took a look around. He saw the 'Nam guy and soon heard that the cop had beaten the snot out of him. Then there were "other things" going on that Brian didn't much appreciate (nor did he want to talk about later).

While waiting to be bailed out, Brian told himself, *I will never, ever work for the Houston Police Department.*

Never say never—because it always comes back to bite you in the ass.

Several months after the ordeal, HPD's Internal Affairs Division (IAD) contacted Brian while conducting a complete investigation into several suspected Vice Division officers shaking down clubs that refused to hire off-duty cops for security. IAD heard Brian had seen some things and was taken aback by a lot of it.

Brian never identified any of the officers, but during the interview process with IAD, he expressed how turned off he was with the Houston police force and how it had soured him about perhaps one day getting into law enforcement there in Houston. There was a chance, he said, that he wanted to get into police work, and Houston had probably been his first choice.

Not anymore.

A week went by. To the credit of the HPD, Harris said later, someone from the department called him. He was impressed.

"We'd like to try and change your mind about the Houston Police Department," the caller said. The officer had read Brian's IAD interview. "We'd like you to take a tour of the department and talk to you."

They obviously cared. There were bad apples in any government business. Perhaps, Brian now considered, he'd had the bad luck of running into all of them at once inside HPD.

Brian explained he was just getting into college and was planning to study criminal justice and law.

After a meeting with the chief—the actual chief of the department had wanted to speak to him—and a tour of the department, a spokesperson turned to Harris and said, "We hope you might change your mind, and when you're finished with school, come back and keep us in mind."

Brian Harris, a skinny kid from the East Coast, was shocked by this statement. What a turnaround. From being arrested to being offered a chance at a job.

In an unbelievable twist ending, Harris went back after school and got himself a job with HPD.

GEORGE KOLOROUTIS WAS one of those guys who couldn't sit around and do nothing. He needed to be involved: hands on. Not only did it help George cope with such an immense loss, but it kept up pressure on HPD to stay focused on the case. George knew the more he pressed, the more headway they would all make. The more he stepped back, the better the chance the case would run cold.

"I just want to be real about all of the emotions," George said, thinking back to this time. "Sure, overwhelming sadness and extreme rage were there and drove my actions. But there were days of fear, too, dictating what I did."

"That Koloroutis could be a real pain in the ass," Tom Ladd later said. "But without him, I'm not sure this case would have ever been solved."

Ladd had a tremendous amount of respect for George, as did most of the law enforcement officers involved.

George had opened up an account for the reward website, which became the Rachael Koloroutis Memorial Fund. On Monday, November 3, 2003, George drove to the Southwest Texas Bank, near downtown, to finish some business with the accounts manager of the fund.

"How are all the memorial accounts doing?" George asked.

She said fine. Things were moving in the right direction. A woman from one of the other families had been to the bank to open a memorial fund account. "She seemed very nervous," the accounts manager said.

"What do you mean?" George asked.

"She seemed more nervous about giving her Social Security number than [the death of her loved one]." The accounts manager thought the woman's behavior was out of character for someone who was supposed to be grieving. She didn't see that this person was "mourning" in the same way that George and other family members had been. The behavior concerned her.

Judgments—we all make them. Who can say how one person responds to trauma and loss as compared to another? People express grief differently.

The accounts manager explained to George that she had asked the relative if the police had any leads, or any idea about who might have killed the kids.

"What'd she say?" George wondered.

The accounts manager lowered her voice, looking from side to side as if to make sure no one was listening. "She said they—the police—knew who did it, but had to keep it on the 'down low' to protect the other children." There was also some indication about this person knowing who it was, but she was too afraid to say anything to the police in fear of other members from her family being the killer's *next* victim. "I think you need to know this, George," the accounts manager concluded.

George had that reputation of being able to get things done—the "go-to" person within all the grieving families.

"Thanks," George said.

"She called back," the accounts manager said, "and I told her I was going to have to tell the police what she said."

"Good," George added, and left.

BRIAN HARRIS STOOD by Tom Ladd, George Koloroutis, several of Marcus and Adelbert's family members, and several police officers as Crime Stoppers announced in front of a small crowd of media that HPD needed help in obtaining leads in the Clear Lake murder case. The press conference was something that needed to be done, they had all agreed.

"The plan is this," George Koloroutis told the *Houston Chronicle*, "collect as much money as possible, put it all together, and set up a supplemental reward contract with Crime Stoppers to get the word out and draw these animals out."

Animals: it was clear where George Koloroutis stood.

The best thing about George leading the crusade to find the killers from the standpoint of the families was his ability to speak to the public as a father and family man, a member of the community, but also as a guy who just wanted to find his daughter's killer. Make no mistake about it: George was not going to stop until those responsible were in jail.

"We are a family in pain," George added. "My wife, Ann, and daughters . . . are having a hard time coping with this. I can tell you, as a father, my heart is broken and I struggle making it from day to day."

Just a few days before the press conference, a benefit concert was staged to honor the four victims and bring awareness to the investigation. The concert, held at the A.D. Bruce Religion Center, on the University of Houston (UH) campus, featured Jennifer Grassman, an up-and-coming local Houston singer-songwriter, who had worked with Rachael for a short time.

"I remember my mom calling me up at work," Jennifer said later, talking about the moment she found out about Rachael's death. "'Honey, I've got some horrible news: Rachael's dead. She's been murdered.' At first, I couldn't process the idea that she was talking about Rachael Koloroutis. I got numb all over. It was a feeling of profound shock, disbelief, and horror."

When she first saw Rachael behind the cash register at Randall's, a local grocery store, where they had met as coworkers, Jennifer was impressed. "She had wavy honey-brown hair, big brown eyes, and an infectious smile. She was the sort of girl that other girls were jealous of, and all the boys ogled. It was high school. Rachael could have been one of those catty, ditsy girls that gossiped and flirted, but she wasn't. She was kind, gentle, and generous."

They got along well, Jennifer recalled. They connected as friends. Soon Rachael and Jennifer were taking their breaks together. They'd sit and talk about family, school, boys, and all the weird customers they dealt with at work. All the guys would run toward Rachael's line because she was so pretty. And yet, to Jennifer, Rachael also had depth to go along with her looks; she never trounced around like some sort of beauty queen. She loved everyone the same.

"I distinctly remember Rachael telling me about church camp, and discussing various moral and religious issues. . . . She asked me about my music once, [about] how I had aspirations of becoming a recording artist. . . . She said, 'When you write songs, do you ever write them about friends? Maybe you could write one for me!' "

Jennifer was "caught off guard," she remembered.

"Sure, why not?" she told Rachael.

The songwriter blew off the notion. It wasn't until a year later, after that painful call from her mother regarding Rachael's death, and a desire to help the families raise money for Crime Stoppers through the benefit concert, that Jennifer Grassman wrote a song for her old friend. The idea came to her when she saw Rachael's photo on the local news one night.

"There was video of a memorial on the sidewalk outside the house in which Rachael and her friends had died."

People had left scores of traditional roadside remembrances: roses, teddy bears, candles, and cards. Looking at it all that day, Jennifer "felt sick." But then she went home and, recalling that Rachael had asked her about writing a song almost a year earlier, she sat and penned the song "White Roses" for her dead friend. It was a way to release her pent-up feelings, a way to pay homage to a friend she had never really gotten to know as well as she would have liked, and also a way to put into song how much Rachael would be missed by the community and her dear friends.

Now, a week after that benefit concert, on November 19, a day before Rachael would have turned nineteen, Crime Stoppers was holding a press conference. The reward, Crime Stoppers announced, which over two hundred donors were said to have contributed to, was the largest cash reward ever offered through any Crime Stoppers organization nationwide. Quite a message was being sent by those who knew the victims and, for that matter, those who didn't.

The reward of $100,000 was a lot of money for the person who could call in a tip anonymously. The amount alone, most were certain, would generate interest and stir the community into action.

If there was one final message by family members related on that day of the press conference, it was that the kids "were targeted" and that "somebody out there knew something."

Hopefully, money would draw that person out of his or her shell.

At the end of the press conference, it was declared that anyone with information about the case should call the Crime Stoppers tip line.

With that, what else was left to say?

As the event broke up, Tom Ladd called George and Ann Koloroutis off to the side. "I want to introduce you to Detective Brian Harris. He's part of the team now working on the case."

Harris stood with a bashful smile. He and George Koloroutis exchanged pleasantries. They had met once before, but not formally.

George appeared to be encouraged: here was someone new, someone with a fresh perspective, someone with some fire in his eyes for finding answers.

"Great to meet you," George said, sticking out his hand, rubbing Harris's shoulder with the other. He liked Harris the moment the officer spoke.

"Look," Ladd explained, "Harris is working on a few leads. He's heading off to Jacksonville tomorrow to check out some things. I can't discuss them with you right now."

This impressed George. Maybe there was a break in the case? George didn't want to get his hopes up or meddle. He never did. He wanted only what was best for the case. He wasn't going to push Ladd into telling him what Harris was onto. When the time was right, George knew, they would come to him and talk about it.

Leaving the press conference, Harris stopped by the office to pick up some cash and a few other personal items he needed for the trip. His plane was flying out that night. Within several hours, Harris would touch down in Jacksonville, Florida, and be on his way to following a new trail.

CHAPTER 18

ONE OF RACHAEL and Tiffany's best friends back in high school, Christine Paolilla, had been bouncing around town after the school year ended. Christine still had another year of high school left. That summer of 2003, Christine was doing what young girls with little direction, a chip on their shoulders, and an erogenous appetite do when left to their own devices. She was working at Walgreens, a job Christine claimed to like, but she was beginning to dabble more and more in a serious side of teen life as each day passed—a side that can grow out of control without warning.

Some of Christine's acting out—the drinking, the dirty sex, the dope smoking, and the pill popping—was said to be based in the fact that she had grown up without her biological father since the time she was two years old. There had not been a male role model figure in her life for what was an important formative time period. Also, Christine's mother was an admitted drug user, fully recovered as Christine headed into her latter high-school years; but, nonetheless, she had not been the best mother to Christine, as a clean and sober mom might have been.

One of Christine's psychological doctors later commented on the girl's overall childhood experience, saying, she "had these great big glasses, growing up from first grade, and she had no hair—no eyebrows, no body hair, no head hair. She was a little girl who just wanted to kind of . . . be liked, like all of us."

The doctor went on to say that Christine also wanted to be like every other child she grew up with and met in school. She was a follower, in other words. Definitely not a leader.

"And those kids would tease her because kids do that. She's got great big glasses. She's got a wig. And they pull and play with that stuff. She just kind of wants to fit in. . . . And she's got ADD. So, she's not like a great student, either. So, she's got no way to fit in."

While her mother was away "getting fixed," the doctor added, Christine went to stay with her grandparents, who were "old [and] they're kind of old-time strict folks."

When Christine turned fifteen, her mother, Lori Paolilla, fresh from rehab and rebuilding her life with a new outlook, asked her daughter for a second chance. " 'I'm a different person now' " was the way the doctor recalled Lori putting it, "and they ship Christine to her mother . . . with her new husband to try and give everybody a fresh start."

Christine had a brother, whom the grandparents "kept," the doctor said.

The implication by the doctor was that Christine had never been raised in a stable environment that would allow her to evolve into a productive teen and young adult.

"She's still looking for a place, somebody to kind of take care of her," the doctor recalled, describing what he said was a pivotal time in Christine's upbringing.

By any standards this would make any kid in the same position grow to be wracked with control and codependency issues. Christine didn't know what a stable environment was like; she had been living with the idea that her father was killed when she was a young girl; and, truthfully, no matter how she turned out later, in Christine's view of herself, she believed her life had been one uphill battle (and disappointment) after another, at least according to this one doctor.

Christine had said herself that as she moved through high school, she always gravitated toward "stray dogs and losers" for boyfriends. It was her sole intention when taking on those lost causes, perhaps subconsciously or consciously (she never said which), to *fix* them, and then move on to the next challenge. The idea was, she couldn't fix her own life or her own psyche, so she'd settle for fixing somebody else's and meet her emotional needs from that. There were additional, mitigating factors involved, that same doctor explained. Because she had lost her dad in that workplace accident (which one source later claimed was brought on by the man's own issues with drug use), Christine feared losing the people in her life more than anything else. She woke every morning with the anxiety of someone she loved walking away from her, or not coming home from a simple trip to the store. She did whatever she could then to keep people in her life. She didn't want to be left alone; it brought back all of that repressed feeling of loss and solitude she had grown up with, so claimed this same psychologist.

Tiffany and Rachael had always been there for Christine through their high-school years. Christine could count on these girls; she could depend on them for whatever problem came up. Christine even wrote about her love for the two girls in her school notebooks. If there was one constant in Christine's life when she arrived at Clear Lake High School, it was that Tiffany and Rachael always had her back and were the cushion for whatever fall she'd have on a particular day. And when we're talking about Christine Paolilla, there seemed to be one drama after the next happening on any given day.

On one piece of notebook paper, Christine had shared with the girls how much they meant to her: *Christine + Rachel* [sic] *+ Tiffani* [sic] *= B.F.F.E.* She dotted the *i*'s in "Christine" with hearts, and wrote *I love you guys* on the top of the page.

Tiffany responded underneath, writing: *Christine, I love you! You have been there for me when I needed you! I really appreciate how nice you are.* -♥-*Tiff.*

If nothing else, Christine could depend on Rachael and Tiffany when all else—and everyone else—failed her. But now they were gone: two more people who had been there for Christine throughout a rough period in her life but were suddenly swept away in a violent, untimely, and unspeakable manner. And Christine, as she went about her days postmurder, was experiencing that loss in ways no one could have ever imagined.

IN JUNIOR HIGH, before she ever met Tiffany or Rachael, Christine had hooked up with a kid whom she liked a lot, but whom she became scared of, she later claimed. The kid, Chris, was pushy and aggressive, which she knew from experience could easily turn into violence. Christine had lost touch with the boy for a time. But at a party one night during the winter of 2003, Christine ran into Chris. It was great to see him. He looked so different and grown-up. Since the school year had ended, Christine had been hanging out with Christopher Snider again, the boy who had, according to her, terrified her so much back in junior high. He was a good-looking man now, with neatly cropped, nearly buzz-cut, short, dark blond hair, which he combed down in front to hide what was a receding hairline. Like many kids of his era, Chris had a barbell eyebrow piercing. Christine liked his striking blue eyes, the color of Caribbean water, the neatly trimmed goatee he kept; yet at the same time, Christopher still had that strange look of confusion about him, which she had noticed years before. He was definitely twisted and mentally agile. Something was going on inside his head, for sure. Maybe not something that Christine wanted anything to do with at this point in her life. Yet, she was drawn in by Christopher Snider from almost the minute they reconnected.

Christopher liked his drugs, mainly whatever he could get his hands on. Christine claimed later that she was smoking *only* pot at the time she met and hooked back up romantically with him, but that he kept pushing other dope on her, demanding that she use it with him.

"He was," Christine later explained, "just, like, a very, uh, hopeless person—yeah, a hopeless person."

Her boyfriend had a certain darkness he kept within. He was definitely depressed and internalized those feelings to a point where the only thing that took away the pain was the numbing effect of drugs. This was one reason why lots of kids felt the urge to do drugs to begin with: that the hardships of life, whatever they might be, would magically disappear if only they could get high enough.

Part of what changed Christopher Snider, family members later said, was an accident he was involved in as a child. He and his sister, Brandee, were playing football in the street in front of their Texas home one afternoon. He was twelve; his sister was fourteen. They were having fun, tossing the ball back and forth. A truck, apparently not seeing the children, came barreling around the corner and struck Christopher dead on. The impact was so powerful it threw him in the air, sending the boy flying across the street, his rag doll body thumping on the tar. Brandee ran over to her brother, scared he was hurt badly. She bent down. Her brother's eyes were rolling back into his head. His was in shock and going into convulsions.

"It seems that he changed a lot after that accident," Brandee later said.

Christine fantasized about having a life with Christopher Snider: white picket fence, kids, boat, two cars, a dog maybe, and that suburban, blissful euphoria every human being chases in their mind at some point. Perhaps she saw an unrealistic juxtaposition between the good job and hard work during the week and the parties and good times on the weekends.

These feelings of running off into the sunset with Christopher Snider came, Christine later acknowledged, when he was at a "begging for pity" phase of his life.

"I'm the type of person," Christine said, "[who has] always dated stupid guys just because, you know, I think I can help them and get them back on their feet. And, you know, all that wonderful stuff that I couldn't do for me."

Christopher was not that much older than Christine; he had just turned nineteen when they reconnected. But the kid had a rap sheet. There were times, according to Christine, when Snider simply snapped, wielding that resource of anger and violence he kept buried within. He had a ticking time bomb, she suggested, a fuse inside him, which was waiting to be fired up by something she might inadvertently say or do.

"When I first met him, he made me feel so special," Christine later said. "And there were times when he would act like a fool. He was just a very *violent* person. His family had called the cops on him a bunch of times, and, you know, I always tried to convince his mom that he's doing better—I was, like, enabling him. . . . I was *lying* for him."

They were at Christine's house in Friendswood one afternoon. It happened to be the same day that Rachael and Tiffany, Marcus and Adelbert, were murdered, July 18. Christine's parents—her mother, Lori, and her stepdad, Tom Dick—weren't home. Snider decided he was going to light up a doobie.

"What the [heck] are you doing?" Christine said. "Put that out!" This particularly upset her because there wasn't any reason for him to be there while her parents were not at home. She was seventeen. They'd freak out if they knew he was even in the house, better yet sparking a spliff on their property. Christopher also knew damn well,

Christine later speculated, "that my mom was a recovering drug addict—and yet he *still* thought it was okay, you know, to do drugs in my house."

But Christine bit the bullet and remained calm.

At first.

"Christopher, look, you know, put that out," she demanded. They were outside in the backyard, standing by the patio; Christine had managed to get him, at least, outdoors, so the inside of her mother's house wouldn't reek of dope. "I don't want that stuff in my house." Christine had smoked weed herself and "experimented," she admitted, but never at home and not on that day. "I would never bring it home. I would never hurt [or] disrespect them (my parents) like that."

(Yes, that might be true, but Christine surely had other ways of showing impertinence toward her parents' authority, will, and overall desire for her to do good in life and become the adult they expected.)

"Whatever," Christopher said, continuing to smoke, as if he didn't give a hoot about what his girlfriend was asking of him. "I'll be done quick enough. This is my last one. I don't have any more. Let me do this *real* quick."

Christine became upset, exploding, "You always have to do things *your* way."

That initiated a loud argument between them, vulgarities and curses flying back and forth like spittle. It was the middle of the day in suburban Houston, people all around, neighbors with their ears wide open.

"Come into the house!" Christine yelled. "I am not going let my neighbors hear this."

"Fine, fine, fine," Christopher said. "Take me home, then! Now!"

"No, Christopher. Don't be mad. Come on." Christine calmed down. Then turned on the lovey-dovey charm. (" 'Cause I didn't want him to be mad at me," she remarked later. "I just wanted him to understand.")

Christopher didn't say anything in response.

"Come on, baby," Christine continued, "I just, like, please just respect my house and my parents." She was whispering, trying to show him that she wasn't into fighting about something that seemed so stupid.

Christopher Snider, on the other hand, didn't much appreciate his girlfriend barking at him as though he was a child. So Christopher did what, according to Christine, he did when someone pissed him off: he went after her.

"I tried to forget about [it]," she said later, describing that day, "[and] there was, like, physical contact."

Christopher decided he was leaving. She wasn't worth the trouble. The argument had gone and ruined his high, anyway. So he walked out of the yard.

Christine didn't want him to go. She ran after Chris as he tried exiting the patio area. She grabbed at his shirt, trying to hold him back.

Christopher snapped, Christine said, and swatted her off him.

She fell back and "kind of hit [her] head on the foyer of the house."

It was marble. Damn thing hurt like hell, too.

Christine panicked. Christopher had gotten physical with her in the past, so she claimed, and she was afraid he was going to let her really have it. That push was a prelude to a beating, she suggested.

So she pleaded with him.

"Now take me . . . home, I said!" he screamed.

"Okay, babe, okay . . . okay," Christine said, trying to appease. Next thing she recalled she was driving in her car with him, heading toward his house, still begging him to calm down, promising that everything was going to be okay. *Just relax, baby. Try to steady your feelings and don't allow your emotions to get the best of you.* And yet that outburst back at the house, Christine Paolilla would later say, was nothing compared to what Christopher Snider would do next.

AS THE FALL of 2003 wound down with the Thanksgiving holiday around the corner, Christine Paolilla was back at Clear Lake High School, going about her senior year, one would imagine, totally numb from the effects of having her two best friends murdered in such a whirlwind of bloody violence. For Christine, life went on. It had to. She studied and she worked at Walgreens. What else *could* she do?

For Brian Harris and HPD's Homicide Division, however, Christine Paolilla was probably someone they would love to speak to, her being good friends with Rachael and Tiffany. Only problem was, Christine's name had not come up in the investigation as of yet. Nor had Christine come forward to talk about whatever she might know, if anything. In fact, what could have been a significant lead this early on in the investigation was sitting in a box, inside a cubicle, inside the Homicide Squad offices. It was a photo that was actually mislabeled. Buried in one of the Clear Lake murder investigation boxes was a photograph of Rachael Koloroutis lying on a couch, wearing a short red top, her six-pack abs quite visible, her hair up in a beehive hairdo. She had a bottle of booze in her hand. Rachael was smiling, a look of sexual flirtation on her face, her right hand over the back of another girl whose head was but a few inches away from Rachael's crotch area. They were obviously horsing around, playing up things for the photographer, whoever—likely Tiffany—she was. This other girl, who also had a bottle of booze in one hand, was smiling, one bare foot on the carpet, the other tucked underneath her butt. She was leaning down and had the hip band from Rachael's G-string panties by her teeth, stretching it out of Rachael's pants. Rachael was staring down at the girl from her leaned-back position.

The photo was marked as "Rachael and Tiffany."

Err, *mis*marked was maybe a better way to analyze this: because that girl with Rachael's G-string panty band between her teeth was, in fact, Christine Paolilla, and no one in the Homicide Division knew this yet.

CHAPTER 19

IT WAS THE middle of the night. Somewhere near two or three o'clock, he wasn't able to exactly recall what time, the phone was ringing. Brian Harris was opening his eyes, acclimating himself to his surroundings at such a late hour. He was bushed, having traveled back days before from that trip to Florida, which did not yield much as far as new leads went.

"Yeah? What is it?" he said after answering the phone.

She sounded frantic and, at the same time, scared. It was Ann Koloroutis.

"What can I do for you?" Brian Harris asked. He was half asleep.

"I had a dream. She came to me in my dream."

Rachael.

Great, Harris thought.

"What happened?"

"Rachael said something about a pocketbook. 'The pocketbook,' she kept saying. 'The pocketbook.' I don't know what it means."

Harris didn't know what to think. At this point in the investigation, with so many dead ends and red herrings and leads that fizzled into dust, the idea that one of the victims was speaking to her mother from beyond didn't seem at all that far fetched.

Harris wrote it down in his notes.

Pocketbook.

CHAPTER 20

THE **TIPS SPILLING** into Crime Stoppers came in at such a continuous clip that you'd have to wonder where all of these people had been hiding since the murders, nearly five months before. In some ways many of the tips bolstered Detective Brian Harris's growing theories; but in others they put the kibosh on what he thought and, simultaneously, opened additional doors that had to be, on merit alone, checked into with as much enthusiasm as any other lead.

One woman called in with a "vision" she'd had of Rachael or Tiffany "having an affair with a married man by the waterfront," though she did not go into great detail about how that vision was actually connected to the murders.

It was taken with a roll of the eyes.

Another tip, from a "white-sounding voice," the report noted, said there was a party for her back on July 17 and Marcus had left with someone there and had bought some weed, and then returned a half hour later. She mentioned a name that would once again become synonymous with the murders as each day turned to night and a new tipster called in.

JU.

A young-sounding female called to say that she had overheard JU on the telephone saying, "You won't go down for it if the cops don't know anything." This gave a bit more credence to the idea that JU had brought someone with him.

Yet, another female called to say she'd had sex with JU on the day *after* the murders, and that when he heard about who was killed, JU "cried." One of her friends, she reported, described JU as a "small dealer," and not someone who could have been involved in something so horrific.

A woman called to say she had heard a local funeral director had had something to do with the murders.

"That was a misunderstanding," the funeral director told Tom Ladd. "I know nothing about the murders other than what the victims' family [members said] and [what] looking at the bodies for my work told me."

Then the tone of the calls shifted altogether. Now the blame was cast on George Koloroutis.

"I think George had something to do with it," said one caller, who identified himself as being related to Marcus.

George Koloroutis had long ago been eliminated as a suspect: He had been in a staff meeting at the time of the murders. There had been twelve senior people from the company George worked for with him at the time. There was no way George Koloroutis could have committed the murders—that is, himself.

Someone called and said George had tried to hire Marcus and Adelbert "to do a thing" for him and that they wouldn't do it.

Still, no one in HPD was on board with the notion that George was behind the murders in any way whatsoever.

Concluding the report detailing all of these phone calls, Harris wrote about the "possible working scenarios" that his department had to contend with as the case carried on into the Christmas holiday. One of the scenarios included the idea that George could have done the murders because he was outraged over Rachael's lifestyle. The other, stronger possibility, Harris noted, was this name "Fats," which came up several times with several of the callers.

"No matter who we were talking about," Harris said later, "George, Fats, JU—any one of them—they all had to be checked and rechecked. No one could be scratched off the list. And the thing was, we were so far off from what truly happened inside that house."

GEORGE KOLOROUTIS WAS all about full disclosure where he was concerned. He had already given his life story to detectives. He kept repeating the same thing every time the idea that he was involved came up: the sooner you get through looking at me, the sooner you can get out there and locate the *real* killers. In meeting Brian Harris, George was enthusiastic about having a new investigator involved in the case. It gave the entire investigation a freshness, which it required, and, with no disrespect to Tom Ladd, a shot in the arm, which it needed.

George had met Harris earlier in the case a few times, but now they were working together on a closer, more intimate level.

"My impression of Harris was good right from the start," George recalled. "Right away, I sensed that he wanted to catch who did this and that he felt he *could* figure it out. I looked at all the cops involved . . . just like I do [my] employees. Their mission is to catch killers. This became a business plan to me, and in order to execute the plan and meet the objective, I had to set clear expectations and provide constant feedback. Of course, I understand that there are others besides me who set expectations and provide feedback, such as their supervisors, their own work ethic, sense of duty, and so on. But all of those other drivers are outside of my control. I was competing with hundreds of other cases. What I *could* control was my own level of engagement—I had only one case to focus on."

In George's view of things, the one item that remained clear about Harris from the get-go turned out to be the idea that Harris was "a winner. I have many on my team in business, people who are simply rock stars, Super Bowl weapons. They produce at a high level, year after year, and do it regardless of the circumstances or challenges." George saw Harris as one of those "rock star" quality producers in life: someone who could get the job done, regardless of the adversity, nepotism, and negativity he faced.

It was clear from the start that Harris didn't care what other people thought, or how others in the department did things. He conducted himself with grace, professionalism, and tenacity. He was a cop to the core. Not that Tom Ladd wasn't interested in solving the case, but Brian Harris came across differently. And George appreciated and welcomed it. The guy was clearly not going to stop until he caught the people who had murdered George's daughters and the others.

"You just know it when you are around him," George said of Harris. "Ladd [was leaving], and so [were] a series of sergeants after him."

Harris became the most important part of the investigation moving forward, and George knew this.

Beyond that, a cop had committed suicide right in the detectives' cubicle area of the Homicide Division; and the Homicide Squad was in the throes of going through a change in retirement plans, which had come from the top, the mayor's office, and it had caused a plague of early retirements. This, mind you, in a division that was already strapped for detectives. Then a series of domestic violence cases were given to the group to investigate. They had countless murders still open. Where, then, did the Clear Lake case fit into all of this?

"This type of environment," George concluded, "makes it hard for an average or below average performer to do well. At the same time, this environment makes a guy like Brian Harris stand out."

CHAPTER 21

A S THE INVESTIGATION INTO the murder of her friends continued to limp along, Christine Paolilla did the same in school. It
is safe to assume that Christine, about six months away from her
eighteenth birthday, was counting down the days as if retirement was
in her near future. On the day she turned eighteen, Christine could
tap into that trust fund insurance money she was awarded after her
father died on the job, sixteen years earlier. And what a pocket full of
change it was going to be.

As she went through her final school year, every time Christine
heard something about what she later called "the murders," she
"wanted to scream." She didn't really get along with many people in
school. "You know, I mean," Christine added, referring to Rachael
and Tiffany, "they were really, like, the only girls that wouldn't stab
me in the back."

Whenever Christine had a problem, she turned to either Tiffany
or Rachael. "I could always talk to them, all the time, without a
doubt, any time at night, you know, they could call me, I could call
them, and I just got mad, you know. . . . [Someone had taken] away
any, like, real friends that I really had. . . ."

Between all those stammers of "like" and "you know," was Christine Paolilla saying that she missed her friends? That here were two
more people she loved who had been taken from her?

It appeared so.

Christine later said that although she and Rachael often messed
around at parties and teased each other about "getting together," it
was all "you know, joking around, but nothing ever sexual."

The deaths of her friends had been so traumatic—bringing up all those repressed memories of her father's death—Christine couldn't even bring herself to go to the funerals. "Too much guilt," she added. "All funerals brought back the death of my father, and I didn't like funerals because of that."

Even though she claimed he liked to get violent with her at times and the two of them together were more like oil and water, Christopher Snider was still a major part of Christine's life during the fall of 2003. He was, in fact, more of an influence on her life now than her schoolwork, which was suffering greatly. And there was something else that Christopher—if you believe Christine—had turned her on to: crime.

In late October, Christine and Chris were picked up and booked for shoplifting. The arresting officer asked Christine her father's name (she was seventeen then, a minor).

"Dick Thomas," she said.

It was not hard for the cop to find out she was lying. A quick check of her address showed that Thomas Dick, her stepfather, the only father figure Christine had ever known, lived at her address.

Christine was able to get out of the shoplifting charge with a slap on the wrist, for the most part, and a promise to stay the heck out of trouble, finish school, and hopefully use all that money she was about to come into to go to one of the local colleges and get a decent education.

But that just wasn't going to be the case. For some time now Christine had been dipping her toes in lawless waters, which apparently felt warm and comforting. Going back to March 2003, Tom Dick had called the police on his stepdaughter for "attacking [him] with her fists." The incident stemmed from Christine's desire to leave home and be with Chris Snider. Lori Paolilla had called the cops on Christine a number of times, once saying, "She thinks she can leave home. I'm having problems with her over her boyfriend, curfew, and general conduct" around the house. The girl believed she could do whatever she wanted and not have to suffer any repercussions for the behavior. That last time she ran away, Christine walked out of the house with her luggage. She said she was moving in with Chris.

A week later, she was back. It was May 2, 2003. The police officer who had responded to the call got ahold of Lori after Christine's return to follow up and see how things were going.

"She's still grounded," Lori told the officer. "All her privileges have been removed. Christine was diagnosed with ADHD, and when she gets depressed, she starts to act out."

Tom Dick told the officer Christine had said she understood what she had done was wrong and was regretful. She was ready and willing, at least superficially, to redeem herself.

Lori explained that (or maybe blamed) a lot of Christine's conduct and acting out on Christopher Snider, whom Lori viewed as a misfit troublemaker, who was only making her daughter's life more miserable than it had to be.

"Chris," Lori explained to the police, "had been 'protecting' Christine." Or that's what Christine had told her mother he had said to her while she was gone with him. "She told us they had been riding around and staying in parks. . . ."

The way Christine played off her relationship with Chris to her parents, you'd be left with the impression that the guy was keeping her against her will and she was under his spell, living in fear, being forced to do anything he said—or else! Those who were around the two of them during this period of their relationship, however, paint a different picture, quite opposite to the "poor me, I can't break free from his influence" scenario Christine had sketched.

For one, Christine was insecure and jealous beyond anything her friend had ever seen, one source later said.

"Pretty much every fight and/or argument between Chris and Christine," added that source, "was over her crushing jealousy."

If Christine ever *thought* Chris was looking at another girl while they were out, she'd fly off the deep end, saying, "What?" She would slap him on his arm or punch him. "Do you think she is prettier than me?"

At times Christine's adolescent, jealous comments exploded into what a source referred to as "crazy rage."

The source said, "Young girls are like that to a degree—insecure. But not anything like Christine."

Chris would go out of his way to avoid fights with her, but he knew they were an inevitable part of the relationship. So he learned to accept Christine for the way she was and put up with her hysterics.

"The psycho," Chris's sister, Brandee, called Christine, and so did the rest of the family. "He was so beholden to her. She was *always* calling our house. They'd spend hours on the phones. She called incessantly. You'd think she'd have to call our house to keep the world going." Christine was always going off the deep end, screaming at Chris for some stupid reason, going up one side and down the other for who knows what purpose. She would later make the claim that he had hit, continually abused, and controlled her. Yet his family saw things differently: they thought it was the other way around. So much so, the main reason why they had referred to Christine as a mentally unstable *psycho* was because she had shown them on numerous occasions that she was out of control.

"She was constantly overriding our lives, constantly around, constantly in our face," a family source said. "She was very hyper."

CHRISTINE HAD CALLED her boyfriend "relentlessly." When they weren't together on a specific night, she stalked him. If they fought and he refused to talk to her, she'd spend the night on the front lawn, sleeping, trying to get into the house, yelling, going nuts, rattling the screen door. "She even threatened to kill my mom, my dad, and even me!" Brandee later said. "She was an absolute cancer to us."

Several times Chris had told his family: "There are two things in this world I am afraid of. The cops and Christine."

The one thing Chris Snider hated was Christine's near-obsessive compulsion with sex—anal sex, in particular. Chris considered sex itself to be "overrated" as a whole. He hated how Christine constantly demanded anal sex from him, as if she wanted him to punish her. Chris thought it was dirty. Yet, he felt he had to serve her needs.

There was a modicum of generally bizarre behavior on Christine's part. One day, as Chris and Christine argued, Christine backed him up against a wall in his house, yelling and screaming in one of her furious fits of jealous insecurity. She cursed him and demanded that he tell her the truth about what had happened. Chris usually took it, said a source who witnessed many of these instances. On this day, though, Christine stopped midway through her tirade. Chris stared at her, and she back at him. Then Christine, without warning, licked his face from his chin up, across his nose and forehead, and shot him a deviously evil gaze without speaking. She spat on the ground to his right and walked away, as if sending him some sort of cryptic message: *Don't ever F with me! I'm a crazy woman!*

NOT LONG AFTER that shoplifting charge, things at home got much worse for Christine. Christopher Snider had a warrant out for his arrest in Kentucky, where he had once stayed with family and had gotten into some serious trouble, stealing a car and taking off. Texas authorities booked him on the shoplifting charge and ran his name through the system.

Christopher Snider, the man who had "taken away my womanhood," Christine claimed, was now on his way back to Kentucky to do some serious time.

This posed a problem for Christine, who wanted to follow her man. But her parents would hear nothing of it. She had been arrested for shoplifting. Christine's mother was no dummy. Obviously, Christine and Chris were stealing to feed other habits. So when Christine balked at the idea that she was not to go running after her crazy boyfriend, Christine began once again hurling obscenities and threats at her stepfather and her mother. Then the police were called back one afternoon when Christine had apparently taken things to a level that perhaps her mother had not seen coming.

When the cop got there, Christine "was very irate, out of control, and being held down on the ground by" Tom Dick, said one report. She was screaming and yelling and kicking her legs. It was Tom who had called the police.

"She's just been released from jail on shoplifting charges," Tom said, looking at the cop, then back at Christine, who was still spastic. "She's on two different medications for bipolar disorder." After allowing Christine to sit on the couch, where she promised to be a good girl, Tom Dick told the cop what had happened earlier and why he felt he needed to call.

Christine walked down the stairs some time before the police had arrived and proceeded to tell her parents that she was going to go see Christopher Snider.

"You're not leaving this house to go see him," Tom Dick told his stepdaughter.

She went for the door, spewing venom about being able to do what she wanted, when she wanted to do it.

Tom Dick stopped her.

Christine ran into the kitchen, grabbed hold of a knife, and put the blade on one of her wrists, as though she was threatening to cut herself.

When Tom told her to stop, Christine "held the knife up in a [somewhat] threatening manner," pointing it toward him, Tom later told police. He described the incident as "semi threatening."

Christine held the knife above her head "for a few seconds"; then she put it down by her side, still holding on to it.

As Christine stood there with the knife, Tom grabbed hold of her. He was worried, he said later, that she was going to harm herself more than hurt anyone else. So they called police.

This incident had upset Lori. As she spoke to the officer in her living room, telling him her version—which turned out to be the same as Tom's—an important point came up.

"It was fifteen years ago today," Lori explained, "that Christine's biological father died. Her medication has been changed recently and hasn't had time to work properly."

Still, Christine could be put in jail for the outburst and the "semi" knife attack. But Lori didn't want that. Neither did Tom.

"We just want her to get some help."

So four EMTs called to the scene transported Christine to the Mainland Center Hospital for psychiatric treatment.

The attack, Christine later argued, was brought on by what had become two major problems she acquired during those days following the murders of her friends: Christopher Snider and drugs. Chris and Christine had started using harder drugs than simply weed; cocaine became an obsession of Christine's, as would heroin in the coming months.

In fact, as November gave way to December, the police were showing up regularly at Christine's house.

"October through December was very turbulent in the house of Christine," a law enforcement source said. "She was mad that her family wanted her to stay away from Snider."

Christine's mother believed Chris Snider was no good for her daughter. The guy had no direction, spoke of the darkest things imaginable—devils and death and blood and guts—and wanted to do nothing but drugs. Christine had fallen for him, and was seemingly using drugs to numb a pain she didn't want to talk about with anyone. It was as if her boyfriend had become another addiction.

But now *he* was gone.

As part of a deal she struck with the court, Christine was sent to drug rehab in San Antonio—where her real problems would begin.

CHAPTER 22

THE NEW YEAR dawned with a certain amount of trepidation for the families of the four. They felt no closer six months later than they had on day one. It was altogether frustrating and intense. Every day they woke up and hoped that the phone was going to ring with HPD on the other end talking about how they had made an arrest. It was one of the motivators keeping many family members from staying in bed all day, with the shades drawn, wallowing in the darkness of having lost a loved one so young—someone with so much life ahead.

Brian Harris knew Tom Ladd was leaving in March, retiring. Harris had that hanging over his head; it would mean one less man on the Clear Lake case. Tom Ladd was focused on the JU angle of the case and was (80 percent) convinced that JU had had something to do with the murders. If not directly, then indirectly. As luck would have it, Ladd and Harris heard JU had been busted recently on a serious drug charge and had pleaded his case to nine years behind bars. JU was serving his sentence in a local prison. Now was probably as good a time as any to head over, get in JU's face, and find out *exactly* what he knew.

"We figure now maybe he'll talk," Harris said later. "We're in a good position with him. Any number of things could happen."

Harris had a unique philosophy regarding interrogation, much of which was rooted in the moral and religious beliefs he took into "the box" (interview suite) with him whenever he went to interview a suspect. Some didn't like the way Harris handled himself in the box.

Others called him "egocentric" and "arrogant." Whatever the case, the guy knew how to get the job done—and one cannot argue with results.

Harris relied on trigger words a suspect used during an interrogation: "sincerely," "honestly," "truthfully." Those adverbs with the *ly* ending were "like a big red flag going up," Harris explained. When he heard those words during an interview, "I'm like, 'Here it comes.'" Those types of words were what Harris referred to as "qualifying statements," generally preceding an admission of something. It was the suspect making himself feel better before laying the blame on someone else.

There was also what Harris referred to as "nonverbal cues." One of any nervous gestures, such as "hair twirling, face rubbing, and, above all, defensive body posture, when a suspect closes himself off or backs away from his interrogator." These physical tics told Harris that the suspect was blowing smoke.

"One nervous indicator," Harris was quick to clear up, "does not imply guilt. It's the totality of the package. You might lean back and be like . . . 'Get out of my face, man. That's not what happened.'" When a suspect did that, Harris pointed out, he or she was creating distance between himself and the interrogator.

That's what Harris looked for: separation. The idea that the suspect was looking to put physical space between him and the cop told the officer that the suspect had something to hide.

If he could, Harris made sure that the box was set up in a way that gave him a psychological edge with his suspect. There should be nothing on the walls to distract the suspect. Make sure the suspect's chair had straight legs, immovable, while the chair the interrogator used had rollers, so he could move throughout the room at his own pace, by his own accord, and come across to the suspect as, well, free.

"I may start off being three to four feet away," Harris said, "but when I feel they're about to confess . . . I may move to within inches."

Going into the interview with JU, Harris had to consider what he had. The room was bare, for the most part, and JU was situated in his own chair. Harris was going to try to get what he could, once and for all. It was time to charge JU, or scratch him off the list. To continue running around in circles with the likes of JU wasn't helping the case. Homicide needed either to dig deeper into JU's life, and see where they could fit him into the murders, or write him off completely. Either way, Harris decided, they needed to move forward.

"JU was always up front with me about his dope dealing," Harris recalled. "He wanted to be this major big-time dope player."

JU was not a tough guy in any respect; he was a businessman. Harris had seen plenty of guys like him. They lived and died by the street, dealing their drugs, ruining lives, creating chaos in the community, without realizing it. The sad thing was that Marcus or Adelbert were not like JU at all. They were young kids in a man's world. They had no idea what they were getting themselves into.

Harris explained to JU that someone JU knew had admitted to being a mule, a drug runner. Harris gave JU the name. Told him a little bit about the guy and how he wasn't necessarily the person JU had thought he was.

JU was shocked by this revelation; he had believed that the guy whom Harris had mentioned was a major player in the drug world.

"He was just transporting the stuff, Jason—and skimming off the top."

"No [way]," JU said, surprised. He couldn't believe it.

"We've been down this road before, Jason," Harris said after they exchanged a bit more small talk. "Tell me about Marcus and the ten grand he owed you."

"I liked Marcus. He was a good friend. It was only ten K. That is *not* a lot of money. It works the same way in this world as it does out in the business world. You have to build credit and work off of that credit."

"Let's go through all of it again."

Jason Uolla conveyed a certain melancholy about him that Harris had not seen or heard before this day. He seemed down. They talked about how JU had been flippant with Tom Ladd and Phil Yochum in the past. He had not been all that forthcoming.

Why? Harris needed to know. What was he hiding?

"I had my head bashed in," JU said, defending himself.

"Yup, I know."

"Man," JU said at one point, "maybe I let him into the game too soon. . . ."

"What are we talking about now?" Harris said, confused by the comment.

"Marcus. Maybe he wasn't ready."

Harris knew they were getting somewhere. "Tell me about that, Jason."

JU rubbed his face. Took a deep breath. "I brought Marcus into this game . . . perhaps too soon," he said, "and, honestly, maybe I'm responsible for his death—but I tell you this"—and here he looked at Harris seriously and paused before concluding—"*anyone* who admits to having *any* part of that Clear Lake thing is a dead man."

"No kidding. . . ."

"Hell yeah! In *this* state?" He was talking about the death penalty. "They'd be crazy to talk to you."

JU had taken a polygraph and had failed.

"Why do you think you failed the polygraph?" Harris asked.

He thought about it. "Because, Detective, perhaps I *am* responsible."

Was this a wink-wink moment, or was JU being sincere in his feelings, marking himself accountable for Marcus's death? Perhaps Marcus's behavior and the drug dealing had gotten them all killed? Was Harris sitting and talking with a drug dealer with a conscience?

In any case, though, JU was finished talking.

Harris left the interview as baffled as he had been before he walked in. JU's body language, he noticed, told him that he was being straight, totally honest.

Why would he say that—"perhaps I am responsible"?

Still, HPD didn't have enough to charge JU, so they were, in the grand sense of this mysterious case, back to square one as far as JU was concerned. Harris was now going to have to explain to George Koloroutis, who was all but certain that JU was their man, that he still wasn't sure about the guy and could not arrest JU under simple suspicion of murder.

CHAPTER 23

MAY 2004 BROUGHT some of that marvelous Texas spring weather the state is known for. As he sat at his desk one morning, George Koloroutis realized—how could the guy *ever* forget?—that he had not heard much of anything from HPD in quite some time. George knew Tom Ladd had retired. The last thing he wanted was for HPD to forget about the case. It was important to keep pressure on the department. That old adage of the squeaky wheel actually worked in some instances, and this was surely one of them.

George called Brian Harris to find out if anything new was in the works, or if any progress had been made since Ladd's retirement and the ambiguous nature of JU's involvement.

"What's the deal, man, *who* is in charge of this now?" George wanted to know.

"I guess I am, George."

Screw it, Harris figured. He should probably take the bull by the horns here and run with his gut. He somewhat knew the ins and outs of the case history. Why not delve completely in and see if anything came up. With Ladd gone, the case needed to have a leader, or Harris knew by experience that it was going to collect dust in cold-case storage.

"I had been assigned to the case," Harris commented later, "so it was my chance to take the ball."

Harris was now running the investigation; he could do things *his* way. Not that Ladd had done things the wrong way, but Harris had his own "never stop" attitude, which would bode well with George (and this particular case). George was becoming increasingly frustrated that the year anniversary was coming up, and they were no closer to solving the case than they were during those all-important forty-eight hours after the murders.

Phil Yochum, still part of the Homicide Division, was interested in other fields of police work. Harris went over to Yochum, who, under normal circumstances, would have been the ideal choice for the lead in the Clear Lake case. He asked Yochum if he could take the files over to his cubicle and dig in. Brian Harris didn't want to step on anybody's toes.

"You mind if I do that?" Harris asked. It was out of respect; after all, the case was still Phil Yochum's.

"No, no, no," Yochum said, "go right ahead. Take it all. Whatever you need."

Solving murders involved passion. Yochum and Ladd had run out of gas long ago. It needed a hungry detective with a fiery spirit.

Going through the reports, Harris came to the same conclusion that Ladd had, and he understood more clearly why Ladd had always come back to JU. The dope dealer's name kept popping up in all the right places. There was no way to deny it, or overlook the obvious, unless you had a solid reason to write off JU. And at this point Harris had more evidence pointing to JU than he did leading away from JU.

"You have to follow the evidence," Harris remarked. "That clichéd statement is true."

HARRIS GOT WORD of a suspect arrested for burglary who wanted to speak with someone in the Homicide Division about the Clear Lake murders.

Here we go again. . . .

The guy was in county lockup. Harris went over to see him. It was May 10, 2004, near ten-thirty in the morning.

Harris waited inside a room at the 174th District Court in Houston. The guy's attorney sat down. This particular witness, Harris learned, was thirty-nine years old; he was a big dude, tough as nails, and hailed from the local Houston area. He was being held on a no-bond charge, serious stuff. He first talked about the number of the cell he had been in, something that would become important. He said he worked in the kitchen inside the jail. He talked about a big guy he had met on the inside. The guy wore glasses and a beard. He was being held in the cell next to him.

"How did you get to know him?" Harris asked.

"Well, you know, white boys in a predominantly black atmosphere."

Simple answer.

"You know, you kind of ride together. We played volleyball on, you know, a self-formed team."

Small talk. Harris understood it was part of building rapport.

The guy explained how he and this guy had gotten "pretty close," as they basically slept in the same pod, ate together, and hung out most days, talking most nights.

"Tell me what happens," Harris said as the guy's lawyer looked on, "how you're watching TV one time, so I hear, and what's on TV?"

"Well, it's either the news or a recording of the news. I wasn't really paying much attention . . . because it's, like, at six o'clock every day they put the Crime Toppers [*sic*] thing on TV, and it lasts thirty minutes."

"Okay."

"And, you know, we're playing a game of dominoes or checkers at the table and then you glance back and forth, catch the headlines, or, you know, and that's how I saw the"—he hesitated, looked at his lawyer—"I saw the . . . what we've been talking about."

So far Harris was half impressed. He kept responding "uh-huh" and "okay," so as not to plant anything in the guy's head. He wanted this informant to tell him what was going on. Lots of guys liked to waste the time of law enforcement and tell stories—boy, had Harris learned that the hard way during this case. Every inmate who came forward, Harris knew, wanted something, some sort of a deal for himself. This guy was no different. He sounded sincere and vague enough in the way he told his stories that he might be believable, yet that unavoidable "but" was coming somewhere down the line.

"When that came on," he continued, referring to the Crime Stoppers nightly report on television, "he said, 'I know. . . .' "

"What came on the news, though? We're on tape here: what comes on the news?"

"They show the reward. They show all the different rewards for all these unsolved crimes, right?"

"Uh-huh."

"And so they show one for four people that was killed in, like, toward Galveston, Pearland, or, I mean, not Pearland, Friendswood."

Close enough.

"Okay."

"He says, 'I *know* these people.' "

Nothing else was said at that time. It was two weeks later, the informant explained, when his cellmate began to talk about Clear Lake and what he actually knew.

"We're lying in bed, you know, talking. . . . And he said the stuff they showed on TV about the four people . . . he said, 'We went in there and Rachael was sitting in the chair watching TV and we pistol-whipped her.' And the reason that brought it to my attention was because he had said 'we.' "

Harris was interested. Details. Somewhat off. But details of the crime scene, nonetheless.

"And then there are two other people sitting on the couch," the informant added.

"Uh-huh."

"He said they didn't beat them all, but he specifically said, 'We beat Rachael with the pistol,' and he carries the pistol under his arm, you know, and he told me that on three or four occasions."

"What kind of pistol?" Harris asked.

"I don't know. . . . Like, he says, he goes [over there] to deliver weed or something, to somebody's house, this girl that he knows in Pasadena, and he'll leave his pistol in the car. . . ."

They discussed the notion that he sold weed and was, in fact, a dealer.

"What else did he say about this *thing*?" Harris asked.

"Well, he said that this girl, Rachael, was staying there. It's like her house or her mom's house, and she left town and left the house on the market, and this girl apparently wasn't even out of school or something, 'cause he said she was supposed to be finishing school."

He had a few things wrong, Harris noted, but the detective was impressed with the fact that the information wasn't exact and the guy was in the neighborhood of what the living conditions actually were. He was obviously mixing Rachael up with Tiffany.

They talked about the girl, Rachael, having a boyfriend in the house—he meant Tiffany Rowell, of course.

"[He] was selling dope for a cousin."

"Uh-huh."

"I assume it's speed they're talking about, because they do speed."

"Okay."

"And he said they owed somebody money. Apparently, they turned the house into a dope house." But he didn't know how much, exactly, they owed.

"Did he say they went over there to collect the money?" Harris asked.

"I assume that's what they went to do."

"Okay, but he never told you that?"

"He never told me that."

"Okay, what else did he tell you?"

"Uh, I mean, that's really, that's about it."

Harris wasn't biting. "Well, see, I might have been sitting in the bed going, 'Why did you kill them all?' "

"Well, I was."

"Uh-huh."

"I really wanted to keep talking, so I acted a little disinterested."

"Uh-huh."

"And then when I asked him questions, he didn't say any more."

They went back and forth, but the informant could not offer anything more in the form of details pertaining to the murders. This alone gave his statement a bit more credibility—the fact that he wasn't laying out the entire scenario.

Turned out the guy who had admitted all of this was someone by the name of "Bear," or "Big Bear."

Brian Harris and Phil Yochum busted Bear out of the county lockup. They sat him down and asked him to take a polygraph.

Bear, they soon learned, had a familiar friend and business partner.

JU.

Bear passed the polygraph.

"That just opened up that whole JU thing even bigger," Harris said.

CHAPTER 24

FRUSTRATED, DETECTIVE BRIAN Harris sat down and wrote a letter to his lieutenant on June 7, 2004. Harris wasn't so much concerned that the case hadn't been solved, but more along the line of information coming in and there weren't enough resources or cops to wade through it all. On top of that, he wanted to let his boss know—officially—that he was interested in taking control of the case. He wanted permission, essentially, to run with it, wherever it led.

This is a solvable case, Harris kept telling himself.

Harris had gone through all of the documents and broke the case down into groups of similar information. He wanted to do this, he wrote in the letter, so that whoever ended up investigating the case and working on it—even for a day—could easily sift through an index and become acquainted with all of the ins and outs of the case. This way, nothing would be overlooked.

One of Harris's main issues was that he believed there were still "numerous people" who needed to be interviewed. He warned that the families had been calling and had become "concerned about the lack of attention on this case." Those family members, Harris noted, wanted to know "how many" investigators were assigned, and what "the latest" had been. George had called a media consultant who had worked for the city promoting events, Harris wrote. The woman knew the chief personally and had already related the families' frustration to him and the need to draw attention back onto the case.

Harris said the families had requested a meeting with whoever was in charge. They had gotten together and were going to be placing billboards up around the Clear Lake area, announcing again the reward and the Crime Stoppers tip line. There was some talk that George wanted those sketches to be put up on the billboards. The message here was going to be that the sketches weren't necessarily the murderers, but the two people depicted in the drawings could maybe clear up a lot of unanswered questions.

That was the idea, anyway. But one had to listen to the music beneath the noise. If those sketches were on billboards, there was no telling what would happen.

Harris wrote that the families wanted to do this before July 18, the one-year anniversary. The idea was to place the billboards up within two weeks and "launch," as Harris put it, the first series of media coverage. Harris finished his thought by explaining how he believed, from speaking with the families, that this case might "generate negative coverage" for the Homicide Division if family members thought they were being "neglected."

Harris concluded that "exhaustive" work had been done on the case, and Tom Ladd and Phil Yochum had done a fantastic job. But more needed to be done. The sooner, the better.

Harris concluded that the obvious motive was dope, saying how he believed he had already "talked to the killers" during his interviews.

"I was basically trying to get the blessing from my superiors to go forth and dig into this case *my* way," Harris said later. "Look, the families were calling, and nobody had any answers for them. I wanted the case assigned to me officially, so I could begin to get some things done."

Harris has always been known in HPD circles as a cop who voiced his opinions. In that respect, Harris was maybe too outspoken for some of his Texas counterparts, who believed in the more traditional old boys' club. Part of that, of course, or at least the part that his adversaries mentioned more often than not, was the fact that Harris was a tried-and-true Yankee; he had grown up back east, on the doorstep of New England. He wasn't from the Texas belt of deep-seated Lone Star cowboys. He might have had a slight Southwestern twang in his voice from all his years living in Texas, but you could never take that East Coast attitude out of the guy.

Regardless of how anybody felt about Harris, most agreed there was one thing that his competitors (and detractors) could not take away: this cop got things done. Most of his colleagues knew it. His boss knew it. And most of the family members of the slain kids knew it. Heck, it was one of the reasons why Tom Ladd, a Texas cop to the core, had recommended Harris to begin with; Ladd knew Harris would not stop until he found out what had happened to those kids.

Upon reading the letter, Lieutenant Nelson Zoch, a man who, Harris said, "deserves two hundred percent credit, got behind me all the way and told me, 'Whatever you need, let me know. I'll clear the way for you.' "

That was all Harris needed to hear.

CREATING A BILLBOARD was not the same as sitting down and sketching out an idea. George Koloroutis felt he needed to get Clear Channel, who owned all the billboard locations in and around the Clear Lake City region, to donate the space. George figured that if he could get billboards of the sketches and the Crime Stoppers tip line phone number, with the $100,000 reward, out there in front of the community, day in and day out, something would happen. The drawings alone would generate some sort of tip that would ultimately solve the case, George hoped. David Gronewold, Marcus Precella's stepdad, helped George with creating the billboard posters and was able to get his employer to donate some money toward the artwork.

Also, Clear Channel agreed to donate the space. George was grateful. The company provided fifteen locations for billboards. Strategically speaking, George wanted to place the billboard images on every road heading in and out of the Clear Lake region. The hope was that a motorist could not enter the community where the kids were murdered without seeing the sketches or reading about the $100,000 reward.

"It was clear to us by then that the male and female were from this area, and they were seen walking up to the house that day," George said.

So even if the two people in the drawings were not the murderers, tracking them down and speaking to each could prove to be the missing link.

George wanted HPD's blessing to put the billboards up. He didn't want to step out and begin doing things on his own, making enemies of the people who had been helping him find his daughter's killer. Talking to Detective Harris, George understood that there was going to come a time for the billboards, but it would be prudent to wait a little longer.

Patience was key, Harris promised.

Eager to go ahead with the billboards, George listened, though, and waited.

THE KOLOROUTISES WERE distraught. Same as all the families, the Christmas 2004 holiday had not been a celebration or time to relax and enjoy family functions.

"Our little girl was murdered," George said. "My wife has a hole in her heart. It is the worst pain life can throw at you."

Through all of this, now was not the time, George knew, to begin butting heads with HPD. He needed them as much as they—perhaps without coming out and saying it—needed him.

CHAPTER 25

CHRISTINE PAOLILLA WALKED out with the Clear Lake High School graduating class of 2004, but she did not have enough credits to earn a diploma. Back then, if you were a few credits shy of graduating, you could stroll proudly with your class, gown and all, under the assumption that you were going to return that summer, finish your credits, and earn your diploma officially—which was Christine's plan.

Nonetheless, Christine Paolilla looked good on that June day, smiling in a photo with her mother, Lori Paolilla. They hugged each other, shoulder to shoulder. Christine held a red rose and an official high-school diploma booklet, which was actually empty. The "Coke bottle" glasses, which had so much saddled Christine throughout her youth and caused her so much grief from the mean kids—a second aesthetic obstacle she had to overcome along with the loss of hair—were gone. Christine wore contacts. The gaudy wigs of her younger days were also a memory, as she had learned from Tiffany and Rachael that there were more appealing wigs she could wear with a smile. And on that day, the sun shined on her back, the sky the same shade of blue as the most beautiful robin's egg, and Christine's auburn hair glistened in the spring sunlight. Her arrest for shoplifting and problems with Christopher Snider were behind her, and it seemed Christine Paolilla was on her way to better days. Her two best friends had been murdered, sure, but she was going to overcome it all and do something with her life. The determination on her face—at least if you look at that photo and try to predict how she's feeling—showed a girl looking to go on to bigger and better things, leaving a past shrouded in chaos and death behind her.

The road Lori and Christine had traveled to Clear Lake was a tumultuous one. They had lived in Long Island, New York, according to an interview Lori gave to ABC News, while Charles Paolilla, Christine's biological father, worked construction in Manhattan. Lori stayed home with Christine and her brother. As Lori told the story years later, "[Christine's] father got up and went to work [one day] and never came home."

It was after that, Lori admitted, that she fell into a life of drug addiction; the emotional pain of losing her husband, in such a tragic, untimely way, was a wound too big to contend with; she found the burden of caring for two kids and the sudden loss of her husband a hurdle she could only jump, with the help of drugs. The numbing effect helped her cope. Helped her grieve. Helped her get through the toughest that life had to offer at the time. Yet, as the drugs took hold of her life, Lori lost custody of Christine to Christine's grandparents. But then they, too, died. Just a toddler, Christine was said to have asked Lori one day not long after: "Why is it that the people I love go away?"

Some experts might speculate that this overwhelming series of losses in Christine's life set up a fear of rejection. This was said to be something Christine carried with her to Texas years later. Rejection (or maybe an expectation of loss), it would seem, became something Christine considered to be a part of life she would have to continually endure. For Christine, one expert later noted, she internalized those early losses, so that whenever she got close to someone, she automatically expected that person to exit her life at some point. Christine could have viewed the situation—subconsciously or consciously—as a way to feel sorry for the life she had been dealt, as though any authority figure in her life would ultimately abandon her and did not care for her. This type of trauma is easily absorbed into the psyche as a child. Let's say you then add the fact that Christine woke up one day in kindergarten to find clumps of her hair on her pillow, bald spots all over her head like a chemo patient, and her view of herself began to diminish.

On top of all that, Lori Paolilla said, Christine had "poor vision" from a very young age, and she was forced to wear thick glasses—the kind that kids made fun of. Most of these personal (albeit social) issues centered on image—and this can devastate a young girl whose life, essentially, is focused on how she looks.

As far as where Tiffany and Rachael fit into Christine's life after Christine ended up in Texas, according to Lori, Christine claimed that Rachael and Tiffany were "the sweetest girls [she had] ever met. She couldn't speak highly enough about Tiffany or Rachael," Lori said later. Christine called them "fun," "loving," and her mother saw a real change in Christine's personality and overall demeanor after they met and started hanging out. One of the things that proved to Lori how serious Christine was about her feelings toward Rachael and Tiffany was that they were the only friends Christine had allowed to see her without her wig on. Some of the other kids at Clear Lake High had walked up behind Christine and had pulled her wig off when she was standing, talking to someone. They publicly embarrassed her. However, she was actually sharing her condition with Tiffany and Rachael in a personal and private way. It said a lot, according to Lori, about the person Christine was when she was around Rachael and Tiffany.

Along the way, though, this spiked-haired, skinny kid, with all sorts of body piercings and chains hanging from his greasy blue jeans, appeared one day and was back into Christine's life. Christopher Snider was, in one sense, a manifestation of what Christine's life had become at that time. She saw something in Chris. He won her heart, and, maybe more important, according to Lori, he developed a hold on her mind. Christine believed she could fix Chris Snider, which was when the problems started for her at home.

"There was something in [his] eyes," Lori Paolilla told ABC. She noticed it from the first moment she met him. That look he had told her that this boy was going to be trouble for her daughter. One of the things Lori noticed, and Christine's stepfather, Tom Dick, agreed, was how Chris Snider began to isolate Christine. He kept close tabs on her, Lori claimed. One of the ways he did this was to show Christine that he was in control of her life—as in, one day, according to Christine, Chris showed up at Clear Lake High, stood around with Christine as she talked with her friends, and then, without warning, yanked her wig off in front of everyone, laughing as he did it. And still, Christine defended her man, cleaving to his side even more; she claimed, she was in fear of losing him. It was as if she expected to be shamed, to be ridiculed, to be put down, because it had been her view of life for so long. Some said Chris Snider would tell her, "No one else will have you but me. . . . You better not do anything I don't like or disapprove of."

Others, though, tell this story differently. One source there on that day later claimed Christine's version of Chris Snider being the quintessential abusive/tough guy, embarrassing her in front of her friends, was nothing more than a faux persona she had dreamt up to cover her own sick and twisted behavior.

Chris and Christine had been flirting back and forth on that day. One of Chris's friends said to him, "Hey, you know she's wearing a wig, right?" Then Chris's friend walked over and pulled it off Christine's head.

Chris felt bad for her. "He kind of just fell into the boyfriend role," a source explained, referencing when they reconnected at the party and hooked up for the second time.

Tiffany and Rachael explained to Christine that she could do better; there was another guy out there for her who would treat her with dignity, respect, and kindness. Tiffany and Rachael were strong personalities, who grew up in supportive, sturdy households, where morals and regard for others had been instilled. They'd had their share of pain throughout life, as most kids do, but they were not about to let a friend of theirs be abused by her boyfriend. They knew better.

Christine wrote it off as not being as bad as it looked. The guy had his good side, too.

Lori and her second husband, Tom Dick, did "everything in their power," Tom later explained to ABC, to keep Christine away from Chris Snider. "There's only so much you can do. . . ."

They grounded her.

Didn't work.

It was hard to keep watch on a teenager and put in a full day at the office.

They took away her privileges to use the car whenever she wanted.

That didn't work, either.

She stole the keys.

Christine ran away.

They went out and found her.

And there she'd be, in her man's arms, Chris Snider smiling that devilish grin, as though he had won a round.

They called the police.

They sat with an attorney.

Neither could do much more than point out the frustration of having their hands tied as parents.

They tried getting a restraining order against Chris Snider, on top of having him arrested (he was two years older than Christine).

Yet, according to Lori and Tom, neither did any good.

They sat Christine down and talked about her life and the trouble they saw heading her way down the road.

It did nothing.

They warned her that her boyfriend was a different kind of player. She could never fix him. She didn't know what the hell she was getting herself into.

Christine ignored the advice.

"He had some sort of mental control over her that we couldn't break," Tom Dick recalled.

And now here Christine was, with the summer of 2004 before her, only a few credits shy of her diploma. Snider was in Kentucky facing charges, doing time. Christine had a shot at a new start. The ball was missing from a chain still tied to her ankle.

Still, the last thing on Christine Paolilla's mind at this time was school. In fact, Christine ended up at a rehab in Kerrville, Texas, a near five-hour, 250-mile ride west of Clear Lake, past San Antonio. And it would be there, in the hills of Texas, where Christine fell into an even darker hole than she had just climbed out from, having been arrested and sent to drug rehab before she was even out of high school. If Christine and her parents thought Chris Snider—finally out of her life, for the time being—was troublesome and a menace to her well-being, the man Christine was about to meet (on top of getting that truckload of money in her hands) was going to put Chris Snider to shame.

CHAPTER 26

BRIAN HARRIS HAD never had total access to the Clear Lake case file, or complete control of the investigation in the way an officer looking to dig in wanted. One day near the first anniversary of the murders, Harris took the boxes of interviews and reports and photographs and wheeled them over to his cubicle. It was time he settled into the case and took a sharper look at everything in its entirety. There was an answer in there somewhere. The Adelbert side of it all that Harris had been working on never panned out. As much as the Homicide Division might have thought there was a connection between Adelbert and Marcus and drug dealing, it just wasn't there. And as a competent investigator, giving into the will to solve the case, you had to, at some point, let go of the obvious and turn your attention toward other ideas, develop new leads and think outside the box.

Part of Harris's strategy was to learn everything he could from the case files. Then meet with the families. Talk things over with them and see if anything new emerged. Homicide needed to do something, Harris was convinced, and it was probably a good time to release the sketches. Get the case back in front of the news media and out in the public eye. Ask people in the community to start thinking about it differently. Let everyone—especially the killer—know HPD was not going to stop until the killers were caught.

As a stage one, new plan of attack, Harris decided to release the sketches during a bona fide press conference. He was well aware that an onslaught of questions would come regarding why they had not released the sketches earlier. The best answer, which turned out to be true, was that HPD had been looking into several different angles of the case and they did not want to scare off potential suspects, had they seen themselves in those sketches. There was the thought that the sketches looked like several people whom HPD had been looking at as suspects.

Now, though, a year after the crime, and not one palpable suspect on radar, to say they were desperate for the public's help might not be something HPD wanted to admit; yet it was absolutely true.

The second stage of this new strategy, which would take place sometime after the sketches were released, was to place those billboards up around Clear Lake City. That was going to fall on George Koloroutis's shoulders. Put the sketches on billboards heading in and out of town, at calculated locations, where motorists had to look at them while coming in or going out of the city.

After the press conference and official release of the sketches, Harris called Michelle and Craig Lackner. He had never really spoken to them. He wanted to follow up. Reading the report Michelle had given on the night of the murders, Harris knew this witness was a detailed person; it was there in her observations. Of particular interest to Harris was that Michelle Lackner had reported that one of the suspects carried a bag. What more did she know?

"Hey," Harris said casually, "do you recall what happened that night?" It was not a formal interview. He was simply calling as a police officer looking for additional information.

Michelle Lackner ran through the entire scenario for him. When she got to the purse, she described it as a "big banana-boat type" of handbag.

Harris was impressed with her recollection. This was going to become important. With any luck, Harris would be able to head out to the Lackners' with a photo lineup someday to show Michelle and Craig. So many tips were coming in since the public release of the sketches that they were having trouble keeping up. But sooner or later, as they went through and checked people off the list, the Homicide Unit was going to be left with a few key suspects. That was when Harris could go to Michelle and Craig, a mug shot lineup in hand, which matched the sketches, and their perp would be one of the suspects in the lineup. If the Lackners could verify without a doubt that they were certain, there would be no question about the killer's identity. On the other hand, Harris considered, he was walking a tightrope: he couldn't run out to the Lackners' every week with a different set of mug shots.

"I thought, 'I am going to get one shot at this,' " Harris recalled. "I cannot risk a misidentification and so I want to make sure that when I show [the Lackners] a photo array, I have verified everything."

Harris had some raw experience with a witness who had shown him just how fragile these sketches and a possible photo lineup were. There was a girl who had been brought in under a tip. She had been obsessed with Tiffany and Rachael to a creepy *Single White Female* point of contention. The tip appeared to be legit. So they brought her in.

Harris showed the girl the sketches.

She took one look at the drawing of the female, freaked out, and screamed, "That's me!"

But as it turned out, it couldn't have been. She had a rock solid alibi.

SO THE SKETCHES were made public and the billboards set to go up.

"Seeing the sketches," Nichole Sánchez recalled later, speaking for her family, "gave us some comfort. We knew then, looking at these two people in the drawings, that the murders had nothing to do with Adelbert."

Calls came into the Crime Stoppers tip line. It seemed several people knew someone who looked like one of the two characters depicted in the drawings. The problem was that the drawings, although fairly detailed, could be put up to literally hundreds of people and made to match. There was nothing distinctive about either of the two people, besides their thin lips and the fact that HPD was looking to talk to a male and a female.

But again, this, too, was about to change.

CHAPTER 27

JUST BEFORE THE one-year anniversary, Brian Harris's boss assigned a second investigator, Waymon Allen, a sergeant, to help Harris, who was an officer at the time. Allen outranked Harris, but Harris knew the case by now inside out. Allen could help, however, dig through what was a mountain of evidence to see if they had overlooked or missed anything important. Allen was a solid cop, a good guy. He knew what to look for. The answer, Harris was convinced, had to be there—sometimes it *is* right in front of you, Harris knew from his years investigating murder. You just need a fresh set of eyes to flesh it out.

Maybe Waymon Allen was that guy.

"Hey, I'd like to be a part of this," Allen told Harris. "Give me, like, a week to read through everything and familiarize myself with it all, and we'll get together and see what we need to do next."

Harris liked the sound of that.

"We're going to reinterview everybody, take another look and talk to some of the witnesses," Harris suggested. "We missed something. We should probably go back forty-eight hours on the telephone records and see what type of timeline and witness list we can develop from those calls the kids made in the days leading up to the murders."

Waymon Allen agreed. It was a smart approach.

(Funny thing was, which truly shows how complicated and subjective police work can be, that if they would have gone back an additional twenty-four hours, making a total of seventy-two, they could have solved the case right then and there. The killer had called

Rachael Koloroutis not *two* days before the murders, but *three* days before.)

Harris and Allen called the families back in. They discussed the sketches. They discussed George's plan for the billboards. It was time to push the public even more.

"I want to put up those billboards," George said. He had been working on them for some time now. It was time.

"Yes," Harris and Allen agreed.

Something was happening; there was an energy to the case now that had not been there for some time. The families, along with Harris and Allen, felt it. HPD had done its job focusing on Marcus and Adelbert and the choices they had made in life. But now it was time to look in other directions, search out other possibilities, flip over new stones and see what was underneath. Harris believed he had gone down every path imaginable as far as the Adelbert and Marcus angle. The answer just wasn't there.

Allen and Harris worked another lead they had just made public. A few nights before the murders, there was a party for Tiffany Rowell's birthday. Allen and Harris knew there was a good chance that someone at that party had information, or that the killer(s) might have possibly even attended the party. In an article published by the *Houston Chronicle* on July 19, 2004, a year and a day after the murders, Allen and Harris set the stage for the direction they saw the investigation taking, announcing that they were planning on reinterviewing everyone involved.

"The goal is to close the case," Harris said as plainly as possible. Nothing less, Harris made a point to note, would suffice. Justice had to be served here. Four kids, no one needed to be reminded, had been mauled by a storm of gunfire, two of them beaten with a pistol. HPD could not allow the case to go unsolved.

"They were all very young, very immature, and on their own [for the first time in their lives]," Waymon Allen explained to the *Chronicle.* "They have exercised bad judgment at times, but certainly didn't deserve what happened to them."

Both cops were hoping to send a message and ignite some sort of reaction from their killer.

The billboards went up all over town, staring down at commuters, community members, dopers, criminals of all types, the victims' family members, subtly reminding everyone that *someone* knew *something*. As it turned out, those billboards would prove to be one of many stars that were about to align, this as one of the killers—there *were* two!—drove by one of the billboards and felt as though he or she was looking into a mirror.

PART THREE

BETWEEN A ROTT
AND A HARD PLACE

CHAPTER 28

TO HIM, SHE looked "pretty" (his word) just sitting there, minding her own business. She wasn't talking, but more or less relaxing quietly, a look of bashfulness and maybe contemptuousness about her. It was November 1, 2004. "Alive" was how he referred to his first impression of Christine Paolilla as she sat waiting for a 12-step meeting to get under way at a community center near downtown Kerrville, Texas, not far from the halfway house she had been staying at as part of her probation and drug treatment program. Christine hadn't gone back to summer school and finished her diploma, after all; she spent most of her time trying to stay out of trouble, fighting off what had become an obvious monkey on her back.

"She was beautiful," he added later, referring to the moment he walked into the 12-step room and set eyes on Christine.

Right away, they locked glances and "flirted," an immediate attraction settling on the two of them as they gaped at each other, a coy smile and a bit of chemistry at play.

It was a coincidence, he speculated, that they ended up sitting next to each other. Yet, right away, he sensed that Christine was like him—that is, a stranger in a foreign place.

"Hi," he said, sitting down in one of those folding metal chairs used at stag parties and church hall bingo.

"Hello," Christine said back.

He went by Justin, but he had been born Stanley Justin Rott. Originally, he was from the Chicago area, Schaumburg, a graduate of Schaumburg High School. He had been in Texas since early 2004. Justin had moved from the upper Midwest down to San Antonio to be with his mother, a woman he'd not had a relationship with since he was two years old.

"And so, I really never *had* a relationship with her," he commented later.

Justin Rott's biological mother had called her boy one day out of the blue and asked if she could begin to get to know him. Not having much of anything tying him down in Illinois, he made the trip to San Antonio, with the hope of starting over. Sadly, though, as he would later tell it, this renewed "new relationship" didn't come packaged with a Disney ending.

"It didn't work out so well," he said. "She had some issues of her own."

Since his early teens, Justin had internalized an itch for numbing the pain of life with drugs. He had done his share up north; but after moving in as a twenty-four-year-old with his mother, the six-four, 195-pound Chicagoan got an idea of where that longing for chasing the red dragon had come from.

"My mother had a history of drug addiction and, also, some depression, and things like that." He thought she had "changed," Justin added, when he met her for what was the first time in 2004. But there was no denying that she had passed down the addict gene—if we can agree that the body produces one—to him.

Stanley Justin Rott had been in the U.S. Marine Corps for about a year and a half as a young man just out of high school. The reason he was forced out of what was the best opportunity he'd ever had in life turned out to be a failed urinalysis. They called it an "other than honorable [discharge], with separation," but there was no hiding the fact that the guy had messed up. He had done some cocaine while on leave and couldn't pass a drug test. So the military gave him the boot.

Justin said he had started using heavy drugs in junior high. In fact, between the ages of fifteen and twenty-one, he admitted, he didn't mess with simple drugs. Maybe weed in the woods behind school, or a few lines of coke here and there at a party with his mates? No. During that time Justin had been a full-blown heroin addict. A damn junkie. In and out of treatment centers and halfway houses for years, falling victim to that revolving-door syndrome many drug addicts can't seem to escape once they get caught in it. Justin later put part of the onus on his family, saying his parents (a father and step-mother) "looked down [on drugs] very strongly." The first time he asked his dad for help, Justin claimed, "he just wouldn't, because it was drugs. You know, a lot of people today will at least give someone a chance. . . . I understand his position . . . [but] it was difficult, at nineteen years old, you know, it was just *hard*" to accept that his own father wouldn't help him.

When Justin left his mother's in San Antonio, after their little reunion in 2004 didn't go over so well, he fell back into his old behavior. This happened after having been sober for a time while staying with his mother.

"I was using," he said. "She was using. . . . I ended up homeless."

He was on the street, a dope addict, with nowhere to live. That was Justin Rott's life then. No money. No job. No future. The guy who loved to play pool, draw, hit the beach, listen to David Sides, watch *House* on television, sit back and put on one of his favorite movies, *GoodFellas* or *A Bronx Tale*, had nowhere to turn, and no one to turn to. *Conversations with God*, by Neale Donald Walsch, Justin Rott's favorite book, full of practical and spiritual advice, didn't have the answers this time. Justin knew what to do, but he didn't have the willpower or drive to do it.

Beaten by the needle again, seemingly no hope in sight, Justin called on a friend, who picked him up and took him to the Serenity House, a detox center in Fredericksburg, Texas, where he spent twenty-eight days drying out, trying to get his act—best he could—together. From there he was shipped to the Norman Turner House, a halfway house in Kerrville, where he worked at his sobriety while living with twelve other men.

Life inside a halfway house is not a slacker's ride of smoking cigarettes and drinking coffee until his heart explodes and the enamel on his teeth is stained yellow. Nor is it a couch potato's orgy of watching reruns of *Sanford and Son* and *The Beverly Hillbillies,* while talking all things 12-step. A resident is required to work, pay rent, attend addiction meetings regularly, do certain chores around the house, stay sober (of course), and participate in community events. It would be nice, too, if a resident went out and volunteered his time at a soup kitchen or at a homeless shelter. Maybe showed by example how grateful he was for, one, being alive, and, two, being able to give back.

Justin knew from past experience that the way to *stay* clean was to keep busy—any addict in recovery, serious about his or her sobriety, will tell you this. Another prerequisite that many sobriety programs, sponsors, and all 12-step programs recommend is that a person stay out of relationships for the first year of sobriety. A recovering addict needs a year sober to be able to slog through the fog of addiction and realize who he or she is as a new and clean human being. Before a person can make the choices a relationship requires, he or she needs to be able to think with a clear mind. Most recovering addicts, however, don't listen to this solid, useful piece of proven, practical advice. Many addicts feel that in order to stay clean they need to hook up with another recovering addict. More often than not, this decision backfires. The results are generally disastrous, more in line with a wick lighting not one stick of dynamite, but a fistful. Two addicts falling off the wagon together—something that routinely happens in this situation—is double the trouble, as they say. An eruption of chaos.

Which was where, for Christine Paolilla, fate—or maybe its opposite: free will—just happened to walk into her life in the form of a drug addict—arguably like her—who knew nothing about staying sober for any length of time. Here was another man—sitting next to her at a 12-step meeting, smiling, giving her a shimmering, if not lustful, eye—for Christine to fix. Someone for her to latch on to and try to shape and mold into the man she had been looking for all her life.

After the 12-step meeting, Christine and Justin talked. They introduced themselves and exchanged pleasantries, surely discussing where they were living. Out in the world of recovery, especially in the same general county, the circle is quite small. People run into each other all the time: in church basements, at sober dances, in meetings at hospitals and treatment centers. Justin and Christine had exchanged glances and swapped a few stories; yet it didn't seem as though Cupid was going to allow them to move past this initial meeting. Justin was some years older (Christine liked that). He probably had other things on his mind. He didn't seem to be interested in some young chick, newly sober, confused, and just out of high school.

But then, a week or so later, there was a belated Halloween party at a local treatment center, and, lo and behold, Justin Rott and Christine Paolilla bumped into each other. Christine had just gotten out of actual treatment, she told him, and was staying at a nearby halfway house, biding her time before stepping back out into the real world for a go at sobriety alone. She was trying to do the right thing by attending sober events and staying connected to the people she had met in "the program."

Justin still had some time left in the halfway house he was staying at, he said, but he was slated to get out soon enough.

What a coincidence.

It was the older man who had spotted Christine standing with some friends at the Halloween party. There was that familiar girl who wore all that makeup, smiling and talking. The music thumped. People stood around drinking coffee and punch. Justin didn't give warning; he walked up with a smile, grabbed Christine by the hand, and said, "You're *going* to dance with me!" And he wasn't taking no for an answer, apparently.

Describing this moment later, he sounded like a smitten boy who was shocked that the girl of his dreams had answered his call: "She danced with me. I took a chance, and she danced."

They spent the night talking and "getting to know each other." There was definitely a connection. Some sort of common ground they shared. Music. TV. Books. No matter what they brought up, the other was into it. They were alike on so many different levels. Despite the age difference of seven years, Christine liked what she saw. Rott sported a redneck beer gut (pear-shaped torso, more Kid Rock than Larry the Cable Guy). He had an Inspector Jacques Clouseau pencil mustache, a bit of black peach fuzz on his chin, and a calming way about him that spoke to Christine's need to be comforted, loved, controlled, and taken care of. There's no doubt Justin Rott made Christine Paolilla feel warm and fuzzy. He was her new protector. And there's no doubt, additionally, that Christine made Justin feel as though he had found his soul mate.

From there the relationship soared into hyperspeed. Justin went into a halfway house "not too far down the road from where she was at." He saw her again after that Halloween party at a 12-step meeting. That encounter turned into them seeing each other every day. They talked, too, on the phone a few times a day. Hung out, Justin said, every night.

"There wasn't a day that went by that I didn't see her or talk to her."

By Texas standards, Kerrville is a small town, populationwise. Justin and Christine were convinced that wherever they went, "people" (those in the program) would see them and gossip—about what, exactly, he never said. The idea was that with a man and a young girl getting together every day, both of whom were living in halfway houses after being in treatment for drug addiction, maybe some would suspect that they were getting together too soon in their sobriety and they would eventually turn back to drugs. If there is one thing many recovering addicts will admit, it's that the recovery scene can become a muddled world of judging and nattering busybodies. Some addicts love nothing better than to go to meetings and then hang out after, smoking cigarettes, drinking coffee, talking smack about everyone else.

"There's not too many places a person can get away [in Kerrville] where the whole town is not talking about it," Justin explained.

Christine and Justin, however, found such a place: an area of town that he later called "the lake."

"It's a place," he said, "where . . . it's almost like back in the days, a place where couples go." Lovers' Lane. Not necessarily for fornicating, Justin noted, but just to get away from what was a nosey small town of big mouths.

As much as Justin Rott wanted to diminish the idea that the lake was a place where he and Christine chose to consummate their relationship, it took him but two weeks to get her pants off. And he couldn't get enough. That aside, Justin said he viewed the relationship as more than a fleeting bed partner to get him from one stage of his recovery to the next. He saw Christine as someone he wanted to be with all the time. He could not stop thinking about her. He could not stop a desire to be with her. And he could not stop considering that he had never before met someone with whom he seemed to have so much in common.

"We would talk for hours," he explained later, describing how the relationship evolved rather quickly from dating to obsessing over being with each other. "We never argued. We never fought. We had the same interests. [We liked] the same music. I've never had that before."

For all intents and purposes, they were addicted to one another.

CHAPTER 29

GEORGE KOLOROUTIS TOOK a call on November 15, 2004. The woman explained that she was Abby Strickland's (pseudonym) mother. Mrs. Strickland (pseudonym) was frantic. Abby, her daughter, had said she'd been friends with Rachael, though George and Ann had never heard of her.

Still, Abby had been acting very strangely, Mrs. Strickland explained. "Her behavior has been spiraling downhill. She moved in with two male friends and is now working at Exotica." It wasn't until after the murders that Abby had moved in with her friends, who wouldn't, Mrs. Strickland explained to George, "let her out of their sight. They are the ones who kept pressuring her to leave the house and go to work at Exotica."

"What can *we* do?" George asked.

"Can you go talk to her?"

Abby's father was a Drug Enforcement Administration (DEA) agent in Boston, Mrs. Strickland said. Abby's mother had called him and he was back in town to help out. There was a swell of concern emerging from the public about the Houston drug culture being involved in the Clear Lake murders, and fear of a possible swarm of potential murders forthcoming. A DEA agent whose daughter was on the forefront of that line was not going to stay put and allow his own daughter to become a target.

George grabbed Ann and drove to where Abby now lived with her two friends. Her DEA agent father was there as well.

"Come on in," he said. "I want to warn you that there is a gun in the house."

Ann, who was with George, looked at her husband. *Okay. . . ,* she thought.

They sat with Abby and talked. "Pleading with her to move back home" was how this part of the conversation was framed in one report.

Abby said she didn't want to go home. She was scared. This apartment, with these two guys, was the best place for her to live right now.

It sounded to them as if Abby believed her two roommates would protect her.

Ann got up and walked around the apartment. She looked at several photos of Rachael that Abby had on the walls. They were not the kind of images Ann wanted her daughter to be remembered by. So Ann took them off the wall.

"What are you doing?" Abby asked. "Come on . . . those are mine."

"You can come to our house anytime and pick out a photo of Rachael," George said.

Abby was crying. She was confused. Although they didn't know her, they could tell something was wrong.

Abby said she would go to George and Ann's house the following day and meet with them, and would talk about things a bit more. The situation, to put it mildly, seemed weird.

The next day Abby brought one of the two guys she lived with to George and Ann's house. Almost immediately George and Ann were "creeped out" by the guy, who walked into the house with a cocky chip on his shoulder.

Lelah, Rachael's sister, was also home.

"You had no right taking those photos off the walls of my apartment," the guy said sternly. He looked at Ann and George.

George stepped in front of the kid, his bulky chest pumped out, a look of *take it easy there, big fella* about his face. "Just relax, buddy," George said. "Cool your jets. As a mother, Ann had *every* right to confiscate those pictures of her daughter."

After that, the man calmed down. Meanwhile, Lelah was in her room talking to Abby about Rachael—and getting a strange vibe from the girl. Then they walked back into the living room, where George and Ann were with the kid.

"It became obvious to us," George said later, "that [Abby] didn't really know Rachael that well. [Lelah] got a really bad feeling about her and sensed she was a liar and was faking her closeness to Rachael."

Why, though?

During the conversation with Lelah, Ann and George, Abby tried to play up how great a place Exotica was to work. The guy she brought to George's house worked at the club, too. In fact, it became clear that he and Abby's other roommate were quasi recruiters for the club, looking for girls to turn into strippers.

"They're really nice people," Abby said of both guys.

"The management is great," Abby continued, trying to convince herself it was the right choice in life. "It's the perfect place to work."

George wondered where this was going.

After a few more insincere words, Abby mentioned that she had spoken to HPD and told them everything she knew.

George didn't believe her.

The *other* guy Abby lived with was worried, the guy *with* Abby explained to George and Ann. "He thinks he gave HPD too much information and that the killers may come after him."

"What else did he say?" George asked.

"He told us Adelbert told him that he owed the Voo Crew money."

"The Voo Crew is a group of Vietnamese from the Seabrook region," one law enforcement source said, "that raced cars and sold a little dope. This idea that they were involved turned out to be a rumor fueled by the likes of [Abby Strickland]," who was trying to push the investigation as far away from her doorstep as possible.

Why are they sitting here telling us this? George wondered, staring at Abby and her friend. He wanted to hear what they had to say, but he also wanted them out of his house.

But then it hit George as he stared at them: *They look just like the people in the sketches.*

CHAPTER 30

AFTER ABBY AND her friend left his house, George sat down and wrote out everything that had been said, on top of everything else he knew about Abby and her two roommates. George, Ann and Lelah had a bad feeling. At the end of his note, which was addressed to a detective in the Homicide Unit, George added: *This is all we can think of. . . . We are not sure of the knowledge they have, but believe they know more than they've admitted to. We continue to have concerns about JU, [a few others], and Miranda Baxter (pseudonym) as well. One thing seems very evident: Whoever committed this heinous act knows the kids were at the house at that time.*

George went on to ask HPD about phone records. He wanted to know if all of them "had been scrubbed"? He was concerned that the media wasn't taking the sketches by the horns and running—very little had been said in the media about the sketches since HPD had released them. Why hadn't there been more media play?

From what I understand, the two in the composite were seen by a neighbor walking by wearing black clothes, George wrote. *They stopped and looked in Tiffany's truck!?!? This [was] all around the time the murders were committed. . . . Were they the killers? Who are they? Shouldn't an effort be made to find out?*

The Koloroutis family's frustrations, much the same as the other families, were there, implicit in every word George wrote to HPD. He thanked those members of the Homicide Division for all their efforts, but at the same time, he wanted something more to be done.

The last thing the police needed now, any of the detectives investigating the Clear Lake case knew, was George Koloroutis becoming impatient and pushy. This was an incredibly protean investigation; it was constantly changing its shape, its feel, and its profile of a suspect.

ABBY STRICKLAND CALLED George at work. The last time they spoke, Abby was at George's house arguing with Ann about the picture of Rachael that Ann had taken from the wall of Abby's apartment. Abby and her roommate didn't much appreciate it.

"How are things going?" Abby asked. George could sense in her tone that she had other things on her mind besides small talk.

"You know," he said, to oblige her.

"I heard you guys know who did it."

"Who told you that?"

"My mom."

"The police have a very good idea and are investigating accordingly. That's about all I can say at this point."

"Listen, I heard that some black guy, who was supposed to be all doped up, one night at a party, he was, like, mouthing off that he had done it. . . ."

"You heard that?"

"I'll try to find out who it was," Abby said.

"Don't do anything dangerous. Please use caution . . . and notify the police or me as soon as you can."

Another week—heck, another year—and another new theory to add to that growing list of possibilities.

George hung up the phone and sat back. Some days were tougher than others. All he could do was take a deep breath, have a good cry, and carry on.

CHAPTER 31

A S THANKSGIVING 2004 arrived, Justin Rott and his new girl
decided to part ways for what was the first time in their near
month-old relationship. Because Justin didn't have any family nearby,
he went with a couple of guys from the halfway house to San Antonio
and spent the holiday with one of their families. Christine drove back
to Friendswood to spend the weekend with Tom Dick and Lori Paolilla.

Christine had been transformed. She was feeling good, looking
good, and comprehending the notion that drugs were only going to
slow her down in life. She saw Justin Rott as the ideal man for her,
mainly because he was gentle, soft-spoken, and, according to her,
nonviolent in every way that she had been accustomed to with Chris
Snider. Justin treated her like a lady, and Christine had never experienced such affection and tenderness from a man. He allowed her to
have her own feelings, think for herself, and be herself. And she truly
felt, for maybe the first time, that a healthy relationship with a man
was possible. She could love someone without smothering him with
insecurities.

Between Thanksgiving and Christmas, Justin and Christine continued to see each other every day. Perhaps against their better judgment, Lori Paolilla and Tom Dick told Christine that Justin Rott was
welcome in their house for the Christmas holiday. No doubt Christine had told them about Justin during the Thanksgiving break. And
she must have worked them hard since then. *Look how great I'm
doing, Ma. . . . He's an excellent guy! I love him.*

In any event Christine approached her new man just before the

Christmas break. "Why don't you come to Friendswood and spend the holiday with us?"

"Of course," Justin answered. "Yes, absolutely."

Justin Rott had some news himself. Just before they prepared to head northeast to her parents' house, he took Christine out to a bridge in Kerrville. It wasn't the George Washington or the Golden Gate, but the small concrete edifice with the murky, muddy water below was good enough to serve his purpose on this day, and perhaps even act as a portent, pointing out what was ahead for both of them.

"I cannot be with you anymore," he said as they stood on the bridge, a slight wind blowing cool winter air.

Christine's jaw dropped. Then the tears came.

Here we go again: more rejection. She thought she'd escaped it this time. But here was another human being she had given her heart to about to walk out of her life and never return. It felt like murder. And if there was one person who knew about those feelings, how much they tore at the heart, it was Christine Paolilla.

CHAPTER 32

GEORGE WAS HOME in his office, working late. He had been feeling as though the case was never going to be solved. It was that up and down, back and forth, hot and cold nonsense that comes with the territory of losing a child to murder, and then becoming actively involved in catching her killer.

In the days to come, George Koloroutis and Brian Harris would refer to them as the "old guys." One of the old guys called George at home. George had been the most visible of the victims' family members. He was on the news and in the newspapers.

One of the old guys decided to phone him with news that sent George's heart racing.

"We think we know who killed your daughter," the old guy said.

George stood up from his desk chair. "You what?"

The old guy repeated it.

They talked some more. The old guy explained that he and his partner, a retired cop, were private investigators. They wanted to help. You know, go over some things the police had already investigated and follow a few leads they had developed on their own.

George set up a meeting and hung up. Why not hear them out?

No sooner had he cradled the phone, than George called Brian Harris and explained what was going on.

"We want to be there," Harris told George, meaning at his house when the old guys came for that meeting.

"No problem."

CHAPTER 33

JUSTIN ROTT KNEW immediately that he'd made a terrible mistake in teasing the love of his life.

"I cannot be with you anymore"—he corrected himself quickly after seeing the tears run down Christine's cheeks—"as your *boyfriend*!"

"What?" she said, perking up. "What did you just say?"

"Christine, I love you. Could you please make me the happiest man and make me your husband, and you be my wife?"

Not so much a smooth wordsmith, but the guy was proposing marriage in his own sincere way.

"Yes. Yes. Yes!" Christine answered. She wanted to jump up and down, but instead she hugged her man and wept some more—this time tears of joy.

They were engaged. Weeks after meeting, while both were in treatment for serious drug addictions, Christine Paolilla and Stanley Justin Rott were planning on getting married. This was no simple train wreck in motion; it was more like a fifty-car pileup on the highway, and a train with a dozen railcars was heading toward it!

"It was one of the reasons," Justin Rott said later, "why she wanted me to meet her parents" during Christmas break.

Both agreed, however, that it would not be a good idea to tell Lori and Tom that they were going to be husband and wife within a few short months. That would be their secret, at least for the time being.

"Well, I mean," Justin recalled, "everybody thought we were kind of crazy because we didn't know each other that long. And that's one of the reasons why she wanted me to meet her parents—because we got engaged."

Both were able to secure the required permissions from their halfway houses to go to Christine's parents for the holiday. They drove down to Houston/Friendswood from Kerrville, arriving a few days before Christmas Eve, with the intention of staying about five days. It was supposed to be Justin Rott, Christine, and her parents. Christine's brother showed up and took the spare bedroom, while Justin was given one of those plastic Walmart blow-up mattresses to put on the floor of the entertainment room, a section of the house, he later added, that impressed him. There was a large-screen television and a nice setup for showing movies.

Christine and Justin slept together on the blow-up mattress. And, according to Justin, neither Lori nor Tom voiced any objection to the arrangement.

During Christmas dinner, Christine appeared depressed, looking down at her plate of food, playing with her vegetables. She seemed to be forever on the verge of saying something that never came out of her mouth. Justin looked on and listened most of the time, knowing his boundaries.

"I miss home," Christine finally voiced.

"We want you back here," Lori said.

Christine smiled. She wanted to come back.

"I can offer you a job," Tom Dick told Justin at one point during the meal. It wasn't pitching bales of hay or picking up horse dung, either. Tom Dick promised Justin he could help get him into the plumber's apprenticeship program. Not too shabby for a dope addict in recovery.

At some point during the dinner, Lori, according to a source at the table, brought up the Clear Lake murders, saying, "How difficult this holiday season must be for those families that lost their children."

They all knew what Lori was referring to. The crime was still something the community, of which Lori and Tom were a part of, had been concerned about and were still coming down from. If four kids could be murdered like that in broad daylight, and the crime went unsolved for as long as it did, what role did the community play in the delay? Not only that, but Lori had met Tiffany and Rachael.

Christine didn't seem to want to discuss the crime, especially since her friends had been among the murdered.

She was still as a stone. Quiet too.

"I think," Lori said next, "that whoever did this to these kids should get the needle."

Such a bold statement.

Justin Rott agreed.

Christine, white as paper, "with a frozen look on her face," Justin later said, didn't respond. She looked at her man, however, with her eyes bulged out, or, as Justin later put it, "just . . . huge." Christine was shocked that her mother had said such a thing.

Justin thought something was up: There was more to the look on Christine's face than someone, per se, reacting to an audacious remark about the death penalty. There was something about the way she protruded her eyes out at him. He made a mental note to continue the conversation with her later, when they were alone.

After a brief moment, Christine pushed her meal aside and complained about not having much of an appetite.

Dinner was over.

The Christmas holiday visit to Friendswood ended without drama or problems for Christine and Justin.

For Justin Rott, it was the first time in years that he had sat down to a Christmas dinner within the framework and closeness of a family environment, and it made him feel great about the people who were going to be his in-laws. He had gotten along well with Christine's parents.

"They were wonderful," Justin said of Tom Dick and Lori Paolilla. "They bought me Christmas gifts. They were polite to me. It was one of the best Christmases I had had in years."

Besides that one instance—Lori's death penalty comment—Christine seemed happy over the holiday. She had matured in some ways and was ready to take on life with a new outlook. And now her stepfather had offered her soon-to-be husband a job. Sobriety was everything they had promised.

When they returned to Kerrville, Christine and Justin took in a New Year's Eve party at *La Hacienda*, a treatment center for alcoholism and other chemical dependencies where Justin had taken on service work in the past with younger kids, helping out classes on

Thursday nights. He knew mostly everyone at *La Hacienda*, had a good rapport with many of the employees and several of the counselors. Introducing Christine to everyone felt good; he had found someone. It was rewarding to show her off.

The party went off as planned, and Justin and his girl had a great time. Christine was so comfortable with her new surroundings, the way of life she now led with her new man, that she even raised her hand and decided to give karaoke a try. Everyone laughed and clapped along as Christine belted out a few pop songs in her squeaky, high-pitched, off-key singing voice.

At some point during that same week, Justin pulled Christine aside and told her: "I want to take that job your father offered me. Let's go to Friendswood together. Start new lives."

Christine was beside herself. Awesome. Another reason to celebrate. Lest they forget, within months Christine was going to be coming into a whopping sum of money from her biological father's death—$360,000.

They could get married, buy themselves a home, and begin to live happily ever after.

Both Justin Rott and Christine Paolilla had to know that happily ever after was truly something written in fairy-tale marriages only, and this about-to-be union between two recovering drug addicts stepping into a ton of cash—well, let's just say that it would turn into anything but a Rapunzel moment.

THE OLD GUYS showed up at George's house. Detective Brian Harris and a colleague sat with George and greeted the two men as they got comfortable.

The old guys brought photographs and reports. They sat and talked about JU and that drug ring connection. They were certain the JU path was the right way to go with the case. It had to be.

All of the evidence pointed to JU and/or one of his drug-dealing cohorts.

"All right," George said.

After discussing it with Harris as the old guys were out the door, heading back to wherever they had come from, George decided to keep in contact with them and see what they could come up with.

To put it mildly, Harris was "unimpressed."

CHAPTER 34

HARRIS HAD A feeling the old guys were either looking to collect on the reward money, or maybe looking to pilfer some quick cash out of a grieving father. Whether one or the other, Harris didn't trust the old guys. But what the detective didn't want, beyond anything else, was to have two Thomas Magnum, P.I., wannabes, who had probably watched far too much crime television, wiggling their way into his case and muddying the waters. If they knew something substantial, they needed to cough it up.

The old guys had certainly known things that only a cop on the inside could have given to them. By talking to them over the course of a few weeks, Harris could tell that much. So the old guys had some good contacts within HPD. What PI didn't have a source inside the police?

In meeting with the old guys a few times after that night, George had come to realize that maybe they could help, but it was clear that they were also, at times, throwing mud against the wall, hoping some of it would stick.

"They were just rehashing stuff that HPD had scrubbed already," George commented. "They were just trying to get a hundred-thousand-dollar reward! In my mind I was going to do what I could. And that was just one more avenue."

Detective Harris had continually met with the old guys and, in George's words, "they just had some stupid stuff to say to him."

At one time the old guys had even made George feel as though *he* was a suspect.

"Guys, I was somewhere else—everybody knows that. I have an alibi."

In a nice way, George was trying to say, *Let it go.* . . .

"In hindsight," George said, "Brian Harris was right. They were a colossal waste of my time and money."

George was a desperate father hoping to find his daughter's killers. Why wouldn't he jump at the chance to grab a rope that two private eyes were throwing him?

Brian Harris was finished with the old guys, however, and running out of patience. He had given the old guys the benefit of the doubt, hoping maybe they could dig something up. But their presence was becoming an irritation and hindrance more than anything else.

Harris had heard the old guys had gotten some information about a pistol—a weapon involved in the murders. He was curious, especially seeing that they hadn't shared the information with HPD. So Harris called one of the old guys.

The old guy was hesitant about giving Harris the info.

"Well," Harris suggested, "let's meet up and talk then."

The indication he left them with was that maybe they could help each other out.

"Yeah, okay," the old guy said.

They met for breakfast.

Harris showed up with a subpoena for any information they had in relation to the Clear Lake murders. He threw it on the table.

One of the old guys placed his hand on Harris's chest. "Brian, hey, man, we don't have to turn *anything* over to you."

Harris looked at his hand. "You have about one second to take your hand off my chest."

They sat down.

A waitress came and Harris ordered coffee. "Listen," he said, staring at the two of them, after she walked away, "you are *not* going to interfere with this investigation, you understand me? I want to see all your notes . . . anything you have!"

One old guy slid his notebook across the table. "Here."

"You don't dictate how an investigation goes," Harris warned. "You operate under the law."

The old guys understood their role. Harris was clear. He would give them leads to follow up on—things he didn't have the manpower to get done himself. But they were not to hold anything back.

Breakfast was over.

CHAPTER 35

CHRISTINE PAOLILLA AND Justin Rott woke up one morning in March 2005 and decided, you know what, a big, traditional wedding, with ushers and bridesmaids, and long gowns and tuxedoes, and maybe those tiny hors d'oeuvres on silver serving platters, wasn't what they wanted. It just didn't seem to fit their character. Hundreds of guests and a big bill didn't sound all that enticing. The time it would take to schedule and send out invitations. Order food. Hire a band. Then sit and listen to people they didn't know clank forks against champagne glasses. Waiting and laying out a bunch of money for a huge celebration—for what?

Instead, they decided then and there, on that cold March morning, that a short shotgun ceremony would best reflect who they were as people and the love they had found in each other. A minister and a chapel, or perhaps a justice of the peace, would suffice.

Nothing more.

They chose March 22, 2005. Just like that, Justin and his girl woke up single and went to bed that same night a married couple. How easy it was to share a life, legally speaking, and turn over half of what you own to someone else.

Christine called Justin one day from the halfway house she was still living in: "Let's get out of here."

"Okay," he said.

And so that was it: they hopped in Christine's car and bid Kerrville, Texas, *adieu*.

The plan was to move to Friendswood and buy a condo. But for the time being, they stayed holed up in a motel, already spending

Christine's cache of cash. The ATM became a daily stop for the both of them.

"No," Justin said later when asked if they had started using drugs. "Not at this time. No."

That was all about to change, however.

Very soon.

In a gigantic way.

HOMICIDE HAD BEEN manning the phones ever since those billboards went up all over town. The Crime Stoppers tip line and George Koloroutis's website had been running on full speed. Now it was just after the two-year anniversary of the murders and HPD and the families launched another public cry for information. The anniversary was as good a time as any to continue to push the case. The past year had developed some leads, but nothing had ever come of them. With the announcement once more, the publication and the airing of the sketches again, came another round of new calls and leads to follow up on. Detective Brian Harris, who had been promoted to sergeant, supervising those men he had worked with (to the chagrin and resentment of some in the department), was working the case by himself by now. There was no team of investigators spending days looking at evidence, following up on calls, interviewing witnesses. Some cases get to a point where the thing that ultimately solves it is that notorious *break*.

That one lead: someone who perhaps courageously steps forward and decides to open up despite the consequences.

The flip side to this, however, is that there must be a system in place to get this lead into the right hands. Moreover, the lead itself might possibly have to mean something to the investigation in order to be useful. And with an investigation that had produced as many red herrings as this one, not to mention hundreds of "tips" and so-called witnesses, only a magician would have been able to pick out the best tip that the Homicide Unit had gotten up to this point as it came across Brian Harris's desk during the summer of 2005.

This crucial information—naming both killers—was called in on July 28 that year, exactly ten days and two years after the murders.

An anonymous caller phoned the department: "While Christopher Snider was drunk," the female tipster told the tip line, "he told me that he and his girlfriend—her name is Christine, I do not know her last name—killed the four people in Clear Lake."

And there it was: laid out on a silver platter, as if the keys to the case were plated in gold, and arrest warrants were there, filled out, signed by a judge, and ready to be served.

The tipster went on to say that Chris Snider, feeling a steady flow of booze wash over him on that day, wanting badly to get this demon monkey off his back, said, "Christine's best friend was raped by the two males that we killed! So Christine and I went to the location and I killed the two males, while Christine killed the two females. We wore bandanas over our faces."

The details of this call fit a later description of Christine given by Chris Snider's sister, Brandee, to George Koloroutis, spelling out things clearly, and in doing so, seemed to make some sense out of the case and the motive behind such violent deaths. The female victims were Christine's friends, Chris's sister had said (a fact that the tipster had not verified).

"I just remember her (Christine Paolilla)," said Brandee, "as being intensely jealous, maniacal, malicious, and controlling. One thing I can say with certainty is my brother would have *never* touched a girl—much less done what was done, to *any* female. He was very protective of females. And the details of the case further showed me that there must have been some underlying jealousy between her (Christine) and [Rachael]. When I saw the photos of [Rachael], I knew instantly. [She] was very beautiful. . . ."

The speculation was that Rachael and Tiffany's beauty "ate Christine Paolilla alive." She was crazy jealous of these girls—and with Rachael's head being beaten in with a pistol, it would certainly bode well for any argument of her killer snapping into an envious rage and taking that anger out on Rachael. Even more, both Rachael and Tiffany had been shot in or close to the vaginal area, another obvious "tell" pointing toward hatred and jealousy. Add to that the theory that Christine had told Chris that the two boys were rapists, and you have some serious theories of motive going on here. Whereas the investigators had believed all along that the killer (or killers) had gone to that house to murder D or Marcus, now it appeared that Christine had, in fact, initiated this crime to take out two of her friends, using a feigned rape accusation to get Chris Snider over there with her.

The informant nailed Christopher Snider's birth date (HPD checked it out) and last known address. She also stated Christine's father's name as "Dick Thomas."

Close enough.

She gave Christine's phone number to HPD.

Again, this was spot-on (although HPD had no way of knowing this then).

There were two problems for Brian Harris as the lead crossed his desk. "The clue did not even come close to the motive we were working with, because it said he told the person (the tipster) that he killed the guys *because* they had raped [one of Christine's friends]. This was nowhere close to the backgrounds of the victims. I searched the reports and phone records for a 'Snider'[after the tip came in] and did not make the connection. He was not listed in any local reports because the stuff he did with Christine was in the county. By then he had been shipped back to Kentucky."

Then there was that phone record check that the Homicide Division had conducted on the girls' cell phones: that forty-eight-hour search backward. Again, if they would have gone back seventy-two hours, it would have all come together. Because Christine Paolilla's number was part of Rachael and Tiffany's records.

Then there was the photograph of Christine and Rachael. That seemingly naughty picture of Christine flossing her teeth with the strap of Rachael's panties had been mistakenly labeled by someone in the chain of command.

The wrong name was on the photograph.

Christine was not even listed among friends of the girls. So neither Christine nor Chris Snider were ever connected to Rachael or Tiffany. And thus, a tip that could have solved the case right then and there remained, for the time being, just another phone call to add to an enormous stack of calls already in the Clear Lake file.

In addition, there would soon be another major hurdle to contend with as August 2005 approached—this one brought on by Mother Nature.

CHAPTER 36

WITH SOME OF that money she had received from her trust fund, Christine Paolilla and her new husband purchased a condo in Webster, Texas, a two-mile trip south of Clear Lake City, her old stomping grounds. Christine and Justin were now back in the neighborhood of the murders that she had helped commit. It was the end of April when the condo deal went through. They had been married for a few weeks then. Nestled comfortably inside their new home (the deed in both of their names), Christine watched television one day in July, right around the same time that latest call had come through the Crime Stoppers tip line. It was the two-year anniversary of the Clear Lake murders. Justin and Christine were upstairs. Christine was in the bedroom, and Justin was inside his studio, working on some drawings for tattoos. ("Justin was an incredible artist," said one old friend.)

"Hey, babe, come in here," Christine yelled from the other room.

Justin got up from where he sat with his sketchbook. He walked down the hall, then into the bedroom.

Christine was up off the bed, staring at the TV.

"What's up?" he asked.

"Look," she said, pointing. She had one hand in her mouth, almost biting on the bottom of her palm. "Oh my . . . Oh my . . ."

On the television screen were photographs of Rachael, Tiffany, Marcus, and Adelbert. These were now familiar faces to area residents. The newscast was talking about the two-year anniversary and still no arrest.

At one point the sketches went up on the television screen.

Christine became "nervous, very worried" at that exact moment, Justin noticed. She paced, walking back and forth in front of the television.

Oh my! Oh my!

She stood in front of the TV as Justin sat on the edge of the bed, wondering what was going on with his wife.

"And she stood there," Justin later said, "and she couldn't sit."

Then the tears came. "Oh, my goodness," Christine said as the sketches stayed up on the screen, "does that look like me? Does that *look* like me?"

She's involved, Justin thought. *She's part of this.* It hit him all at once while watching her freak out at the sight of the photographs. Several comments she had made to him subtly over the past few weeks. That Christmas dinner. Her knowing the two girls. It was coming together for Justin as though he couldn't turn away.

"I couldn't deny it anymore," he said later, talking about that moment as his wife sweated out the broadcast of the photographs. He realized, for the first time, that he had married a murderer. "There was something. . . . There was *truth* to something."

CHAPTER 37

A S THE END of the summer approached, a storm brewed, a lit-
eral tempest, that is. Katrina had started out as a Category 1 hurricane, over the Bahamas, on or near August 22 to 23, and by the
time it hit land, this prodigious tropical depression had manifested
into a devastating Category 3 hurricane. The storm surge alone was
enough to send thousands of New Orleans residents out of that
bowl-shaped supercity, heading for dry (upper) land, an area of
which turned out to be Houston. And yet Katrina wasn't the storm
that had sent Justin Rott and Christine—"I didn't want to change my
last name"—Paolilla running from their new condo. Hurricane Rita
had made a near direct hit that September on Houston/Galveston,
which pushed Rott and his wife, as well as scores of other residents,
toward safer ground. For Justin and Christine, it was his parents'
house in Arlington, Texas—they had apparently relocated from the
Chicago area, too—that he chose.

He and Christine ended up spending two days waiting out the de-
struction and devastation of Rita. This had worked out for Justin: he
had wanted to introduce his parents to his new wife, anyway.

By now Christine and Justin were fighting that terrible itch, that
subtle yet substantial urge to get back into the game. That money
they had was burning a hole in their sobriety, telling them it was okay
to fiddle a little here and a little there. That demon on their backs
was now on their shoulders and speaking: *Maybe a bag of dope on
the weekends. A few beers. Then back to real life on Monday until
the following weekend. Yeah . . . we can do it right this time.*

A savage disease hibernated inside of Justin Rott, one that Christine had no idea how to defend herself against. Justin was a recovering heroin addict. He had fought legions of demons, not a solitary devil. The guy was constantly on guard against the biggest dragon of them all—sitting there, waiting, dictating to him how to live life. Once that needle was stuck back into his arm, there was no turning back. And with what seemed to be unlimited funding, that sleeping giant, who had sat dormant for some time now, was ready and waiting to pick right back up where Justin had left off the last time, when he wound up homeless.

From Arlington, shooting dope "not every day, but close to it," Christine and Justin drove to San Antonio.

Why?

"To use drugs," Justin said later. A good dope addict goes to where the best dope is—and he had a dealer in San Antonio.

They had actually started using before the trip to Arlington. If Justin had to put a motive behind the reignition of his drug habit, and introducing Christine to the needle, he said he'd be lying if he pinpointed a specific reason. There had been no precise, calculated decision, or an exact moment. In other words, it didn't happen after an argument or a brush with police. A drug addict doesn't have to be sent over the edge, or necessarily *pushed* off the wagon; the disease of addiction is always there, always plotting and planning, always playing games with the mind. One weak moment is all it takes to burst like a blood blister and begin to control once again every aspect of an addict's life.

Justin knew this.

They had decided before leaving his parents' not to stay in San Antonio. Yet, they had no ties, really, back at the condo. They had purchased a dog, and the dog was traveling with them, so there were no pets to attend to back home. They had money. What seemed to be, at the moment, an endless supply of cash. They could roam from place to place, providing, that is, there were drugs wherever they wound up.

"So," Justin explained, "at first, supposedly, we were just going to go there (San Antonio) for a little while and then go home."

As they drove, the subject of the murders and Christine's involvement came up inside the car. By now the newlywed husband knew that his wife was involved; although they were not necessarily openly talking about Christine being some sort of runaway fugitive who needed to be hidden. Christine had told him just about everything. Where it happened. Somewhat how it all went down. And her version of why.

"Just be quiet about it," he said when she brought it up during the car ride to San Antonio. He didn't want her talking to anyone else about it in the same manner as she had been doing with him. He was on edge; they were both withdrawing from the dope and needed a fix—hence the trip to San Antonio. He didn't want to hear about anything besides when that next bag of dope was going to be entering his bloodstream.

"We'll talk about it later," he said to Christine at one point. It seemed it was all she wanted to talk about now.

"Rachael . . . ," Christine said. She started crying. "I can sometimes see her."

"What?"

Christine was having flashbacks. She once explained how, when they'd watch a movie, she'd see someone get shot and think of Rachael, her "friend." She'd stare into the mirror while combing her wig or brushing her teeth and see Rachael's face. It was consuming her, she told Justin. She couldn't handle it anymore, which was where the amnesia drug of choice—smack—came into play: the all-powerful numbing agent.

Christine had now found her new best friend—*cheeba, chiva, chieva*, whatever else you want to call it—to be all she had been searching for. A true love affair had begun. Christine didn't need all that much convincing to take off with the drug and run as fast as she could. She had the genes. The past history. The foundation for such an affair was bursting inside her already.

One thing about Christine that emerged as her life unfolded throughout this period was an inherent willingness to adapt, but in her own narcissistic way. For example, like her mother, Christine had chosen not to take on Rott's last name. Lori was Lori Paolilla, not Lori Dick. Not because she didn't like that last name, but according to Christine, it was a mere nuisance to change over bank accounts and driver's licenses, et cetera.

Christine, Justin Rott later said, "did the same thing" as her mother. "We were going to do it (change her name) at one time. We had just opened up bank accounts and . . . we used that excuse for a while . . . that we didn't want to change everything around. If anyone has ever done it, it's kind of hectic, all that change. One thing led to another," Justin finished, "and it wasn't an issue, really."

And in defense of those who don't share a last name, it generally *isn't* an issue.

Justin and Christine began a tour, essentially, of hotels and motels throughout the San Antonio region, paying with credit cards and cash from Christine's rapidly dwindling trust fund account. And this trip wasn't anything close to a honeymoon or extended vacation that some couples might take; it was about doing as much drugs as they could, as fast as they could, and staying as high as they could.

Truly, as time would tell, this was a bender to end all benders.

CHAPTER 38

HURRICANES KATRINA AND Rita stalled just about everything to do with the Clear Lake investigation. Nearly all HPD detectives were now in uniform, working the Houston Astrodome and other places around the city where that huge influx of "Katricians" had settled in the state, and more crime than HPD had ever seen began to consume all of their time and energy.

"By the end of the summer," Brian Harris said later, "our caseload was picking up."

That would be a gross understatement. The murder rate in the city skyrocketed nearly 27 percent, with what Homicide called "the Katrina murders." Any tip that might have come in concerning the Clear Lake case, including that tip in July regarding Christopher Snider and his girl, Christine, was placed in a notebook and saved. With all the post–Katrina/Rita crime taking place in the city, tracking down Clear Lake tips was certainly not on the top of the Homicide Division's list of things to do in the Clear Lake case. Add to that, that Clear Lake's number one advocate, George Koloroutis, had now moved his family—because of his job—to Kansas, near Kansas City, the Clear Lake murder investigation was about as cold as it had ever been.

And wouldn't you know, this happened precisely at a time when it could have been easily solved with a small amount of gumshoe police work.

BEFORE THAT TRIP he took with Christine for Christmas dinner, Justin Rott had never been to Houston. Justin had not heard about the Clear Lake murders before his wife introduced him to it. Those types of crimes were not something Justin had made a point to follow in the news. It's safe to say that Justin Rott was concerned with his sobriety at times and finding dope at others. He might have seen a news story about it, but he didn't know anything until he met Christine.

And now he was married to one of the murderers and they were shooting dope together as if the poppy fields in Afghanistan were in jeopardy of drying up.

As he thought about it later, little hints that something was wrong had been there all along, though Justin was not attuned enough with the situation to know what they meant. There was one time, after they had first started dating, when Justin and Christine prepared to part ways and go back to their halfway houses. Christine had broken down for no apparent reason inside the car. "We were just sitting there," Justin said later, "and she just started crying hysterically."

"What's wrong?" a concerned Justin Rott asked his then-girlfriend. "Talk to me."

"There're some things," Christine said through tears, "there's . . . um . . . there're some things that I want to talk to you about and tell you, but I'm afraid."

Justin had never seen his girl this upset. Her body trembled. Something had rattled her cage. She wanted to spit it out, but for some reason she couldn't.

"Tell me, Christine," he begged. "Come on." He was trying to say that there was nothing they couldn't handle together. They were a couple now. They loved each other.

She continued to cry. "There're some things"—Christine looked out the window—"there're some . . . things that happened in Houston that I am scared people will find out."

Secrets. Not a good thing, Justin knew from experience, for a drug addict trying to stay sober to keep stuffed.

He was curious, but he decided to let his girl talk. It was the best thing to do. Justin Rott was a good listener; he truly cared about what a person had to say and made the person feel that while she spoke. There can be no doubt that Justin consoled Christine with sincerity, not having any idea that what she was talking about had to do with her murdering four people. He was staring into the face of pure evil, the pure machinery behind psychopathic behavior, trying to help this young woman as much as he could.

"It was an ex-boyfriend of mine," Christine said. She kept pausing. Crying and sniffling.

The pain was immense, Justin believed.

"I was involved . . . ," she continued.

Justin didn't know the ex-boyfriend's name then. Christine kept referring to him as "Chris." Chris this, Chris that.

"It was at the house," Christine said in vague descriptions of that day, not making too much sense. Justin didn't push the matter, for fear of turning Christine away.

"It's okay, Christine."

"Chris and me, we were at my friend's house, going in there, looking. We were going to buy drugs, get high, and some things, you know, like, some things . . . happened, and some people ended up dead."

"And some things I didn't understand," Justin said later, referring to this moment. "And I really didn't question her much. I really didn't believe it. . . ."

Justin wondered who Christine was talking about.

"Two males," she said at one point. They were still sitting in her car outside the halfway house where Justin was staying. "Two females, Rachael . . . Rachael. We were really good friends." He presumed she meant her and Rachael. "We all went to school together. We were all friends."

Justin sat inside the halfway house after Christine took off that night and thought about the conversation. It was strange, sure. She was upset, definitely. But what was she actually saying? He had no idea.

"I thought maybe she knew of something that happened," he explained later. "I really didn't believe that she was involved in anything. You know, people say stories—and she was so vague about it all. And, you know, I thought maybe something had happened to one of her friends and she knew something and she didn't go to the police."

What Justin was certain of when later asked about this moment was that not once during the conversation, as Christine tried to explain to him that she was there on the day her friends had been murdered, did she *ever* give any indication that she had been brought to the house *against* her will, or that she was forced to go into the house and kill. Furthermore, she never said that anyone, specifically Chris Snider, had threatened her on that day or anytime afterward.

CHAPTER 39

AS THE END of the year approached, Justin Rott was doing drugs with his wife—at times they had done so much dope in a day that they were hardly ever in the moment—and he was thinking back to the strange things his wife had told him about the Clear Lake murders. The situation was compromising for him. He was pandering to a murderer, if he knew what she had done and did not turn her in. There could be some charges involved. At times he would stop, think about calling the cops, but then would convince himself that he loved his wife and maybe she was making it all up. Perhaps she had been there, but was not part of it? So many excuses darted through his heroin-brined mind that Justin didn't know what to think anymore. And whenever things became too much, all he had to do was shoot more drugs, thus making it all dissolve into a hazy fog of being perpetually high.

Near Christmas 2005, Justin and Christine had managed to get their act together enough to go visit Christine's mother and Tom Dick. During that week they were in Friendswood, they went out shopping one afternoon by themselves.

"I want to show you something," Christine said. Justin was driving. They were on the I-45, near the 2351, close to the Baybrook Mall. Only about five to ten minutes away from Christine's parents' house.

Christine was in the passenger seat, giving him directions: *Turn here. Turn there. Drive over there and park the car near that building*. She looked around as if someone might be following them, obviously paranoid.

Finally, after all that turning, Christine told Justin to get out of the car and follow her. They needed to walk across the street toward a brick building and stand in this one particular spot she had picked out.

There, above them, stood one of the billboards with the sketches and Crime Stoppers info staring down.

"I didn't think anything of it," Justin said later, "until we pulled up and she asked me to park on the side. There was some building in front of it." She demanded Justin "park on the side of it." She wanted to make sure the car was hidden.

Christine acted suspicious and jumpy. She didn't want anybody to see her car near the billboard.

After settling down, she turned to Justin, who was standing, staring up at the billboard, wondering why they were there. "Hey," Christine said, "let me ask you. Does that look like me?"

Before they had taken off to go shopping, Christine had pulled out a photograph of Chris Snider back at her parents' house and showed it to him. It was part of a collection of photos her mother had around the house. "That's him there," Christine had said, referring to Snider, pointing to the photograph. "That's Chris, my ex-boyfriend." In fact, Christine was still talking to Chris Snider. He was gone, back in Kentucky, sometimes hanging around Houston, but she was still in contact with him. There was one time when Christine had spoken to Chris in front of Justin. Chris had just gotten out of jail and Christine wanted to get him into a halfway house in Kerrville. She turned and asked Justin if she should help him out as an old friend.

"No way," Justin said. "I don't want your ex-boyfriend near us." ("I was jealous," Justin said later.)

Out of respect for her husband, Christine left Chris alone after that.

"So, does it look like me, or what?" Christine asked again as her husband stared at the billboard.

"No," Justin said. "I don't *think* so." (And it didn't.)

"Okay," Christine said, "but does that look like Chris?" She was referring to the male sketch.

Justin studied it. He thought back to the photographs she had shown him at the house.

"Matter of fact," he said, "it does. That looks like him." Thinking about it more, he said, it looked "*exactly*" like him."

Definitely. The sketch was a spot-on representation of Christopher Snider.

Christine had a concerned look, shocked by Justin's response.

"I'm worried," she said as they walked away from the billboard, "that it looks like me, and people are going to think it *is* me."

But it was her.

"Look," Justin said, "don't talk about it to anybody and don't bring anybody over here."

Justin didn't want to believe—although all the cards had been turned over in front of him—that his wife had anything to do with such a horrible crime. It was easy to deny it. He loved her. He was in the throes of a double addiction: the drugs and Christine.

Christine started to say something more about it.

"Just be quiet," he snapped.

She thought about what he said. "Okay. Okay."

There was a time after this when Christine pulled Justin aside and admitted, "You know, God is going to punish me one day for this by taking you away."

Believers would say God had others things on His mind where it pertained to Christine Paolilla and her involvement in the murder of four human beings.

CHAPTER 40

THERE CAME A time when Christine Paolilla sat her husband down and decided to come clean about what had happened in Clear Lake. She wanted to admit everything she could remember (or, rather, her first version of the events). By this time they were doing so much heroin and cocaine (speedballing) that the simple daily ritual of taking care of themselves hygienically became an impossible chore. They were sleeping and shooting dope, eating enough to stay alive, and not doing anything other than making sure the curtains in whatever hotel room they stayed in were drawn and there was enough dope on tap to last days or even a week at a time.

Christine looked like one of those big-eyed aliens common in Area 51 popular culture. She had no eyebrows. Her hair (what was left) was generally propped up in a bun. Her skin was white as the dope she shot. Her eyes were bulging and sad and tired. Her lips were red as a heart. She was skinnier than an anorexic: a nineteen-year-old heroin/cocaine addict shooting enough dope for three junkies. It was incredible that she was still alive.

Christine said she and Chris Snider had gone to the Millbridge Drive house with "no intentions of anybody getting killed." As the evidence later proved, though, they had brought along enough firepower to wage a small war.

Anyway, they parked on the side of the road down the street from Tiffany's and "walked up to the house." This, so far, boded well when placed against the Lackners' description of seeing a male and female dressed in black approaching the Rowell residence from the road, walking up the driveway.

As they advanced toward the outside foyer of the front door, Chris Snider stopped and turned to his girl, according to what Christine told Justin Rott: "Take this," he said, handing Christine a gun.

"It wasn't even planned," Justin later told police, "you know, Chris and her. Chris got the guns, which were his father's guns, as far as I know."

Christine placed the weapon in her purse. She did not fight with Chris or question him: *Why do you have a gun? What the hell is going on here? Why do I need a gun?* Instead, she took the weapon, saying, "Okay." They were there, said Christine, to rob the four of any money and drugs they had in the house. Christine mentioned "marijuana, [a] bunch of prescription pills, some cash, just like an assortment of drugs, Ecstasy. . . ."

One of them knocked on the door. Christine didn't say who.

Rachael or Tiffany—"one of the girls"—answered the door, Christine explained to her husband. Then she said that Chris knew everyone in the house, yet he was not "friends" with any of them. Acquaintances. They had seen each other out partying and said "what up," but did not necessarily hang out together on a regular basis.

Chris and Christine walked into the house. Rachael, Tiffany, Marcus, and D appeared to have been watching television together.

"Tiff," Christine said as they walked in, "can you take me upstairs?" (Because the living room was sunken, they referred to the main level of the house as "upstairs.") Christine made it clear she wanted Tiffany to take her to her room.

"Sure," Tiffany said. She popped up off the couch and told Christine to "come on." Christine explained that Tiffany thought she knew what she wanted, why they were there: to buy drugs. Tiffany and Marcus kept "it" in their bedroom inside the dresser. Christine knew this.

According to what Christine told Justin, before she and Chris had walked into the house, he had told her, "We're just going to take the drugs." None of the kids were drug dealers, Christine added. "They're just some kids that, I guess, have extra, and sometimes they'd sell it to friends. . . ."

"Okay," Christine said to her boyfriend, going along.

"And any money, too," Chris added.

Christine apparently nodded in agreement with this also.

While they were inside Tiffany's bedroom, Christine made it clear that they were there to take the drugs.

With Christine and Tiffany out of earshot and sight of the others, Chris was alone in the living room with D, Marcus, and Rachael, who was sitting on the floor in front of the television.

Back in Tiffany's room, Christine started to cry. "I'm sorry," she said. "I'm so sorry."

"What are you talking about?" Tiffany asked, opening the dresser.

"I'm . . . so . . . sorry," Christine repeated, crying harder.

Tiffany was confused; she had no idea what her friend was talking about.

Meanwhile, Chris brandished his weapon and held the three of them—all of whom were relaxing comfortably, unafraid of this guy they had seen Christine with before—down on the couch and chair. He stood and pointed his gun at them all, going from one to the other, telling them "not to move." It was now clear that Christine and Christopher were there to rob the kids.

Christine and Tiffany returned to the living room, and Tiffany saw what was happening.

"Why?" Tiffany asked.

Rachael and the others echoed Tiffany's sentiment. "Why are you doing this?"

"Get over by the couch!" Chris said to Tiffany, waving at her with his gun. "You," he said to Christine, "take out your gun."

According to Christine, she did as she was told.

Chris and Christine stood in front of the four, holding them at bay.

"The first time she explained it to me," Justin later said, "she said . . . Chris shot first."

Per Christine's first version of this mass murder (there would be several varying accounts of the same story in the coming months), Chris Snider pointed his gun directly at Marcus as he stood by the fireplace. D sat on the couch; Marcus was to D's right.

Marcus pleaded with Chris. "Please, man, take whatever you want and leave. Take it all. Go ahead. Take it." He was sincere, nonthreatening.

The others said the same thing, essentially begging for their lives.

Chris wasn't hearing any of it, though, according to Christine. As Marcus pleaded, Christine told Justin, Snider shot him.

As D went to stand, Snider popped him in the head, sending D backward.

This seemed to be what a male might be thinking at the time: take out the biggest threats first—the two males. Chris Snider was not ignorant with regard to the rules of the street.

As he shot D, Christine claimed, it was almost as if that second shot initiated hellfire. "They both started shooting," Justin said Christine told him. The way she explained it, she seemed to say that the gun in her hand had gone off by itself; she didn't have any control over it. She claimed to be crying as she shot both the girls and put more bullets into the boys, firing blindly in the direction of the three of them. (Marcus was already on the ground, probably dead.) Meanwhile, Rachael was trying to run out of the room.

Rachael . . .

Justin explained how that name alone would later haunt Christine. "She brought it up all the time. . . . 'Cause that was the last one she remembers . . . she had nightmares all the time about her."

Before they opened fire, "both of the girls, they were asking why, why are you doing this, just pleading. . . ."

Justin said Christine couldn't recall exactly, but she thought she had shot Rachael and Tiffany, while Chris Snider continued to fire rounds into the boys.

"I don't really think she paid attention to who she was hitting."

Maybe so. But there were not many misses. So somebody was paying attention to where he or she was firing.

As Christine told the story, she went "back and forth," Justin later said, "between hysterically crying, to just having no emotion."

Imagine, admitting to killing four people, and there were times when she showed *no emotion*. . . .

Christine had never come out and said it, but it was clear that she and Snider kept firing until they ran out of ammo.

"Then they left the house."

Outside, they hopped into her purple Geo Prizm. Christine got into the passenger seat; Chris drove. This was part of the plan.

Why? Because Christine had to go to work.

Before Chris started the car, however, Christine said: "We have to go back."

"What?"

"I have to make sure they're all dead." Christine was under the impression that one or maybe two of them had lived through the barrage of gunfire. She was concerned about this.

Snider said no way.

Christine got out of the car and ran back into the house.

Walking in the front door, seeing blood everywhere, she spied Rachael on the floor in front of the television. Still alive, Rachael was crawling.

Christine stood over Rachael, staring down. As the evidence later proved, Rachael was reaching for her cell phone or had it in her hand and was trying to dial 911.

"And [Rachael] was choking on her own blood," Justin said later, describing how Christine told it to him, "She was gagging."

Christine stood stunned. *Rachael is still breathing.*

"Why?" Rachael repeated over and over. "Why would you?"

Christine took out her pistol. She leveled it over her head, holding it by the barrel like a hammer, and began, in a whipping motion, pounding on the back of Rachael's head, bashing her skull in, making sure she was dead, no chance of coming back. As she did this, Rachael "was crying the whole time." One of the two girls who had taken Christine under her wing, and had taught her how to dress and buy wigs and wear her makeup so she didn't look like Tammy Faye Bakker, was pleading for her life, wondering why her friend was killing her. Christine continued to pound the butt of that weapon into Rachael's skull repeatedly.

Over and over.

Spattering blood all over the walls, the carpet, and even up toward the ceiling.

Satisfied that Rachael was dead, Christine Paolilla ran back out that same front door and jumped into her waiting car. With Snider at the wheel, they took off.

From there, Christine didn't run out and do a bunch of drugs to forget about the vicious quadruple murder she had just committed with her boyfriend. She didn't look to drench those bloody memories—so fresh in her mind—in a pool of booze and sex inside a seedy hotel room. She didn't demand that Chris take her somewhere so they could talk about it and get the heck out of Clear Lake City. Instead, Christine turned to her boyfriend and demanded, "Take me to work."

He drove to the Walgreens and dropped off his accomplice so she could make her shift.

Christine walked into Walgreens and clocked in at 4:23 P.M. (she would clock out for a break at 6:59 and back in at 7:29 P.M., and clock out to go home at 10:35 P.M.); she put on her work apron, washed up in the restroom, and then stood behind the makeup counter, waiting for her first customer of the evening. She was nervous. But okay, considering what had happened.

As Christine got settled behind the counter, she happened to look down.

There were specks of blood underneath her fingernails.

CHAPTER 41

TIME. DETECTIVE BRIAN Harris knew all about it. Such an expressive word, something no one seemed to have enough of these days. Yet time, in its universal splendor, was about to take on new meaning for Harris as the winter of 2006 settled on Houston. *Time* magazine had interviewed Harris for an article about New Orleans transplants and the new (massive migratory) wave of crime HPD had contended with over the past six months post-Katrina. That article, in which Harris was quoted, on top of an award Harris had never asked or lobbied for but received, was about to cause the young, new sergeant a bit of a stir with some of his colleagues.

Harris had been part of a team—the newly formed Gang Murder Squad—that had arrested eight men, all from New Orleans, suspects in eleven murders. It was a major accomplishment—something the department could be proud of amid all the bloodshed that had been spilled since Katrina.

"Of twenty-three Katrina-related homicides in Houston, we linked nine to just two groups from New Orleans—the 3 'n' G and the Dooney Boys," Harris told *Time* magazine. "You see a spike in homicides in New Orleans in July and August, then the hurricane comes and they are displaced to Houston and elsewhere."

Utter chaos was what the city of Houston had experienced. But Harris, along with scores of other good cops, had made an impact on the Katrina-related gang crime and murder, thwarting a solid portion of it all. In addition, many of the Katricians were heading back to where they lived, which was a blessing all by itself. Harris was proud of his men, himself, and anyone else who had helped. Why shouldn't he be? Most in the Homicide Division (Harris included) were hard-working, type A, go-getter investigators who didn't wait for an opportunity. This wave of crime had truly brought out the best in most everyone on the force.

Although HPD now had somewhat of a handle on the Katrina cases, more murders and crimes were coming in every day. Things would settle down, and boom! Another crack dealer beat a lady of the night; another gang member took revenge on a young user who owed a debt; another turf war turned into carnage. And then every so often, Harris looked over to the side of his desk and the Clear Lake case stared back up at him.

Oh, yeah . . . that.

The case was continually poking at him. At this point he was by himself as far as investigating Clear Lake. Everyone else had been slammed with cases, on top of what had been that promised rash of Homicide Unit retirees. An additional blow weighing on Harris was that he had been voted supervisor of the year by the department in 2005. This did not sit well with some of the guys around him. One comment he heard from a particular cop was "A monkey could do this job" (meaning Homicide Division work).

"Really?" Harris said. "You gonna call that guy"—he pointed to a Homicide cop with thirty-three years on the job—"a monkey after his three decades of service?" It was an insult. Personality reigned over principle, duty, and integrity. Some cops stood out on their own merits. Some jumped into the spotlight, brushing their hair first, shining their badge second. Some liked to voice their opinions. Harris was not one or the other; he did his job and let the chips fall.

Every time Harris had a success, that same cop—the monkey comment guy—approached him and pointed to the Clear Lake boxes stacked up on the floor next to Harris's desk.

"If you're such a *hotshot,* why can't you solve *that* one?" the monkey comment guy said one day.

"Buddy, if you think you're big enough," Harris responded, "why don't you jump on board?"

But maybe the guy was right, Harris thought on those days when things seemed to be too much. Was this case, now heading toward its three-year anniversary, ever going to be closed? Did it even have the potential anymore?

The one positive the case had going for it was George Koloroutis; he was not going to allow his daughter's murder to fall by the way-side. George had called Harris's captain one day not too long after the second anniversary, when the Katrina crime exploded. "Look," George had said, "the case has been bounced around, nobody taking any ownership. It's been passed from one group to another, and the only one who has shown any interest lately is Harris. Can you at least allow him to stay on it until there's some closure, or you guys know for sure that it just isn't going anywhere?"

A promotion within the ranks of law enforcement usually meant the guy or gal who received that promotion was transferred to a place in the department where he or she was going to be more use-ful. You didn't want to promote an officer to sergeant and then allow him to stay in the same unit he had been in, obviously, for fear that he or she would show favoritism to those officers he or she had be-friended while one of them. It is almost unheard of that an officer stayed within the same unit after a supervisory advancement.

It was back at the promotion ceremony, Harris recalled, when one of the assistant chiefs from the department put into perspective how unique a situation Harris had found himself in. The assistant chief had made a comment to Harris regarding how rare it was in law en-forcement circles that an officer who was promoted stayed in his unit. The assistant chief approached Harris after the ceremony con-cluded and stuck out his hand. "I need to shake the hand of the man who walks on water!"

Harris was taken aback. "Excuse me?"

"All I'm saying is a man would have to walk on water before his su-periors would ever allow him to stay in the division."

CHAPTER 42

NO ONE EXPECTED it to happen the way it did. But in the end, when you look at the ebb and flow of the investigation from an unbiased point of hindsight, you can truly see how the entire Clear Lake investigation led up to this one moment.

It was 2:02 P.M. on July 8, 2006, ten days before the third anniversary of the murders. A call came into Crime Stoppers. Sergeant Eddie Diaz was manning the desk.

"I overheard Christine Paolilla talking about the murders in Clear Lake, back in July '03," the tipster said. "Christine was in the Starlite rehab in Center Point, Texas, back in '04 and I was in the same facility."

It's important to note here that although the anonymous caller was male, it was *not* Justin Rott (as many would later speculate). Justin had never been in the Starlite Recovery Center, and at the time the call came in, he was actively using drugs with Christine, both embroiled in the disease of addiction on a level snowballing out of control.

Diaz asked for more info.

"She claimed that she helped her boyfriend commit the murders," the male tipster continued. "I have no idea who the boyfriend is, but his name might have been Chris. Not sure. Christine, though, was a friend to one of the girls who was killed."

In a report of the call, HPD pointed out: *The caller was very forthcoming, not shy, and didn't express any fear.*

Christine Paolilla, apparently under the auspices of sobriety and maybe guilt, had opened up to the tipster. They were alone one afternoon in the rehab, sitting together, talking. Christine started the conversation by posing a shocking question to the tipster: "Have you ever killed anyone?"

"No," he said.

What a damn thing to ask someone.

"*I* did," Christine said, as if proud she had it in her. "And it wasn't something I thought I would ever do."

She proceeded to explain, in graphic detail, what had happened that day.

"She and her boyfriend," the tipster told Sergeant Diaz, "killed the four to get large amounts of money and X pills stashed in the home. She said they used a forty-five-caliber and nine-millimeter weapon. I [later] overheard her say that they got the guns from a safe inside the boyfriend's father's house. And she also said that the guns were put *back* inside the safe after the murders," and her boyfriend had wiped both weapons clean of any prints.

As the tipster talked through Christine's confession, this new version added details to Justin's description. For one, the tipster said Christine talked about her telling Chris Snider she thought they (Marcus and D) had a gun inside the house, and she didn't, at first, want to go through with robbing them.

"She said she got sick to her stomach while walking up to the house and lost her nerve." But Chris Snider convinced her to go through with it. (A comment that spoke of premeditation.) "They then went . . . inside and opened fire."

Christine even gave particulars: "One male was shot on the sofa and died instantly." She had no idea who shot whom. She didn't know if she shot the girls, or if he shot the boys, because they fired at the same time, as soon as they entered the house. It sounded as though they rang the doorbell and barged in while unloading the chambers of their weapons.

Shoot first, search for the drugs and cash after.

Those kids never had a chance.

"She also said that after leaving the scene, she became scared and worried that one of the victims could still be alive and that the surviving victim could ultimately identify her and her boyfriend. So she walked back into the house. I am not sure if the boyfriend went with her. But one of the victims was still alive, and this person was crawling on the floor. She was out of bullets and had to beat the victim to death with the [butt] of her gun."

(In a later version of this same moment, Christine said that Rachael, while crawling and pleading for her life, had her phone in her hand and was trying to dial 911, which ended up being consistent with Rachael's bloody fingerprints found on the numbers 9-1-1.)

The tipster spoke of Christine working at Walgreens; he said Christine and Chris changed clothes after the murders and "she went to work." He had "no idea" where Chris and Christine might be these days; but the last he knew, Christine was at a halfway house in Kerr-ville, Texas.

"She claimed to no longer be with the boyfriend . . . that he had moved somewhere in Kentucky, but he still calls her from time to time. She said he usually calls her to threaten her by telling her he will kill her if she ever tells anyone about the crime."

One of the most interesting aspects of the confession for police was that Christine had told the tipster, "After the shots they did not get hardly anything they wanted." Christine and Snider had assumed that Marcus and D had a wad of money hanging around the house, along with a major stash of drugs. And this sort of pissed them off. They had killed four people, essentially, for nothing.

The call into the Crime Stoppers tip line came in on a Saturday—and wouldn't you know, Brian Harris was on vacation that week, out of touch until the following Monday morning.

CHAPTER 43

IT WAS JULY 11, 2006, before Brian Harris and his new partner, Detective Tom "TJ" McCorvey, were located. Harris was with Mc-Corvey, it turned out. They were at a gas station fueling up.

"Frank Poe from Crime Stoppers," the caller said to Harris.

"Yeah?" Harris said.

Frank Poe explained the call Diaz had taken. Harris knew right there it was a turning point and the call that they had been waiting on all along. He could feel it. As Harris listened, the evidence left behind came to mind. It all backed up what the caller said.

Harris got back into the car. Looked over at McCorvey. Turned the ignition key. "Hey, TJ, buckle up, partner—we're in for a hell of a ride!"

Yet, hearing that Crime Stoppers had taken a call about the Clear Lake case should not have been something to get too excited about. It's safe to say that Harris had been jaded by this point and was not going to jump up on his feet and pump a fist because a tipster had phoned in.

Tom McCorvey researched this new name connected to the Clear Lake case: Christine Paolilla.

Christine had just turned twenty. Almost immediately, Chris Snider's name came up as being connected to Christine. In the system it showed that Snider and Paolilla had been arrested together back in October 2003 "in the same part of town where the murders of Millbridge Drive took place."

A viable link . . . finally.

What also showed up was that Christine had been ticketed several times while in Kerrville by law enforcement (Kerrville being another indicator that the tipster was accurate with his info). After that, McCorvey found out that Chris Snider had a Kentucky state identification number indicating that he had at one time been handled by Kentucky law enforcement. More info consistent with what the tipster had reported.

It was all fitting together.

Harris had a thought when he heard about all this new information: that tipster calling HPD back in 2005 and giving them Chris Snider's name and his girlfriend as "Christine," with no last name.

Now it made sense.

Harris went through the file and pulled out that photograph of Rachael and the other girl, the one who had Rachael's panty band in her teeth. They now had a driver's license file photo of Christine Paolilla.

A match.

The photo had been mislabeled.

Damn it all.

Harris called Lelah Koloroutis. He explained the photo of her sister and the girl he now knew to be Christine Paolilla.

"Yeah, that's Christine," Lelah confirmed. "She and Rachael were friends. Rachael used to carry a photo of Christine in her wallet."

There was a photo in Rachael's purse. Christine had written Rachael a note on the back.

Damn we've had some crazy memories. . . .

This suburban home in Clear Lake City, Texas, was the scene of a brutal quadruple murder during the late afternoon hours of July 18, 2003. *(Photos courtesy of the Houston Police Department)*

Shell casings from two weapons were found in the living room foyer, directly in front of the door, suggesting that the killer started firing immediately after entering. *(Photos courtesy of the Houston Police)*

Spent bullets were found outside the house after exiting through back windows.
(Photo courtesy of the Houston Police Department)

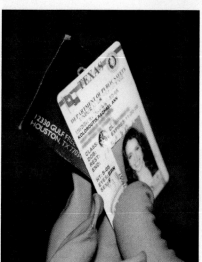

One victim was identified by her driver's license—which had a bullet hole through the center of it. *(Photo courtesy of the Houston Police Department)*

This arched bullet pattern on the living room wall shows how the killer fired at some of the victims as they ran for cover. *(Photo courtesy of the Houston Police Department)*

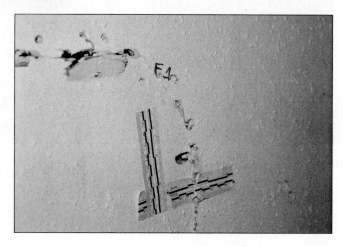

This blood spatter pattern near the ceiling told police that at least one of the victims had been pistol-whipped. *(Photo courtesy of the Houston Police Department)*

A spent bullet found inside a section of fence proved to be an important piece of the homicide puzzle—but not until three years after the murders. *(Photo courtesy of the Houston Police Department)*

These two phones gave police plenty of problems as they began investigating. Bloody fingerprints on the numbers 9-1-1 on one of the phones showed a victim tried to call for help. *(Photos courtesy of the Houston Police Department)*

Two victims were found on this couch, both shot in the head and in multiple places throughout their bodies. *(Photo courtesy of the Houston Police Department)*

Rachael Koloroutis was an outgoing youngster. *(Photo courtesy of George Koloroutis)*

Rachael's father, George Koloroutis, was instrumental in keeping the case in the media and a top priority for the Houston Police Department's Homicide Division. *(Photo courtesy of George Koloroutis)*

Rachael graduated from Clear Lake High School weeks before she was shot and beaten to death. *(Photo courtesy of George Koloroutis)*

A middle child, Rachael (left) was adored by her siblings for her restless, gentle spirit and cheerful, positive demeanor. *(Photo courtesy of George Koloroutis)*

Rachael Koloroutis and Tiffany Rowell (right), victims of a calculating and cold murder plot, were best friends. *(Photo courtesy of George Koloroutis)*

Adelbert "D" Sanchez (left) and Marcus Precella (right), who died on that same July 18, 2003, afternoon, were cousins and best friends. *(Photo courtesy of Nichole Sanchez)*

Adelbert was an aspiring rap artist with dreams of going to college and a future in the music business. *(Photo courtesy of Nichole Sanchez)*

This is one of the Sanchez family's favorite photos of Adelbert Sanchez. *(Photo courtesy of Nichole Sanchez)*

Without the tenacity of HPD Detective Brian Harris, the Clear Lake murders may have gone completely cold and unsolved. *(Photo courtesy of the Houston Police Department)*

Detective Tom Ladd was adamant about catching the people responsible for killing the four youths, but retired before the case was solved. *(Photo courtesy of the Houston Police Department)*

Detective Brian Harris questions 20-year-old suspect Christine Paolilla three years after the Clear Lake murders. *(Photos courtesy of the Houston Police Department)*

Even when these sketches of potential suspects in the Clear Lake City murders were released a year after the crime, it took two additional years before the case was solved. *(Web page courtesy of George Koloroutis)*

WANTED For Questioning
In Murder of
4 Clear LakeTeens
Up To **$100,000 REWARD**
For Information Leading to
Arrest and Charges Filed In Case.

 713-222-TIPS

A Public Service Message of Clear Channel Outdoor

This poster design was used to create billboards, which were placed around the Clear Lake region. *(Photo courtesy of George Koloroutis)*

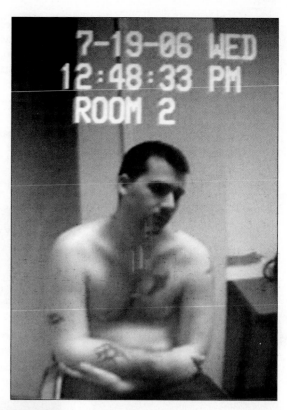

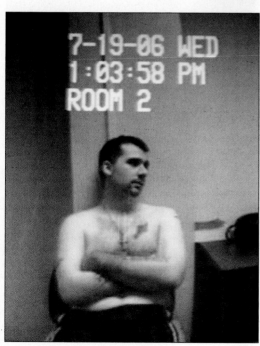

Justin Rott told police he suspected his wife, Christine Paolilla, was involved in the Clear Lake murders. *(Photos courtesy of the Houston Police Department)*

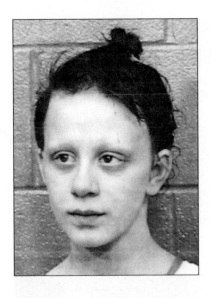

Murder suspect Christine Paolilla, shown here without eyebrows, suffered from alopecia. *(Photo courtesy of the Houston Police Department)*

At home in Texas, Chris Snider smiles just after getting his eyebrow pierced. *(Photo courtesy of Brandee Snider)*

Christopher Snider would ultimately escape legal justice as Christine Paolilla's partner in the murders. *(Photo courtesy of the Houston Police Department)*

Snider loved his dog, Paco. *(Photo courtesy of Brandee Snider)*

Christine Paolilla was often mocked in school, called a clown, and ridiculed for the wigs she wore and the abundance of makeup she layered on. *(Photos courtesy of Clear Lake High School yearbook)*

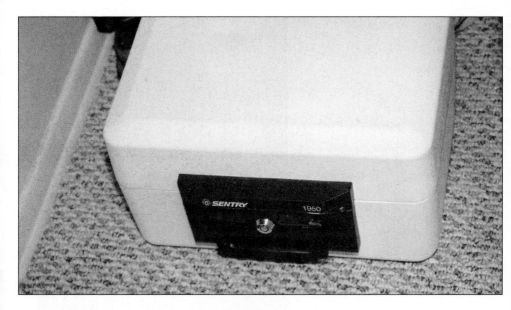

While police questioned Christine Paolilla, the case came together on the forensic side, as a safe containing several pieces of evidence was discovered.
(Photos courtesy of the Houston Police Department)

These guns—one found in the safe, the other in a dresser drawer—proved to be the murder weapons. *(Photos courtesy of the Houston Police Department)*

This photo shows how deeply involved with drugs Christine Paolilla became. Dozens of needles of heroin—some ready to be "booted"—were found inside the hotel room where she was holed up, numbing the memories of killing four people. *(Photo courtesy of the Houston Police Department)*

With help from Rachael and Tiffany, Christine Paolilla was able to make herself beautiful. Yet she murdered the girls she called her best friends.

CHAPTER 44

JUSTIN ROTT AND Christine Paolilla had found a new home at La Quinta Inn on the I-10 in San Antonio, not too far away from one of Justin's suppliers. The hotel was nearly on the corner of Vance Jackson Road and the interstate. They had been there for about seven or eight months, paying for the room every two weeks by calling in a credit card. In fact, Christine was so terribly consumed by the drugs she was injecting, that since they had rented the room back in December 2005, she had never left it.

"Not once," Justin said later.

Their life together—that love story they had both dreamt of and jumped into back in Kerrville, falling hard and marrying without giving sobriety a chance—had come down to eating boxes of Cheez-Its, packages of Reese's Peanut Butter Cups, drinking bottled water and soda, along with $250 worth of heroin and $250 worth of cocaine (that "speedball"—the same deadly combination of poison that had killed actor John Belushi) per day. They were shooting $500 worth of drugs into their veins every day. Justin's routine consisted of getting up, hitting the local gas station food mart across the street from La Quinta to purchase cigarettes, snack food, maybe a magazine, and then the ATM for their daily drug money.

On the dresser next to the only bed in the room was a mishmash of used Reese's wrappers, plastic cups, alcohol swabs, packages (empty and full) of Marlboro Reds, bottles of rubbing alcohol (it was always good to make sure you had a nice clean vein to tap so as not to get an infection), and over one hundred syringes, some ready to be booted, others used and tossed.

Scattered on the floor around the bed were animal feces from the dog they kept in the room, alongside dirty clothes, towels with bloodstains, vomit, any number of bacteria, and plain old-fashioned garbage. This was what drugs did: sent you down on your knees to the lowest depths of hell. If they didn't have a dwindling bank account (nearly tapped out now), both would have probably been homeless, living in Christine's purple Prizm. The only difference between living on the street like the junkies they were and having a roof over their heads was some cash in the bank and several credit cards in Christine's name.

There was also a laptop computer in the room. And lo and behold, near this same time, George Koloroutis had taken a call from his source tracking the hits on the website he had put up with the Crime Stoppers number and the sketches: "There's one address repeatedly hitting the site," George was told. Every day. The same IP address, it would turn out, belonging to that computer in Christine and Justin's hotel room.

Christine Paolilla was getting high and visiting the site devoted to catching her.

CHAPTER 45

TOM MCCORVEY WAS a down-home Texas "country boy." Called a "big muscle-type cowboy" by a colleague, McCorvey is that Texan with the unmistakable native drawl you recognize immediately if you're not from the region. Tom liked to wear the finest clothes and always showed up to work wearing a tie. He bowled. He golfed. The kind of guy who takes care of his father, and still finds it within himself to refer to the old man who raised him as *Daddy*.

Harris had a good partner in McCorvey. They made the perfect team, at least for this nagging Clear Lake case. And now, perhaps more than ever, Harris needed a cop like McCorvey by his side; someone he could bounce ideas off to see if he was being overzealous or heading down the right track.

"I want to take a photo lineup to the Lackners," Harris told McCorvey one day after the recent tipster phoned in. "What do you think?"

Now was as good a time as any.

McCorvey and Harris arrived at Michelle Lackner's work with a female and male lineup of six photos each. They sat down. Michelle Lackner viewed the lineup. She took her time, studying each male suspect with guarded curiosity. Then she pointed to one particular photo.

"That's him," she said, sure of herself.

The photo was of Christopher Snider.

Harris placed the female lineup in front of her.

Michelle Lackner took her time again, studying each photo carefully.

"That's her—the woman I saw carrying the purse."

Christine Paolilla.

When they met with Craig Lackner later that same day at his place of employment, he took a look at each lineup and agreed with his wife.

IT WAS A day later, July 14, the middle of the afternoon, when Crime Stoppers called Harris and told him to phone Officer Frank Poe immediately. Poe had someone on the line. He said he wanted Harris to listen.

Poe was talking to a male, who was whispering. Harris was patient. Poe repeated whatever the caller said.

"I'm calling from out of state. . . ."

Poe repeated it.

"I'm not familiar with Houston," the caller said. "I'm scared. I was with a dude named Chris Snider last week in a nightclub. Chris had been drinking. He told me that he and his girlfriend, who he called 'Chrissie,' had killed four people a few years back. It was somewhere in Houston called Clear Lake. Chrissie, I guess, knew these people and had bought some dope from them in the past. Chris said he used a nine-millimeter gun and still has it."

"Do you know what kind of other weapon they might have used?"

"No," the caller said. "Chris told me that he killed two and Chrissie killed two. But that they didn't get the money they wanted."

Harris pulled the phone records. He reviewed Tiffany Rowell's cellular calls to and from her number. On Tiffany's number list was the name "Christine," along with her phone number. The last time Christine had phoned Tiffany before the murders was late into the night on July 14/15, 2003. This phone, which was always thought to be Rachael's (found near Rachael's head) had dialed 911 at 3:12 P.M. on July 18, 2003. This was the exact time, Harris knew, that Christine Paolilla was beating Rachael Koloroutis to death with her pistol to make sure she was dead.

The following day, July 17, 2006, two arrest warrants—one for Christopher Snider, the other for Christine Paolilla—were signed by a judge and given to Brian Harris.

Now all they had to do was locate Snider and Paolilla, an effort that would soon prove to be almost as difficult as solving the case.

Finding Christine wasn't a problem. HPD sergeant Guillermo "Will" Gonzales and Harris County District Attorney investigator Johnny Bonds tracked down Lori Paolilla at the University of Houston, in Clear Lake, where she now worked.

They advised Lori that they were looking for both Christine and her husband, Justin Rott; had she seen them? Harris had looked Christine up in the system and found that she had gotten married to Justin Rott, who himself was no stranger to law enforcement.

"She got married without our blessing," Lori said. She sounded disgusted by the thought of it. They liked Justin, sure, but as a husband? Lori knew better. "She met him at a halfway house in Kerrville."

"You have any idea where they are?" one of the investigators asked.

"Christine has been able to access her trust fund since she turned eighteen"—two years ago—"but since September of '05, we haven't heard from her at all." It was clear to Lori—she could only guess—what Christine was doing with her money. It was so unlike her not to communicate with her mother or Tom Dick for such an extended period of time. "We have, though, spoken to Justin."

"What's going on with him?"

"He would send us text messages."

Lori was able to track down the location of the ATM machine they were drawing money from and gave it to the investigators.

"We tried to help Justin. My husband gave him a job as a plumber's helper, but he didn't last. Then they moved away from Houston." Lori looked concerned. And why shouldn't she be? She knew what Christine and Justin were doing. But why were two investigators looking for her daughter?

It didn't take detectives long to figure out, with a bit of bank and credit card searching, that Justin Rott and his wife were holed up at La Quinta hotel in San Antonio.

Harris assembled a team for the long ride west to San Antonio. It was time to go kick a door in and get Christine Paolilla under a spotlight in the box to see what she had to say.

PART FOUR

THE PROMISE

CHAPTER 46

IN MARCH 2006, Haley Dawkins (pseudonym) met Chris Snider while trolling Myspace. Haley was in the market for a "Russell Crowe look-alike." Apparently, Snider fit that bill. Haley was older than Chris, who was closer in age to Haley's daughter. But Haley liked younger men, she later told police. Chris didn't care. He didn't want to work. He wanted someone to take care of him, give him money for drugs, feed him, and shelter him.

Those who were around when this relationship began later observed that from Chris Snider's view, Haley Dawkins was an "older version of Christine. She was a real done up, girly-girl type, and needed male attention badly." It was not but five days, according to one source, after she and Chris met on the Internet that Haley flew from South Carolina to Texas to visit him.

"That creeped us out," a source said.

Five days talking online, the next thing Chris knew, Haley was standing at his doorstep.

A good-looking woman, Haley felt comfortable within Chris Snider's world. For him, one family member later said, Chris undoubtedly looked at Haley and thought, *What can I get out of her?* ("He just wanted to do drugs and mooch off somebody. And anybody who is going to fly to your house from across the country is going to want to take care of you—she was another mother figure for him.")

Haley and Chris had a nice first visit. They bonded. She flew home. He went back to his life. As the days passed, they talked on the phone, chatted online, and e-mailed. Then Chris was on his way to South Carolina, all on Haley's dime. A few days later, he returned home with a smile on his face.

"Are you in love with this person?" a family member asked him. "Or are you just using her?" It didn't seem right, Chris using the woman and not loving her.

He shrugged.

"Well?"

"Hey, she gives me money, okay," he said. "Whatever."

Near the end of June, about six weeks into the relationship, Haley found herself nestled comfortably in the seat of a plane once again on her way to Houston. Chris had been in Kentucky staying with family since the murders (on and off), spent some time in jail late in 2005 until early 2006, but he had gone back to Houston because of his probation.

Not long after touching down in Texas, Haley and Chris were driving back to South Carolina, arm in arm, on their way to living together. The only problem with this plan for Haley was that she had no idea she had fallen for a man whose mind, essentially, was as twisted as the quadruple murder he had helped commit.

When she stepped off the plane and met Chris Snider in person that first time, Haley realized almost immediately she was dealing with a different person from whom she had met on Myspace. Snider was "very paranoid," Haley noticed as soon as she was around him. Haley had tried to arrange several jobs for him when they got back to South Carolina. But he said no way, refusing to take any of them. "They will turn in my Social Security number and realize that my transfer of probation has not been approved."

Chris wasn't allowed, under the law, to move to South Carolina, but he went, anyway—and Haley was about to find out that the guy she'd scooped up via a website was anything but her knight.

CHRIS SNIDER LIKED to draw; it was one of his passions. He was not bad, either. Chris was no wordsmith, as his writings later proved, but the guy didn't have any trouble putting his feelings and the dark nature swirling about his soul, and inside his head, into an art form on paper. For example, in a drawing he titled "I won't become the thing I hate," a promise he intended to keep, Snider sketched a truly scary demon-faced character (in the same fashion popular culture depicts Satan—only much darker) with dragon wings and a scorpion's tail with a sharp pointer. Snider's Demon Man was crucified on a cross, blood dripping from where the demon's hands were nailed to the cross. In its totality and simplicity, this drawing screamed of a man whose life had come down to a series of demonic deeds he believed he would be punished for one day.

In a similar drawing, with a similar creature crucified to a wooden cross like the Christ, a second Demon Man, with the same scorpion's body, was secured to the cross, but by the bodies of two large snakes, whose heads pointed directly away from the demon's head at the top of the cross. The image itself was disturbing enough. Yet the additions Snider had made to it would make one wonder just what was going on inside his head: Facing drops of blood protruding from the demon's crucified palms were two large flies, both of whom had long tails—akin to umbilical cords—with two strange-looking, naked, chubby babies attached to the ends. At the top of the cross, walking down toward the head of the Demon Man (unbeknownst to the demon, apparently), was a dragonfly, two pinchers poking out in the front of its body, a three-pronged devil's pitchfork tail curled upward.

"Disturbing" is the word that comes to mind when looking at this particular drawing. And yet, as you worked your way through Chris Snider's portfolio, what he was feeling—or maybe suffering from—became obvious. There is an emotional torment and torture apparent in every drawing.

In one drawing Chris depicted himself as a standing man, looking straight ahead, a single bullet hole through the center of his head. The man looked very much like Chris. In two pictures accompanying the standing man on the same page, off to the right of the man, a barrel of a gun was placed up against a head, the top of the head blown off (bits of flesh and brain matter flying through the air) by a bullet protruding from the barrel; the picture on the lower right side of the same page showed a head, a bullet entering below the chin, splitting the face in two.

All of these drawings were done in jail, on the back of Snider's monthly inmate account's receipts.

The next two drawings spoke to the true disorder (and perhaps chaos) swirling around Snider's idea of his life, up until that point. The first showed a fat man who looked to be dressed in a leather mask and leather pants, who had been electrocuted and tacked to a cross (that religious theme again). Although Snider failed to depict how he was placed on the cross, the fat man's arms were stretched out in a *come-to-me* gesture that a parent might use when teaching a child to walk for the first time. The electrocuted man's stomach was torn open and snakes with long forked tongues exited from his insides. Beside him was an abnormally large-headed snake, a solitary demon head above it, another demon head with a scorpion's tail to its right, the pointed end of the tail emitting a single drop of blood like a tear coming out of a syringe that was about to stick into a large fuzzy fly. The right arm of the cross seemed to be connected to a line, which led down to a fire or series of lightning bolts (it's not clear which). In several other similar drawings of scorpions, Snider made their tails out of syringes, obviously trying to say how lethal getting involved with a needle was.

The next two drawings explained a lot about how Chris Snider felt toward Christine Paolilla. On the left side of one page, he depicted himself as a tall man with short, military-style, buzz-cut hair shooting straight up like inverted icicles, a goatee, and one arm—his left—reaching out toward a female on the right side of the page (a caricature of Christine). With his right hand, the man held on to the center of his chest (his heart), which was drawn as a missing puzzle piece. The female, all the way on the right-hand side of the picture, far away from the male, held that missing puzzle piece in her hands, but she was lighting it on fire. Both the male and female in the picture are looking straight ahead.

Regarding these puzzle piece drawings, family members said this was Christopher Snider's way of showing how Christine Paolilla had held him hostage after the murders. There was one day, a Snider family source noted, when Christine told him, "Look, if you *ever* try to leave me, don't forget that all I have to do is get a gun, come up and knock on your front door, and blow your entire family away."

In the next picture, the man is standing in the same position, his arm stretched out toward the female (like in the previous picture), but she is facing him now, with a look of utter hatred on her face. She is holding the puzzle piece in front of him, with that lighter in her hand, and the puzzle piece is almost entirely engulfed in flames.

Snider's drawings speak to a part of him that felt a close connection to the evil side of his life. Anybody who could walk into a house and kill four people for drugs and cash truly had no appreciation (or conception, honestly) of the importance and meaningfulness of a human life. There was no value there for family, for self, for the impact that killing one person would have on the community and the victim's family, better yet four. Some would categorize this person as a sociopath/psychopath, and might be spot-on with that assessment. Yet, there is much more at work here. Paranoia, coupled with the chronic use of drugs and alcohol, on top of an upbringing steeped in dysfunction and loss (most of which Snider talked about at one time or another), creates an unpredictable adult capable of things that others cannot imagine. Risk taking becomes a daily part of life for this person. The stakes are not as high. There's no conscience, essentially. Morality is not something measured in a way of life. This person develops an intense dislike for not being able to move forward in life under his own standards of living and begins to blame others and harness and suppress an intense rage for those not aiding him, which builds up to a point where an explosion of emotion (in the form of rage) occurs. At the time Snider and Paolilla committed these murders, their drug use was on the rise, while their self-esteem and self-worth were on the decline. In this situation the person has trouble controlling impulses, good or bad.

According to some estimates, drugs (and alcohol) are factors in up to 70 percent of homicides.[1]

Chris wrote to "M" in January 2006 (M is likely his mother, if you look at the way he addressed similar letters to a woman he said was his "only motivation to do anything good!"), shortly before he was released from jail and met Haley Dawkins. In that letter it's clear he was not in a good place—mentally—and also that the murders he had committed weren't necessarily the source of his anger and confusion in the days after (he was, one could easily discern from read-

---

[1]This statistic is from Dr. Jonathan H. Pincus's *Base Instincts: What Makes Killers Kill?* (p. 115). Pincus's book, expertly written, I should note, makes the point that killers kill for reasons, and yet some of the reasons they commit these acts that we view as heinous might not be what we assume. Pincus argues that class, social status, and race all play a role in the reasoning behind some murders. After all, some people are evil, willing (and able) to do things we may never understand: and we may never uncover the *why* we are continually searching for when studying these cases.

ing his writing during this period, obviously beyond the murders by then). As time went on, it became clear that he was learning how to live with what he had done.

He started off by saying how the price of stamps was going up and he needed extra money in order to keep writing. He wanted to thank his dad for sending a money order. Then he broke into a rant: *Let's see, just some of the things wrong with me.* It was a poor-me pity party that seemed to be directed toward drawing sympathy, which inmates, generally speaking, look to do. Chris was pouring it on, trying hard to guilt those on the outside into thinking that he had it bad, taking no responsibility for the behavior that had put him behind bars to begin with.

He talked about an ear infection in both of his ears, which "ached all day and night." He was pissed off because the nurses weren't giving him antibiotics every day and the infection kept coming back and wouldn't go away. He had some sort of rash on his stomach that looked like spots or blotches. The doctor whom Chris had seen for his shoulder, which was hurting him lately, was an "idiot." He said the doctor told him it was nothing more than a few "ripped tendons," but the bone was sticking out and it hurt, so he was certain there was a conspiracy against him to see that he was in the most pain possible. He was worried that he looked "deformed." However, he didn't want to show the doctor the injury again, because the prison would restrict him from the gym, and lifting weights had become one of the only outlets in the joint Chris had during those days.

All told, he complained that there was a lot of "bullshit" to deal with in that nasty place.

The only solace Snider had found in jail was his music, which consisted of bands to the tune of Nine Inch Nails, Tool, Marilyn Manson, and the Deftones—that dark, thumping, and thrashing heavy metal with evil and gloomy themes involving child abuse and rape and murder and torture and many other negative things. He liked to sit and copy the lyrics of the songs he liked most. He also asked his mother to send him lyrics from several songs he named. He *needed* to have these lyrics, he said more than once. They were important to him. All of this music obliged that inner hatred Chris had for not only himself but for the world around him. The music allowed him to make sense of the tremendous noise inside his head; it was all one big theme song to a life mired in crime and murder and drugs and anarchy, which he had been involved in since junior high. The lyrics fed an appetite he had to hate himself and the life he had led up to that point. The music certainly wasn't to blame. It was more akin to a man finding a pair of shoes that fit him as though they had been designed and stitched together just for him. One recurring phrase Chris used often when he tried his hand at writing songs and poetry, which he looked at after writing and thought little of, was an idea that there was "no love in me." He went back to this theme again and again: He considered himself "shallow" and empty and without a desire to care for his fellows. He wondered where it came from. He was trying to understand it. He was a man who could not "find his way" in life and had no reason or purpose to go on. Becoming a murderer, in the fundamental essence of what it had done for his sense of himself, solidified the person Snider had thought he was *before* he committed the murders. In firing that weapon into the bodies of the four, Chris Snider was acting out on the *thing* he had seen himself turn into long before that day—or, as he put it himself, he was a "disease" with "no cure."

HALEY DAWKINS AND Chris Snider were living together in Greenville, South Carolina. Snider felt good about being so far away from a place where he had committed a crime that could ultimately put the type of needle in his arm, administered by the state of Texas, that wasn't going to get him high. Now he had Haley, who was, by standards Chris Snider had placed on himself regarding girlfriends of his past, a homecoming queen—the woman who could make him, he was certain, a better man.

"I knew that he was on probation," Haley later told police. Chris had shown her a newspaper clipping written about him that previous January, when he was in jail on burglary charges. "Texas won't leave me alone," he had told her, playing it up as though he had a bull's-eye on his back with the Texas law enforcement symbol in the center. He was convinced—and maybe he truly believed it—that he could do nothing right in the eyes of Texas law enforcement. He felt HPD was out to get him.

"He would never drive a car," Haley recalled.

He also didn't have any friends, Haley said, besides a Vietnamese guy he called "Tommy."

Chris's troubles, according to an interview a sibling family member later gave police, began when he was thirteen: marijuana and gasoline. He smoked one and sniffed the other. From there he developed a serious dislike for school and homework; and his mother had to continually discipline him about his lack of desire to get up and go.

Things never really got any better as he grew. Chris despised school. By the time he was fifteen, Snider had graduated to smoking marijuana cigarettes dipped in formaldehyde or embalming fluid. This drug wreaked havoc on the teenage mind, especially the developing brain of a fifteen-year-old. When Chris couldn't find wet joints, he settled for acid and mushrooms, sometimes all three. The one constant in his life, besides the use of drugs and his getting into trouble with the law, was a gradual desire to end his own life, a suicidal tendency. One of the more recent times he had been arrested (while trying to steal a car), he had left home that day saying he wanted to get caught committing a crime so the cops would shoot him: suicide by cop. Instead, he was pinched and put in jail.

But now he was out of jail, spending his days with Haley Dawkins, his Internet romantic interest.

Meanwhile, a team of police officers was preparing a nationwide search for the guy.

CHAPTER 47

IT WAS THREE years to the day when the search warrants came through, signed, sealed, and ready to be served. Brian Harris, Tom McCorvey, and Detective Breck McDaniel were ready to jump into a car and head west for San Antonio.

Harris needed to make one phone call before they hit the road, however. It was something, Harris knew, that had to be done. The guy had been there all along, praising the Homicide Division when they were on the right track and screaming through a bullhorn when they weren't. George Koloroutis needed to be brought up to speed.

George had been in Washington, D.C., attending a meeting. On this particular day George stood at Ronald Reagan Washington National Airport waiting for his flight back home to Kansas. His cell phone rang. George looked down.

Harris?

"Hey, listen, you gotta promise me you won't say a word about this to anyone," Harris began. "I need that promise from you." Harris hated to have to say it, but business was business; George was a guy who understood that—maybe more than most.

"Course, Brian, what's up? What's going on?" George could feel that pulse rise inside him. He could not recall hearing Harris sound so different.

"We know who did it," Harris said. Was there any other way to put it?

"You're kidding me!" George responded.

"Yup . . . it's this girl named Christine Paolilla."

The name did not ring a bell with George as he stood in the airport, people shuffling by, going about their lives, hurrying from one experience to the next.

"Do you know who she is?" Harris asked.

"No. But let me call Ann and find out if she does."

"Okay. But again, not a word. Tell Ann and [Lelah] not to say anything to anyone. We still have not arrested her yet. We're about to go get her. We understand she's in a hotel."

Harris explained that there was another person involved, a man named Chris Snider. George said he had no idea who that was and had never heard the name before.

"We're going to get her first—and then we're heading to Kentucky, where we think he is."

George stood stunned, his legs numb, standing in the airport with this immense burden being slowly lifted from his heart. It was as if the world stopped for that moment.

They got 'em!

All that work. The interviews. The misinformed tips. The lies. The red herrings.

JU.

It was all over and done with now. Homicide had figured it out.

"Ann," George said, the elation and the pain equally prevalent in his voice, "they got 'em!"

George explained all he knew. He told Ann not to say a word.

Ann understood.

Then: "Do you recognize the names?" George asked.

"Oh, my God . . . that [animal]," Ann said, referring to Christine. "There's a picture of her in Rachael's wallet!"

"Take out that picture. Go get it. Read to me what it says on the back."

Ann went to get the photo. As she pulled it from Rachael's wallet, a memory hit her: that dream she'd had long ago. Rachael had come to her and told her about a pocketbook. Ann had called Harris in the middle of the night to explain the dream.

Chill bumps.

Rachael had spoken to her mother in a scene right out of Alice Sebold's *The Lovely Bones*.

George waited. He needed to hear what his daughter's killer—at least one of them—had written to her months before taking her life.

"Only a demented person would write something sincere and then murder that person," George said later. It was important for this father to get to know who the person was in reference to Rachael. It was part of a process on the road toward healing, toward quelling that anger George had built up all these years, that frustration and pain that at one time had been driving him in his desire to kill the people who had killed his little girl.

Any delight about their daughter's killer being found was now gone. Anger settled on George and Ann, the people who had loved this dead child. As they talked, the hate for their daughter's killer rose inside them.

"We spoke for a short time about what we would love to do to Christine Paolilla, had we the opportunity to be alone with her," George said later.

Then it was back to business: "I have never heard the other name," Ann said, speaking of Chris Snider. Lelah, who was in the background with Ann during the call, said she had never heard of him, either. But she *did* know Christine.

And now that phone call from Harris asking her to identify the girl in the photo made sense to Lelah.

This was not another one of those get-your-hopes-up moments they had all gone through so many times throughout the investigation; this was the real deal.

CHAPTER 48

WEDNESDAY, JULY 19, 2006. Noon. Room 111. La Quinta motel. San Antonio, Texas. Just off Interstate 10, at the intersection of Vance Jackson. It sounded like the dateline to a news story, but that was the information Harris had bouncing around inside his head as he stepped from the car. He, Tom McCorvey and Breck McDaniel were here, together with their counterparts—the local tactical unit—in San Antonio. Christine was in room 111 with her husband, Justin Rott. The search warrant they were going into that room under was actually for "the body of Justin Rott."

San Antonio's tactical unit had already set up on room 111 and had surveillance set up around the entire perimeter of the hotel, not to mention a bead on the only door in and out of the room.

Harris, McCorvey, and McDaniel stood with the team and watched. There was no movement for quite some time. Justin and Christine were sleeping off their high, getting high, or preparing to get high. Either way, Harris had that warrant for Justin, who had an outstanding charge of theft pending. The warrant, essentially, was also for the room itself, a way for them to legally search for the body of Justin Rott. It was a slick move by law enforcement to get inside the room and take Christine Paolilla and Justin Rott into custody to see what they knew about the murders. Heck, for all the detectives knew, Chris Snider and Justin Rott could have easily been mixed up—perhaps it was Justin who had committed the murders with Christine. Perhaps neither had done anything and this was one more dead end! Harris had put his money on the case being solved here, but one never knew what was beyond a door.

The plan, which Harris had designed with his San Antonio colleagues, was to bust in while screaming, *Homicide, Homicide, Homicide—Houston PD!* Yell that, over and over, to see what type of reaction they got. Homicide and drug busts were two different things. Even hard-core drug addicts knew that much.

And that's exactly what they did.

Boom.

The door was kicked open. And in went the troops screaming and yelling and pointing their weapons, flak jackets, goggles, gloves, the works. Just like on television. It was designed this way to intimidate and make it known that this wasn't some sort of drill or a simple drug bust going on here.

It had taken two solid hits with the boom to bust the door open, then a good kick. That provided a warning and enough time for Christine to realize that trouble was on the opposite side of the door and soon coming in. She had jumped out of bed and, nearly naked, nestled herself into a corner of the room on the floor. She was, of course, shaking and crying and shivering, mumbling to herself, "What's happening? Why are you doing this?" Lines very similar to what Rachael was pleading as Christine kept bashing her skull in.

The dog barked. Cops stepped in dog doo-doo and flanked around the bed. They had Justin Rott and his wife cornered. They were not going anywhere.

The room stunk of feces and body odor and garbage. It was disgusting. Drug paraphernalia was scattered everywhere: needles (used and unused), bags of dope (empty and full), soda cans and bottles, empty chip and snack bags, cigarette butts, you name it. There was also a large amount of blood spattered around the room (on the sheets, the rug, towels, on the damn walls, all over Christine's filthy nightshirt).

Harris took Rott, handcuffed him without allowing him a chance to put a shirt on; then he led him out the door toward a waiting patrol car.

"I know what this is about. . . . I know what this is about," Rott said, turning his head, whispering behind his back to Harris.

"Okay. Okay. Take it easy," Harris advised. "You play your cards right, man, everything will be okay."

Now was not the time to talk.

Harris called McCorvey over. "You take Rott and interview him. I'll grab her."

"Right."

The entire operation took a few short moments. By 12:38 P.M., Justin Rott was sitting inside the San Antonio Police Department. It took him no time at all to "summon" investigators, saying, "I wanna talk."

They knew why.

TJ McCorvey sat with Justin Rott inside an interview room at the San Antonio PD, in the Homicide Division headquarters. Rott was dressed in only pants and sneakers. He came across fidgety and nervous, more from using heroin and cocaine than anything else. He had no trouble dropping a dime on his wife. Within a few minutes of sitting down, right after giving McCorvey his vitals, Rott laid it out: "She told me that she was, uh, dating, like, uh, a guy by the name of Chris Snider and, uh, all . . . the whole group, I mean, four of 'em, you know, Rachael, and all of them were friends. . . ."

From that point on, it was hard to stop Justin Rott from talking. He told McCorvey everything Christine had related to him vis-à-vis the murders.

Detail after horrifying detail.

"Dude," Rott said at one point, "it was just so brutal, what she told me, you know, what they, it was all in close range, you know . . . and then, you know, just beating her over the head, over and over again, just, you know, I couldn't believe it."

McCorvey peppered Rott with inquiries concerning dates, times, names, all the essentials that would help them when Harris got his crack at Christine—an interview that was about to get under way in the room next door, a box that was being prepped as they spoke.

What Rott said was going to paint a picture of what had happened inside that house. Within that framework of stories, the truth would eventually emerge, without Justin Rott or Christine Paolilla realizing it.

Near one o'clock, Harris entered the interview room, where Christine sat on a chair, her legs crisscrossed, and her feet tucked underneath her butt. She hugged a bright yellow blanket around her shivering body. Christine came across as a chronic dope addict in the throes of an addiction that was potentially at its peak. She wore a white nightshirt stained with dried blood from all those times she or Justin had stuck a needle in her arm. All told, considering what she had been through, and how much dope she and Rott had shot over the past half year or more, she didn't look or sound half bad. She was coherent. She knew what was happening.

Donning a bright blue shirt, his sleeves rolled about elbow high, Harris sat in a chair with wheels. He came across a bit wired and anxious, likely because he was finally facing the yellow crime-scene tape at the end of the finish line, literally just around the last bend of a three-year-old marathon case. Christine was moving back and forth, hugging herself, yawning, staring at the floor. Her hair was up in a bun, her eyebrows gone, leaving these two white bumps jetting out from the bottom of her forehead. Her skin was as white as the Styrofoam coffee cup sitting on the table to her right. The room was rather bleak: gray, not too much light; a computer monitor turned off; a video camera facing the two of them, its red light letting them know Harris was recording every word and action.

It was close to two forty-five by the time Harris pulled out a card and Mirandized Christine, who kept responding rather politely, "Yes, sir," whenever Harris asked if she understood. It was clear from the video that Christine was not yet withdrawing from the massive amount of drugs she had injected that day, nor in a state of needing a fix—not yet. She was in junkie limbo. There is a period between bags of dope when the junkie is quite coherent. The point being that Christine knew exactly what she was doing and why she was sitting, speaking to an HPD Homicide Division detective; and once she got herself acclimated and worked up some tears, she had no trouble feeling comfortable and talking.

"Do you understand you have the right to terminate this interview at any time? You know, just say, 'Brian, stop.' And that's it. Do you understand that?" Harris said.

"Yes, sir," she answered, her voice cracking. An avalanche of emotion was rumbling. This was clear from Christine's facial expressions. She was feeling the weight of killing four people and the consequences of that crime, which were right around the corner.

Harris leaned forward, a foot or two away from Christine, put his elbows on his knees, and spoke with his hands. "Look, in order for me to understand what happened, for you to speak about the emotions you say you've been going through, you have to waive, give up your right, so I can hear what's going on, what happened."

Before he could finish, Christine broke down, bawling like a child, pulling that raincoat-yellow blanket even tighter, as if she could somehow disappear inside it.

"Do you understand? I know you're scared. But are you ready to tell me what happened?"

More tears. No words.

"Let me ask you this," Harris said. "I see that you're crying, okay. When we talked earlier about justice and mercy"—this was one of Harris's themes to get a suspect to understand that he (the cop) was not there to judge or condemn, but only wanted to understand and get to the truth—"you remember that?"

Christine nodded through more tears. She looked down. Stared at the floor. The immensity of this horrible crime was implicit in the way she squirmed.

Harris spoke about people getting what they deserve—*justice*—and others getting what they need—*mercy*. He explained how important this was within the context of what he and Christine needed to get into. Before the formal interview started, Harris had spoken to Christine about his philosophy behind mercy and justice, and how this would decide what type of person she was and what type of penance she was going to ultimately receive. Christine had a chance at mercy, Harris had explained in no uncertain terms. She had a moment here where she could ask for and receive compassion, at least from him. It would not save her from any potential penance. But Harris was clear that we all had a choice when facing that mountain of judgment; and Christine was there, standing before it. She could climb over, or turn around and walk away.

"Do you believe," Harris asked after Christine refused to say anything for a few beats, "that you deserve justice or mercy?"

She was interested in this. He could see her eyes light up. She squeaked her answer through tears, stretching out the word "M-e-r-r-r-c-c-c-y," while nodding her head to Harris and repeating it.

"Okay," Harris said. He sat back.

"Yes," she said, again nodding. "Yes, yes. Very much so."

Harris found an opening.

"Okay . . . I'd like to be able to understand *why.* . . . Can you give us some insight as to what's going on? Okay?"

This seemed to lighten Christine's load. "Justice for *him?*" she asked. "Justice for him and mercy for me? Or justice for *him?*" She sounded confused.

"Well, when you mean 'for him,' who are you talking about?"

"Justice for *him,*" she repeated. "Mercy for me."

"Okay," Harris said, raising his voice, "when you say justice for 'him,' now who do you mean?"

"Chris Snider."

"Okay, now mercy for who?"

"Me."

"Okay, okay. Well, tell me why, then?"

With that, Christine broke into one of those chest-thumping crying fits that moved her entire upper body up and down. She did not say anything right away.

"Look, all I can go by right now," Harris said in a cop-type authoritative voice, "is what other people have told me and"—he paused—"and what *Chris* has told me." Another pause. Then: "I mean, you don't have to tell me anything. I'll just go with what we have."

They had not spoken to Chris Snider. In fact, HPD had no idea where he was.

"Do you understand?"

"Yes, sir," she said in a high-pitched voice, nodding.

"Okay. What happened?"

Christine sat still for a brief moment. "He can't have contact with me, right?"

"Excuse me?" Harris asked. "He cannot contact you. . . ."

"I don't want him to hurt my family. . . ," she said, crying harder, "or *anybody* to hurt my family."

"Has he threatened your family in the past?"

Christine looked off to her right, as if the question hurt her.

"Let me ask you. Tell me what kind of person Chris was?"

"Um . . . he was very . . . just . . . um . . . very"—she looked at the floor, thinking, going back, or maybe trying to come up with something that would suffice—"um . . . hopeless. Just a hopeless person." Then she broke out of her shell a bit: "He was begging me for all that pity, you know. I am the type of person . . . you know . . . I have always dated, you know, stupid guys, just because, you know, I think that I can help them. Get them back on their feet. You know, all the wonderful stuff that I could never do." She reached across the table (startling Harris) to grab a tissue. "But then . . . like . . . you know . . . but then . . . there was times, you know, when I meant *everything* to him. But that was when, you know, whenever I was giving him whatever he wanted. You know, towing him when he wanted . . . sticking up for him, lying to him, or lying *for* him. . . ."

She carried on about how she had always felt alone and that everyone was against her and out to get her, and that Chris Snider had made her feel special for the first time in her life.

Harris explained that they needed to talk about her family, Chris Snider, her entire life, why she had been estranged from her mother for so long, and all things *Christine*; but first, before they could get into any of that, Harris stressed, they needed to go back to July 18, 2003, and get that out in the open.

"So tell me?" Harris asked.

Christine slumped. This was the classic tell suspects gave when they were ready to confess. Her body curled into a question mark. She stared at the ground, this time intently. She did not cry.

Christine was focused. Thinking. She was back in the Rowell house on that day. In the moment.

Then it came out: "We were at my house," she began, "and it was just . . . me and him there." They were hanging out. Dating at the time. She talked about Chris smoking some weed at the house. She didn't want him to. "Put that out," she had told him. "I don't want that stuff in the house. Listen," she then said to Harris, as if it was some sort of admission, "I am not going to lie. I smoked some, too. But I would *never* bring it into my parents' house."

Next she talked about the fight she and Chris had on that day.

"I was nagging at him and yelling at him," she said. "He was like, 'Fine, I'm gonna leave then. Take me home.' I was like, 'No, no. . . .' I finally just gave in, whatever, and, you know, and . . ." She couldn't finish.

The tears came back.

The horror.

Memories of murder.

"You were *seventeen* and thought you were in love," Harris said.

Christine took a moment to regroup. Then explained—finally—how she and Chris had left her house and driven to his house. Snider was acting crazy by then, she said, referring to him as "psycho guy," and she didn't want to know what was going to happen next, so she went along with whatever he said. Part of dealing with Snider on that day, Christine suggested, was going along with a plan he had to steal some drugs from Marcus and Tiffany. It was a plan, she explained, that she neither knew about beforehand, or had any role in developing.

CHAPTER 49

THE WAY SHE described the murders to Harris on this day, you'd have to believe that Christine Paolilla was in a state of panic, fear, and under the Manson-like control of a madman who was going kill her and her family if she didn't go along with him and keep this terrible secret.

Christine was in Chris Snider's room, inside his parents' house, about an hour from Clear Lake. She thought he was in the kitchen, searching for another joint to smoke. He became increasingly hostile and angry because she had made him douse his last bit of weed, and now he wanted more.

According to Christine's first "official" version of the murders, Chris came out of his father's bedroom (not the kitchen) and said, "Take me to Seabrook."

"For what?" Christine asked him.

He didn't answer.

"Why, Chris?" she said. "Because you *ain't* got no more dope here and you need to get over there and get some?"

"Just take me," he said.

"We were kind of, like, talking about normal stuff," Christine explained to Harris. "But it still seemed like, you know, something was on his mind."

Christine did not want to fight with her boyfriend, so she jumped into her Geo Prizm and told Chris she'd take him to Seabrook, if that's what he wanted.

As they drove, he said, "You know what, um, don't go over to

Seabrook. Take me to your homegirl's house or whatever, and I'll see if, uh, Marcus is there."

"Why? Why do you have to go *there*?"

"You know, I heard Marcus got some good shit."

Christine claimed that this statement upset her. They had been over at Marcus and Tiffany's a few weeks before that for Tiffany's birthday party. There was some indication here that Christine didn't appreciate Chris going over there, talking to Marcus and Tiffany, or, especially, Rachael, without her. She was jealous. Chris had admitted that he had hooked up with Marcus a few times after that party without her knowledge, and the thought of them together without her had infuriated Christine.

"Are you on that [stuff] now?" Christine asked Snider in the car. She assumed he had taken some pills back at the house—some of that "good shit," he was referring to—and she didn't like it.

Christine pulled her Prizm into the subdivision opposite the Millbridge Drive neighborhood where Tiffany lived, she told Harris. She parked down the street, sort of in back of Tiffany's house (although she never said why she did this).

"And he was like, 'Come on, come on.' Just like rushing me."

"What the hell, you know, what the hell have you got there. . . ?" Christine asked Snider as they sat in her car. He was in some sort of a daze, she claimed. "I thought, honestly, I know it sounds real stupid, I thought that maybe he had, you know, messed around with one of the girls or something, you know, and he wanted to see them or something."

So he'd ask his girlfriend, a good friend of both girls, to drive him over there? That didn't seem like too likely a scenario to Harris as he sat and listened. However, he allowed Christine to talk her way through her version of the day.

Christine wanted to start the car, do a K-turn, and hightail it out of the neighborhood.

"I'm late for work already," she told Snider.

Her shift had started at three o'clock. It was just after that hour.

Snider screamed "at me, you know, like messed-up crap."

"Get out," she yelled back. "Get out of this car! Go do what you want."

Snider slammed the door and started walking.

Christine said she sat and waited. "I just wanted to leave him there and go to work."

But she didn't. Instead, she waited.

At some point, though, she claimed she started the car, turned around, and started driving out of the neighborhood. Her home was a mere two miles away. Yet, instead of driving home, Christine said she pulled down Tiffany's street for some (unknown) reason and drove toward Tiffany's house, eventually parking her car nearby, a few houses down the block from it. The idea she was obviously trying to convey here to Harris was that Snider had gone into the house by himself, apparently to cop some drugs or to visit one of the girls he had a *thing* for, and she had decided to wait for him.

"And then I saw him, like, walking in the opposite direction of the house."

So she pulled up. Beeped the horn.

Chris hopped in. "Just drive, just drive! Come on . . . just drive," he said frantically. There was something different about him now, Christine claimed. He was all hyped up and anxious, more than usual. Totally flipping out, according to Christine's version.

"He looked at me with this *look*."

He pulled out a bag of drugs from his pocket, she said. "I was like, good. I thought he had hooked us up. But I know he didn't have the money for [the amount] that was there."

"I jacked dem fools! I jacked dem fools," Snider said as Christine drove. He flashed the drugs at her inside the car.

("I started freaking out, you know, because they knew me," Christine editorialized to Harris.)

"Why did you do this?" Christine asked. "Why, Chris?"

Her boyfriend reached over and turned on the radio "really loud." Then he started screaming the lyrics to a song by the band Nine Inch Nails, yelling at the top of his lungs.

Christine turned the radio off, letting him know she didn't approve. She had never seen him like this.

He reached down and felt his leg near his shin. He uttered a stream of expletives and then said, "You gotta go back. Go back *right now!*"

"What?" she asked, startled.

"You gotta go back."

"No way."

"You don't know what happened. . . . Go back!"

"What did you do?"

"I forgot something. . . . I forgot something. You gotta go back. Right now!"

Why would he want to go back if he just jacked those people? Christine thought.

Against her better judgment, she turned around and drove back to Tiffany's house. "I was gonna, you know, just pull over in front of the house. 'Cause if I had to, you know, apologize for him, you know, he's gonna get his butt whooped."

"No, no, no," he said as she pulled up in front of the house. "What are you doing?"

"What are you talking about?"

"Don't pull up in *front* of the house. I just jacked these mofos, you know. Are you . . . stupid?"

"No! I'm *not* fucking stupid!" Christine yelled. That comment pissed her off.

She screamed some more at him.

He yelled back.

"I'll go right in there now and tell them you're *right* here!" Christine threatened.

She got out of the car.

"Get back in here," he said from the window. "Or you're going to . . . regret it."

Christine hopped back into the car, turned the key, and prepared to drive away.

But Snider jumped out, she claimed, as she started the car, and ran into the house.

She turned the car off and watched him.

Brian Harris pleaded with Christine at this point. She had broken down during this part of the interview and didn't want to continue. Harris said, "Okay, be the voice of justice for [Jesus] Christ, give him (Snider) what he deserves—what *happened*?"

Snider came running back out, Christine continued. At first she didn't know why, she said. "And he came running out with the gun— with one of the *guns* in his hand."

This had been the first time Christine Paolilla had ever mentioned a gun was involved—and Harris knew, right away, from the way she had said it (first *gun,* then *guns*) that Christine Paolilla was implicating her boyfriend and extricating herself. She was placing the burden of the murders entirely on Snider by working this weapon into the mix.

But she had made a Freudian slip.

Guns.

They both sat inside the car. "I didn't say anything to him."

Total silence. They both sat still as stone.

"I need to go to work," Christine said, breaking the silence.

("I was so scared," she told Harris, "to say *anything.*")

"Some people," Snider told her in a soft, cautious voice, "are just at the *wrong* place at the *wrong* time." He emphasized that word, "wrong."

"What is going on? What the hell are you taking about?"

Christine said she thought about calling Tiffany on her cell to see what was up inside the house and if she "would talk about it."

"Are you . . . stupid?" Snider said when Christine expressed a desire to call Tiffany.

Silence again.

"I am in so much trouble," he said, repeating it a few times.

"What? Why? What did you do?"

"I took all of Marcus's [stuff]."

"What did you do?"

"If I tell you, don't be mad at me. Promise me that."

"Okay, okay," she said.

"I shot them."

During this first interview, Christine said, "I was not in the house. I've been thinking that I was not in that house."

Harris asked if she was ever in the driveway, not telling her that the next-door neighbors had placed her and Snider together in the driveway. "Yes," she said, "I wasn't in the driveway. The only time I was close to the house was when I drove up because I was gonna— he had to go back for something, I don't know, then . . . And then I got out and I started walking toward the house 'cause I was gonna tell, uh, Tiffany and Rachael that I had nothing to do with, you know, him jacking them."

Christine explained what happened inside her car next as she and Chris sat, talking about what he ("alone") had done inside the house. "He had no sympathy at all for what happened and what he told me he did, explain like, you know, what happened. He told me he was, like, you know, say this if the cops are, like, asking you anything. You tell them that you did this, or whatever."

All Snider said about what had happened inside the house was "I shot them," according to Christine. She made it sound as though she was in no position to press him for details. She claimed that she slept with her mother for a week after he murdered her four friends. But that she never told her mom anything. Never told friends. Never told anyone.

"Christine," Harris asked, "you were with him for at least three months after that, so within that three months he tells you details, okay? You saw news clips. You saw things. What were the details he told you that happened?"

"Nothing was really said after it happened, but there was times when the news came on and, like, they did say that, um, like, they weren't just beat or something. You know, I always asked him questions and stuff, you know. It made me feel real . . . I couldn't tell anybody. I felt I didn't think it was real, you know. I thought usually he was trying to show off, and I didn't want to . . . He always checked my phone."

The truth was that Christine Paolilla called Chris Snider incessantly after the murders, at all times of the day and night. It got so bad, Chris's mother later said, "I had to keep buying phones, because our phone was drained so much it wouldn't recharge." And the idea that Christine was scared of Snider was further quashed by a statement Snider's mother later gave in reference to their relationship before and after the murders: "Chris was so sick to death of Christine, but would always answer her calls, and meet with her. I asked him one day, 'What does she have over/on you? That Christine is crazy.' "

Chris responded, "Mom, you have no idea."

Harris wasn't buying this version, either. He was beginning to press Christine for more detail, hoping to pin her down to a version HPD could later tear apart.

"In order for that road toward mercy," Harris said, going back to his original (spiritual) plea, "I need complete honesty."

"I am! God, I'm telling you," she said.

"And sometimes that's some of the bad with the good, okay?"

"I'm being *honest* with you."

Harris went into some of what Justin Rott had told HPD (in the adjacent room), without giving Christine too much detail. "Why would your husband tell us . . . that one of them was crawling on the ground and that you admitted to striking Rachael?"

"I never said that. I've talked to my husband about the situation . . . and all I ever told my husband was that I'd tell [him] what had, what the news had said, that they did say she was on the ground."

"When you went in there?" Harris asked, trying to catch Christine in one of her lies.

"Went in where?"

"When you went there, when you went in the house, your husband is telling us that you pulled Rachael out, okay, initially?"

"I did *not* go into that house."

After they discussed blood under Christine's fingernails that someone had reported (Christine denying that also), Harris lied: "Now, you understand that Chris is saying that this was all your idea and that you had a lot of pent-up frustration toward Rachael that he thought that you thought that he was having an affair with her and that's why—"

But Christine wouldn't let him finish, butting in: "I would have never."

Harris explained that if she was telling the truth, she would have to be much more specific about what had happened and what Chris Snider had told her he did inside the house.

"I'm trying so hard," Christine said.

"And try to remember what happened to the gun afterward."

"I don't know what happened."

CHAPTER 50

BRANDEE SNIDER WAS at her aunt's house in Pasadena, Texas, when she heard that her mother and father's house was being "raided" by police. Chris Snider had been staying with Brandee before he made that move to South Carolina. Snider's mother and father were living in Louisville, Kentucky, where they had moved about two months before. It was close to noon on July 20, 2006, when she (Chris and Brandee Snider's mother) stepped into the shower inside her Kentucky home.

With the help of Louisville police, HPD went into the Sniders' house while Mrs. Snider was in the shower. As they filed in, detectives and tactical officers yelled and screamed pretty much the same thing the officers had back down in San Antonio a day before.

After realizing that Chris Snider was not inside the house, they produced the paperwork for their search warrants and proceeded to get busy searching the house. The main mission here was to find Snider himself, whom his mother, after getting dressed, explained was not living with her. Still, as they worked their way into the bedroom and started snooping around, a safe was uncovered inside a closet, and then a pistol in a dresser drawer.

Inside the safe was a second weapon.

Both of these guns would soon be connected to the Clear Lake murders and proven to be the weapons that had killed Marcus, Tiffany, Adelbert, and Rachael.

"Do you think this has anything to do with the murders?" Snider's mother asked when she called Brandee in Texas and told her what was going on. The cops who had stormed into the house were somewhat vague in describing why they were actually there. It was quite obvious they were looking for Chris; but beyond that, nobody knew what was happening.

"What?" Brandee responded. She had no idea what her mother was talking about.

About three weeks prior, Brandee had gotten into some trouble attacking her boyfriend and tossing his computer into a public pool. In fact, it was the last time Brandee had seen Chris. The day before she was arrested and placed in lockup overnight, Brandee and Chris had gone shopping. They spent a great day together. But when Brandee got out of jail the following day and moved in with her aunt in Pasadena, Chris had already taken off with Haley for South Carolina. In speaking with her mother about the search of the Kettucky house, Brandee assumed that the *Robocop* assault unit busting into Mom and Dad's was in response to her throwing her boyfriend's computer into the water. She thought maybe her boyfriend had called the police and had made up a story.

But murder? What was her mom talking about?

"Yeah, the murders."

Brandee hadn't thought about the Clear Lake murders crime in years. Not since it was breaking news. She'd had no reason to.

But then Brandee put the thought into her mind and juxtaposed it with what had been going on with her brother and the conversations they'd had over the years. She then considered Chris's severe depression and total withdrawal from society, along with the increasing, monstrous appetite the guy had developed for getting as high as he could. Then there were those times (several of them) when Chris had tried to commit suicide over the past three years. Something had been bothering him, Brandee knew. No doubt about it.

"Oh my, I hope it's not that," she said.

"They took the guns," Brandee's mom said.

The other little factoid Brandee got from her mom was that the cops were on their way over to Brandee's aunt's home in Pasadena, and would be arriving anytime to interview her next. It seemed someone had said Brandee was involved in the murders, too.

Later that same afternoon, in Greenville, South Carolina, Chris Snider's aunt called him. This occurred after Brandee had explained to her what had happened in Kentucky.

Haley Dawkins felt this call was strange, she later said, from the first moment she saw the number on her cell phone and noticed the Texas area code.

His family never calls him, Haley thought as she stared at the number.

This was speculation on Haley's part. Brandee and her brother, along with their mother, had been in contact with Chris ever since he left Texas. Snider's father had given him $1,000, in fact, to help him get on his feet. The Sniders weren't the Waltons, but they held close ties.

Chris was outside playing basketball when Haley took the call. Haley distinctly recalled him wearing black tennis shoes, a black muscle shirt, and gray shorts. He seemed to be in a good mood. He had purchased the clothes during a shopping trip he and Brandee had taken shortly before he left for South Carolina. Brandee had picked out the sneakers for him.

Haley picked up the ringing phone. "Hello?"

"I need to speak with Chris," the aunt said. The urgency in her voice was clear.

Haley handed Chris the phone. He was out of breath, sweating. "What's going on?" he asked, wiping himself with a towel.

Haley shrugged. She had no clue.

"The cops are looking for you on murder charges," the aunt said.

"What? What? Stop joking with me," Chris said into the phone. Haley later said he used "a panic type of voice" while speaking to his aunt.

"I'm not joking around here, Chris—this is *very* serious," his aunt said.

"How could a murder be pinned on me? Don't call here," he said. "Don't call me back." He hung up.

The aunt called back.

"Don't call me here, I said!"

"This is serious, Chris." They talked for about fifteen minutes, according to one police report.

"No, I cannot call Mom," Chris said. "Look, the cops are going to come here and catch me. Every time you call, they could be closer to the house."

Snider's family was trying to tell him it was too late for all that.

The police knew where he was, and they were on their way. There was nothing he could do now but tell the truth.

After he hung up, Chris ran over to the computer he was using inside Haley's house. He logged on to his Myspace account and searched frantically through the site links and icons for directions on how to delete his account.

Haley didn't know what was going on. She assumed it had something to do with Chris ducking out on his probation.

"How the hell . . . do . . . you do this?" Snider asked, tapping keys; he was frightened and nervous. "The police are going to find me through Myspace."

Brandee Snider called her brother after getting off the phone with her mother. By this point, Haley had left the house. Brandee was never told why. Regardless, Brandee needed to speak with Chris right away. She had been thinking about his Myspace account, too; that if the cops were smart, they'd log on to Myspace and see that he was in Greenville, South Carolina, living with this new girlfriend. Brandee needed to delete the account for him and, also, ask him point-blank what this was all about. They were close in age and had always been tight. She knew her brother—and the guy she knew was not a murderer. But Brandee also realized that Chris had changed over the past several years. Something wasn't right with him. She needed to know if he was involved in this vicious crime, or if it was all some sort of misunderstanding.

"Chris, Houston Homicide cops are looking for you, *really?* Come on. They pulled Mom out of the shower and were looking for the *guns* in Dad's bedroom. Did you *kill* anybody, Chris?"

"No," he said.

"Chris?"

"No," he screamed a second time.

"Are you sure you didn't kill anybody?"

"No," Snider yelled.

"Well, I don't know what's going on, but I need your Myspace password because you have where you're living on there." Brandee told him she'd delete the account herself; she knew he wouldn't be able to do it.

"I don't know what it is. . . . I don't know what it is," Snider said, referring to his password. He was freaking out.

Brandee had helped her brother set up the account. She remembered the password—BOOGER1—and got into the account. Then she handed the phone to her aunt, and the aunt spoke to Chris while Brandee went in.

Chris was going crazy. He knew that the police were on their way.

"No, [Haley's] not here. . . . I don't know what to do." His mind raced.

They talked a few moments more and hung up.

Brandee called back after she completed the computer task. Some time had passed. Maybe an hour or two.

"Where's my brother?" Brandee asked.

Haley had picked up the phone. "I don't know what the hell is going on," she said. "But Chris was running out of the house as I came in."

"Where did he go?"

"I have no idea. . . ."

"None?" *Come on,* Brandee wanted to say, *you don't know where the hell your boyfriend went off to?*

"No, but I can tell you that he took all of my prescription pills . . . but left three hundred dollars in cash, his cell phone, wallet, and everything else of his here."

This stunned Brandee. Stopped her in her tracks. She knew her brother—and also where he was going.

Game over, Brandee thought as she hung up with Haley.

For Chris Snider, Brandee later said, there was no way he could have come to the conclusion that at that time he could have sat down with police and maybe turned in Christine and told his side of the murder tale. There was no way Snider would have thought that far in advance, or decided on taking life without parole and giving the police Christine. He just didn't have the mind capacity, Brandee explained.

"He had a very childlike mind," Brandee said respectfully. There was a sadness in her voice toward a brother who never really seemed to find his way in life. Chris Snider was a guy who used drugs to fill a hole in his soul, compress any emotional pain, and stuff any feelings of inadequacy he had about himself into a ball, deep down. Chris never thought of himself as anybody, somebody, anyone, or someone. To him, he was nobody, a person whose life was nothing more than gray clouds. Getting up in the morning was a chore for Chris. Facing life was an uphill battle *all* the time. He was constantly running to stand still, going nowhere.

"You can see how he misspelled words," Brandee added, "in the letters he wrote. And the way he talked was kind of baby-fied."

Where this all came from was a mystery. Chris Snider and his sister had a good upbringing in a good home. They were loved. They loved their parents. They didn't get to know their biological father until they were both adults.

"And what a disappointment that was," Brandee said.

The guy was a drug addict and an alcoholic. There was no mystery where Chris had gotten that taste in his DNA for drugs; it had been inherited. But he had never grown up in a household environment strewn with drug use, abuse, yelling, and screaming. They were a happy family.

And now he was on the run—again. This time, Brandee feared, heading to a place where he would never have to chase the dragon or run from the police again. Christopher Snider was finished looking behind his back, his sister knew. As Brandee hung up the phone with Haley, she considered how he was going off like a wounded wild animal to die in the woods somewhere, alone—that is, if HPD didn't find him first.

CHAPTER 51

NOT LONG AFTER Brandee Snider spoke to her brother, she looked out the window and saw a "huge SWAT van" backing up to the door of her aunt's apartment. From there, Brandee and her aunt watched "these militant cops" file out of the van as if they were zeroing in on a 9/11 suspect. One after the other, they jumped out of the van, Kevlar vests, rifles, goggles, just like at her parents' house in Louisville, under the impression that Chris Snider was hiding out in her aunt's home.

"Don't move!" the first cops in the apartment shouted.

Brandee and her aunt were not going anywhere.

They looked under mattresses, in closets, in drawers, everywhere.

"It was crazy," Brandee said.

When they were finished, one of the investigators pulled Brandee aside and told her that she was going to have to go with them "downtown."

"Whatever," she said.

"Let's go."

"Can I at least put on some deodorant and change my clothes?"

Silence. Then a wave of a pistol and nod of the head as an officer followed her into the bathroom first, her bedroom second.

This is nuts. . . . There must really be something going on here, Brandee thought as she got ready.

Once they got Brandee down to HPD, she was put in the box. Brandee thought she was going to be interviewed as part of the investigation into whatever her brother might have gotten mixed up with; but within a few moments, she realized that was not the case.

Brandee referred to the investigator who "interrogated" her ("I refuse to say 'interviewed,' that'd be way too nice," she stated later) as "some really sharp-dressed man."

According to Brandee, the detective told her, "Look, if you don't tell us the truth, the truth we already know, you will be charged as an accomplice and possibly be put in prison for life."

"What?"

The questioning soon turned to where Chris Snider might be and where they could locate him. Brandee gave up Haley's name. She said she hadn't spoken to her brother in some time. He might be on the run.

"I think [my boyfriend] made all this up about Chris to get back at us for what I did to him." Brandee told them all about the Myspace account, her brother saying "no" he didn't do what they were claiming he had done, and just about everything she could recall. Near the end of the "interview," Brandee took a deep breath and accepted the idea that maybe Chris had committed murder.

She told the officer, "If this is true, then my brother is dead."

It felt cold and numbing to say the words, but Brandee knew her brother.

"Christine Paolilla told us that you had something to do with this," one of the interviewing officers said, according to Brandee.

Brandee had no idea what they were talking about. She felt like a murder suspect. A criminal. Brandee was the first to admit she had some pockmarks and the police knew her name, but a quadruple murder?

Come on.

Brandee said HPD kept her under the light for six hours, questioning her about things she didn't know anything about. After repeatedly asking her what amounted to the same series of questions, Brandee giving them the same answers, "they realized," she recalled, "that I didn't know anything. Then they typed up a statement, had me sign it, and took me back to my aunt's house."

In defense of HPD, they had four dead people, a case that was three years old, the end in sight: it was unfortunate that Brandee Snider had to be subjected to such rigorous questioning, but if it could help solve this case (and maybe save her brother from hurting himself), it was part of the process.

Brandee's mom called from Kentucky after hearing what had happened. "If you want to come out here to Kentucky, I'll send you a plane ticket."

Brandee said, "Yes. Yes."

CHAPTER 52

ONE STORY CHRISTINE** Paolilla failed to share with Brian Harris—or anyone else—as she began to talk about her role in what had happened on July 18, 2003, took place the day after the murders. She was at Chris Snider's parents' home in Crosby, Texas.

There was a part of Christine that viewed her relationship with Chris Snider as a "Bonnie and Clyde" type of romance, both of them connected by the crimes they had committed *together*. Some later said Christine had planned the murders of her friends so she and Chris could have this one interrelated bond between them that Snider could not sever—the ultimate secret, in other words, keeping him from ever walking out on her, like she presumed everyone else throughout her life had done.

Some evidence pertaining to this theory was the fact that Christine and Chris were routinely taking off to Walmart or another retail store with a strategy to rob the place. Snider later reported that during one afternoon postmurder, he and Christine took a trip to Walmart (she always drove; Snider never owned a car) and boosted two DVD players. They went back. Christine became manic inside the store, as if she was in her element, an elated state of grace to steal. She loved it. "Hey, babe," she'd said to him while they were walking through the CD section. "Come here." Chris walked over. Christine took a quick look around. Then, happy no one was watching, she stuffed his pants with CDs, laughing. There was a glistening look in her eyes.

The ultimate heist, though, took place on July 18, something both

Chris and Christine could not help but to boast about twenty-four hours later. Brandee Snider was at home on this day, July 19, sitting on her bed inside her room. She heard her brother and Christine stumble into the house loudly, as they often did, making their presence known to anyone around.

Next thing Brandee knew, the door to her bedroom was flung open. There stood Christine and her brother, ear-to-ear grins on their faces. Chris was holding something.

"Look . . . what . . . we . . . have," Christine said proudly, a look of euphoria on her face. Certainly not the dark and troubled gaze of someone who was overwhelmed by the fear of watching her boyfriend kill four people, worried he was going to kill her and her family (as she had said repeatedly in the months afterward).

Chris raised his eyebrows.

Christine now held the bag—the size of a pillowcase—full of pills.

"X," one of them said. "An entire bag of X."

Thousands upon thousands of dollars' worth of the drug.

Brandee flipped out. Jumped up off her bed. "There's only one way, Chris, that you could have gotten this." Brandee was upset and angry. She didn't understand what her brother wanted with all those drugs, enough to put him in jail for decades.

Chris and his girl stepped into Brandee's room, closing the door behind them. Chris knew his sister. She couldn't keep anything from their mother. She was honest like that, to the core. She would tell. But he went ahead, anyway, and showed her the bounty he and Christine had just burgled.

"What is all this? Are you guys crazy?"

They smiled over such a huge score.

"What do you think?"

"You've *got* to get rid of that right now," Brandee said.

"Come on," Chris told his girlfriend. He took the bag and walked toward the bathroom. "We're flushing it."

"What?" Christine responded, shocked. "No, Chris. No."

Brandee stood by as her brother flushed the pills, handful by handful, down the toilet, the clear water spiraling dollar bills into the city sewer system. This was a major hurdle for Snider to overcome in the relationship, family members later said. For Chris to turn and tell

Christine what they were going to do (especially with drugs) was out of character for him.

Later, Brandee found out that she should have stayed and watched them flush it all, because she heard from her brother that they had flushed only half of the bag and kept the rest.

CHAPTER 53

DURING HIS FIRST interview with Christine Paolilla, Detective Brian Harris felt that she was placing the onus of the murders entirely on the back of her accomplice, Chris Snider. The young woman took no responsibility whatsoever for anything having to do with killing Rachael, Tiffany, Marcus and Adelbert. In fact, per Christine's version of that afternoon's events, she had never even gone *into* the Rowell house. Yet, Harris was not going to accept Christine's story at face value. He knew from her posture and demeanor, as she talked her way through the murders, along with the interviews he had conducted throughout the case, and the interview going on across the hall with Justin Rott, that Christine was lying. She was trying to pull one over on HPD and remove all of her culpability for this horrendous crime.

"Christine," Harris said at one point, repeating himself for what to him seemed like the umpteenth time, "in order for mercy to work, I need to have *complete* honesty from you."

Christine stared at him blankly, her leg bouncing nervously, a bite of her lower lip. She was undoubtedly scrubbing through her options—all of which were just about running out.

"Christine, what did he say he did with the guns? He would have had that conversation with you. What did he *say* he did with them?"

The suspect stammered. Harris had her on the ropes.

"I don't . . . I—I . . . don't . . ."

"Christine?"

"I don't know. He did not . . . I swear!"

"Whose *guns* are they?"

"I guess they're his dad's."

They went back and forth. Christine, in a desperate attempt to plead her case, tried to absolve herself. But Harris could see that her story was falling apart.

"Why didn't you go to the funerals?" Harris asked out of nowhere, trying to catch her off guard.

"I don't like going to funerals. . . . Anything, I don't . . . ," Christine said, dredging up some tears, mentioning that now tired story of her dad dying when she was two years old, and how funerals brought all that pain up for her.

Harris shifted in his seat, thought for a brief moment, and then broke into the "Prodigal Son" story from the Bible. He explained to Christine that her life story reminded him a lot of the bad son in that popular Bible tale. The bad son had squandered all of his inheritance on partying and on the luxurious and wasteful things life had to offer during the days of Jesus Christ. It was a good analogy, probably perfect in the situation that Christine had found herself sitting in, having blown through—in $500-a-day increments—close to a quarter of a million dollars that the death of her father had given her. It was almost laughable to watch her sit there and cry about a father she never knew, a man who had died when she was barely old enough to walk and not yet out of diapers. She was crying, allegedly, for this young child who she once was, but blowing all of the money, which his death had given her, on heroin and cocaine didn't seem to make one bit of difference.

Most human beings, Harris noted aloud, when confronted with a traumatic/criminal situation in which they played a role, generally tried to minimize their part in order to allow themselves to feel better, to make a nice cushion for mercy to fall upon. That, Harris said, wasn't the right road to travel if Christine's goal by sitting and talking to HPD was to acquire redemption and, hopefully, be shown some mercy for doing so. If Christine wanted to redeem any part of her involvement in this evil act, the murders "that bastard," Harris called Chris Snider, had committed "all by himself," Christine was not going about it in the right way. She needed to provide him with details, Harris said rather loudly. Christine and Chris had been together for months after the murders, Harris knew. They had spoken on the phone routinely after the murders. Throughout that time, Harris pointed out, again and again, they had talked about the murders. If Chris Snider had gone into that house by himself, how in the world did Christine know all these details she had given to her husband and to others?

"Because," Harris added near the end of his little "Prodigal Son" rant, "*nobody* can open up their arms to you, *Christine!*"

And on that note, Harris stressed, her time was running out.

Now or never.

Christine Paolilla shrugged. Then she said: "Uh-huh," as if what Harris had just spent minutes explaining had been spoken to her in Swahili. It was as if she had not understood one word.

It was difficult to keep Christine focused on one particular subject because the signs of feeling the heavy burden of having murdered two of her best friends, and needing to talk about it, had begun to wear her down. She'd drift off, stare at the wall or floor, and Harris would have to say, "Hey, stay with me here, Christine . . . come on."

Harris brought up the caliber of the weapons.

Ignorantly, Christine said she had no idea what a caliber was.

Harris became excited: "How would he (your husband) *know* the caliber of guns used in the murders?"

Christine found herself backed into a corner. She sat for an extended period of silence, thinking. Then, suddenly, "I know how," she said with excitement, as if *aha, I figured it out!* "Because we had"—she paused, looking puzzled—"right, yes, we talked about it. And it was . . . it was something that had come on the news. That nothing had been found yet. And then I went on the website."

She was all over the place. As she spoke, Harris dropped his head, saying with the gesture: *Give me a freakin' break here. . . . Do better than that!* But he figured he'd amuse her sensibilities and play along for a few beats, asking, "One of the *websites?*"

"That's how he knows."

"How does he know about [the caliber of the weapon]?" Harris wondered, making a point that the caliber of the weapons used was never mentioned in the news reports or on the website.

"I believe the website told what guns they were."

"Okay, okay, how would he know this fact—that *Rachael* was in a crawling position, had a cell phone by her, and y'all believed she was dialing nine-one-one, and that it was a *good* thing that you went back in there?"

Only a person in that room with those dead and dying kids could have known those facts as Justin Rott had explained them.

Christine seemed shocked by this revelation. Her appearance conveyed: *How did you find* that *out?*

"I never, never said that to anybody," she said.

"And how would that person [now referring to one of the tipsters] be able to relay certain details," Harris said, ignoring her answer. Then Harris tried another one of his tactics specifically designed for this situation: remove the blame from the suspect, place it on something other than her conscience. "But the good thing about that is *that* person says that you were sick to your stomach, and you didn't want to do this. You felt like you were *forced* into it. You didn't want to do it. And then when it happened, okay, I think you know what I think happened. I think Chris did what he did and you did run up the driveway, okay? And I think that you went into the house and saw what he did, and you went, 'Oh, gosh,' that . . . he's running behind you and then you see him make sure that they're all dead, and then he looks at you and he says, 'Now you're in this with me!' And he manipulates your mind that way. You see what I mean?"

Harris continued for another few minutes, doing his best to persuade Christine that she wasn't the one to blame, that it was Snider, the "psycho bastard," Harris called him, who had manufactured this entire crime.

Christine wouldn't bite: "I was *never* in that house."

Harris asked what she was wearing that day—if she could recall that simple fact.

Walgreens work clothes, she said.

"Did you have anything on your head?"

"I'm feeling sick right now," she said.

"Did you have anything on your *head*?"

Harris was losing her. Christine wanted a nurse. Her skin was pasty, white as vanilla ice cream. She had dark bags and half circles underneath her eyes, but she was alert and coherent. She knew what was being asked of her and, in turn, responded by asking intelligent questions.

It was 4:45 P.M. Harris could see his subject was breaking down. Her head kept falling to one side.

"Can I see a nurse?"

"Let's take a break, okay, and let's get you . . . get you together."

Christine asked for a nurse again.

Harris explained that someone would be summoned to have a look at her. "Take some water," he said; then he got up and walked out of the room.

With Harris gone, Christine lay back in her chair, curling herself up in that yellow blanket, hugging it tightly, her head falling to one side. She moaned some, and looked uncomfortable. Totally still, Christine just about passed out—that is, until she heard voices outside the room, which startled her awake. She sat up, listening. Then she dropped her head on her right shoulder and passed out.

A door slammed in the background. More voices. One of them was Justin Rott's. This piqued Christine's attention.

Harris barged into the room. "Look," he said, standing over his suspect, pointing at Christine angrily, "I'd like to take you back to Houston so you can be closer to your mom, but I can't do that if you're going to be all [messed] up and gonna pass out and all that other [stuff], okay?"

Harris was angrier now than he had been since they began. He was frustrated and tired and quite unimpressed with the line of crap Christine was giving him.

She looked at him and appeared to be startled by his demeanor. With her image facing the camera directly, it was easy to calculate the toll the drugs had taken on Christine Paolilla; she appeared skeletal and ghostly, ashen-faced, having been deprived of any natural nutrition or fluids. She looked weak and tarnished, a fragment of her old self.

"I'm gonna be sick," Christine said, ". . . if I could just see a nurse and she could just give me something, not like drugs or anything, but . . . I'm not saying I'm gonna OD or anything. If I could just see a nurse."

Justin Rott was outside the door. Harris walked back out and spoke to him. Christine heard her husband's voice and brightened up; some red color even washed back into her face. She leaned forward in her chair to get a closer look outside the door.

The voice got closer and louder. Harris walked in front of the box door and Christine could hear him clearly saying, "Hold on . . . hold on . . . hold on . . . okay" to someone in the hallway. Then Harris walked back into the interview room and, pointing at her, addressed Christine: "Come here."

"Okay," she said, getting up languidly.

"Come *here*!" Harris said sternly, with force, telling her to hurry the hell up.

She got up and walked out into the hallway.

"Stand right here," Harris told her. Then to Justin Rott: "Tell her."

Justin sounded as though he had been crying. He said something none of them could understand.

"This is her *life*," Harris said with force. "You're worried about *your* stuff? This is her *life*!"

They didn't speak.

Harris looked at Justin: "Did you tell us the details of what happened?"

Justin spoke, but Harris couldn't understand him.

"Tell *her* to *tell* the truth."

"Just tell the truth, hon," Justin said after a long pause.

"Go on back in there," Harris ordered Christine, who wanted to stay in the hallway with her husband. "Come on, go back in there. . . . Go *back* in there. . . . Go back in. . . . Sit down."

Harris closed the door behind Christine after she sat. He stood in the hallway with Rott. Christine walked sluggishly over toward her chair and leaned on it without sitting. Then she turned and walked back to the door, placing an ear up to it so she could hear what they were talking about. Could this have been Harris's plan the entire time?

Harris was reading Justin Rott the riot act, finishing many of his sentences with, "Do you *understand* that?" They were close to arguing. "Here's the problem," Harris said at one point, laying out the situation for Rott, who had by then given HPD everything his wife had ever said to him about the murders.

As they talked back and forth, Christine opened the door slightly and said, "Sir?"

"What?" Harris said sharply, letting her know she was interrupting.

"Can you please, I *need* a nurse."

TJ McCorvey was there, too, out in the hallway. "Do what?" he asked.

"I need a nurse," she said again.

"What?" McCorvey said.

She said it again.

"She needs to see a nurse," McCorvey repeated to Harris.

Christine doubled over and held her stomach: "Please, I'm bleeding. I'm bleeding."

"We're getting one," McCorvey said as Christine seemed to rock back and forth on her heels while holding her stomach. "Just sit down in there."

"I love you, Justin," Christine said, changing her tone.

"Just *sit* down."

"Please . . . I can't move . . . please." She held on to the door.

"Sit *down!*" someone yelled.

"I can't move from this spot," Christine claimed.

"We'll get you some help," Harris said.

"She said she can't move," McCorvey told him.

"I'm bleeding," Christine repeated, not saying from where she was bleeding.

McCorvey stepped into the room, picked up her chair, and placed it over by the door. Then he told her to sit down. Help was on the way.

"I'm bleeding. . . . I'm bleeding."

CHAPTER 54

CHRISTINE PAOLILLA DID not give herself up during that first interview with Detective Brian Harris. He tried. But Christine had an unwavering unwillingness to come clean regarding her role in the murders. On top of that, Harris later admitted that he had probably screwed up the interview.

"Yeah," he said, "I should have gotten together with Tommy [TJ McCorvey] when I left the room, before I spoke with Justin Rott. I should have said, 'Tommy, this is what I want to do. . . . This is what Christine is saying. . . . What do you think?' Tommy was down the hall. I thought Justin would come down and say, 'I told them everything,' but that kind of backfired. I should have had Tommy do it (convince Rott to speak with Christine). Justin looked at me like, '*Who* the heck are you?' Once he heard Christine say, 'I love you, Justin,' that was it. It wasn't a mistake 'casewise,' we still had plenty of chances left, but tactically, yes, a mistake on my part was made. I should have gotten together with Tommy."

Christine was taken to the hospital because at some point her addiction to heroin and cocaine was going to catch up with her body; and then after a period of detoxification, she was cleared by doctors to be extradited back to Houston. But HPD could not take her without first putting Christine in front of a San Antonio magistrate. This was not going to be all that simple, once San Antonio law enforcement got involved. Ego runs through police departments like water in the pipes; some officers feel the need to flex their administrative muscle when the chance arises. Still, Brian Harris, Breck McDaniel, and TJ McCorvey were going to bring Christine back with them, one way or another. To make the trip easier, Harris ordered a small state police plane to meet them at a nearby airstrip—that is, as soon as they could get Christine in front of that judge and get the proper paperwork in order.

At the hospital Christine was feeling better. She said she was willing to talk; there were a few things she wanted to share.

Harris hoped she was finally ready.

After being asked, Christine explained that she thought Chris Snider had put the guns "back in his dad's safe."

She next brought Snider's sister, whom she did not name, into the picture, saying that she believed Brandee had had something to do with providing the guns to her brother. After that, she went into a story about how Snider had said he "pulled the gun on them and, like, they started arguing." He later told her that he had gotten into a fight with Marcus.

Harris knew this was an incredibly weak attempt at trying to place the blame on her co-conspirator, for the simple reason that if Chris and Marcus had gotten into a fight, Adelbert would have backed his cousin up. It was ridiculous. Pathetic. But typical.

Harris allowed Christine to talk, nonetheless. Sooner or later, he knew, she was going to trip herself up.

Christine continued to paint a picture of Chris Snider killing the four while she waited in the car. She said she did talk about the crime to some friends, but not in any detail. All she had shared must have come from what she had seen or heard on the news. And from there came a series of excuses and explanations as to how and why Christine Paolilla knew what she knew but had never gone into the house with Snider.

She said that she and Snider had fought in her car over the drugs he stole from the house ("weed"). She asked him to get rid of the drugs, but he refused.

She said he showed "no human emotion" or "sympathy" for what he did after he admitted killing the four. And this made her sick to her stomach.

She said he liked to correct the news when a story came on by saying, "That's not how it happened." This also made her uncomfortable.

She said he was always trying to "show off" and brag about what he had done, like he was some kind of "playa," now that he had killed four people.

After that, she and Harris talked about the wigs Christine liked to wear (black and auburn).

They talked about her being in rehab and meeting Justin Rott.

They talked about how Christine felt that Snider had threatened her life and how he had told her routinely that she was just as guilty as he was because she had driven him to commit the murders.

They talked about the fact that, according to Christine, Snider said he would kill her parents (or have someone else do it) if she ever went to the police.

Harris eased his way into saying, in not so many words, that Christine was full of nonsense. Harris lied to her, saying that they had spoken to Chris Snider and he had placed her in the house with him. Harris wanted to know how that was possible, and what did Christine think of Snider's accusation.

So Christine went through the details she had given Harris the day before, again describing how she had waited in the car *outside* the Rowell home.

Harris didn't let up. He explained to Christine that everybody carried DNA around with them and that it was easy to leave a DNA sample, haphazardly and unknowingly, wherever you went.

She said she understood.

Harris asked, "How would we explain your DNA *inside* that house?"

"Well, I've been to that house before."

"Uh-huh . . ."

"Like, you know, I was there for her birthday, and, you know, people are always at her house—"

"All right," Harris said, "I figured that, okay. But how would we explain a *smudge* mark on her clothing? On Rachael's shoulder, all right, and, um, and it kind of makes sense now, okay, a foreign hair." He was trying to say they had uncovered a hair in the living room. "A lot of times when we're being hit, we do this"—Harris put his hands over his head like he was protecting himself from falling debris— "and we cover our head." He was mimicking what Rachael was likely doing when Christine went back into the house and beat her to death with the butt end of the weapon Chris Snider had given her.

All Christine said in reaction to that was: "Uh-huh."

Then Harris switched tactics. In a comforting tone, coming across to Christine as someone who was on her side, protecting her, the detective said, "See, what I mean is, how would we explain that [hair] being on or about Rachael? See, I don't want you to get jammed up—see what I mean?"

Whenever he said "we," it took the "you"—that accusatory finger being pointed at Christine—out of it, and placed Christine in charge of her own destiny, all with the feeling that Harris and the HPD were her allies. It was a smart strategy. Become her friend and she would, sooner rather than later, trip over herself. From the littlest differences in her stories, Harris could tell that Christine was making this up as she went along. Liars, he knew from experience, always expose themselves by the sheer process of telling more lies.

Christine said something Harris couldn't understand. Then, "We shared clothes," meaning she and Rachael. "I don't know if that would have anything to do with it."

Harris next talked about oils on the skin. How, per se, if Christine had placed her hand over his hand, she would, effectively, sandwich the oils he had on his skin and seal them to his skin, concluding, "How do we explain *your* oils being on those guns we recovered in Kentucky? See what I mean?"

"In Kentucky?" This was surprising to Christine. A big uh-oh.

"Yeah."

"I never been to Kentucky."

"No? I know you have never been to Kentucky. But how do we explain *your* oils on that gun?"

"There was oils on the gun?" Christine felt the itchiness of that noose scratching.

"In other words, all that stuff you see in *CSI* about dipping into bleach, about wiping it down? It's like when you melt a piece of cheese, right? Does the cheese go away? No. It sears into the bread, right? It's the same thing with body oils. That's why *CSI*'s a joke, okay? It seals things in, okay? There were attempts by Chris to, number one, wipe it down, to get them off so his dad wouldn't know it—"

"Okay," Christine said. She was paying careful attention to what Harris was saying.

"—but those oils sear in, see, okay? At what point in time, did *you* touch those weapons?"

"Um . . ."

"You got to explain that."

"When I was in my car that day, we were fighting and—"

"Okay, tell me about that."

"I never, you know, grabbed the gun from him, you know, like there was only one that I saw."

"Tell me about it."

"Then I was, like, all, 'Get out of my car.' Like, 'I need to go to work.' I just wanted to go to work, to get away from him. At the time I wasn't even really thinking. I was, you know, I was just—I just wanted him to leave."

They had hit a critical point of the interview. Harris knew he had Christine in a tight spot. Truth was, they had not even caught up with Chris Snider yet. Word was coming back that no one could find him. Harris was involved in putting a team together to begin the hunt for Snider, once he was able to secure Christine's extradition to Houston.

In responding to how her oils might have gotten on the guns, Christine made up a story about how she and Snider got into a fight inside the car, and that possibly she grabbed hold of his jacket, where he was storing the weapon (which she had earlier said he had stored in the pant leg pocket of the parachute pants he was wearing that day), and she might have inadvertently touched the gun. As far as when and where, exactly, this took place, or what was said as they fought, she couldn't recall.

Harris changed the subject. He asked about "any specific detail" Snider might have told her about the actual murders and how the argument between him and the boys had started and then turned into bloodshed.

She said something about Chris "trying to act cool" while he was inside the house, and Marcus picked up on it and they started to have words.

She could know that only if she was inside the house herself, Harris thought, staring at Christine.

Harris asked if she had heard anything while she was outside sitting in the car, you know, like gunshots?

She said she didn't hear anything. A neighbor, though, Harris knew, one house away, down the block, had heard the shots, loud and clear. How was that possible?

They discussed the murders a bit longer. Christine did not really add anything more to what she had said already, besides offering up a few names of dopers that Chris knew from Seabrook, one being "Jason Uolla."

Interesting, Harris thought.

When Harris made a mistake and called one of Chris's friends by a different name, Christine laughed at the error. Amazing that she could find humor in all that was going on.

Harris asked about the supposed "special relationship" Christine might have had with Rachael.

"It was nothing," Christine said.

After that, they discussed a few inconsequential items, and Harris ended the interview, saying that the batteries in his recorder were running out of juice.

Christine could breathe easy; she had gotten through a second interrogation without giving herself up. As Harris considered things, however, he knew she was holding back.

"She was cunning. She tried to explain away everything, which told me that any 'withdrawal' from drugs was not affecting her ability to try and save her own ass."

AS THE LEAD investigator, Detective Sergeant Brian Harris now faced the problem of getting Christine Paolilla back to Houston, where he could continue to work on obtaining a confession. Harris knew she was there, inside the house, and quite possibly had pulled the trigger herself. He just needed Christine to tell him that. The San Antonio Police Department, nevertheless, needed to release Christine first, which would take a visit in front of a magistrate. All HPD had was a probable cause warrant to hold her.

As they prepared Christine for her appearance in front of the magistrate, Harris later said, he was stopped by one of the San Antonio police officers who had helped them bust in and take Justin and Christine into custody.

"You can't take her out of here. We need confirmation from your court that this is a valid warrant."

"Come on. Are you serious?"

The officer could have allowed them to take her without a hassle.

The idea was to place Christine in front of a San Antonio judge, who would then order her held on probable cause for an additional day or more, which would allow HPD to transport her back to Houston. It was supposed to be a simple court appearance.

But San Antonio was not going to release her that easy.

Tom McCorvey stepped up in front of the officer's face: "Are you crazy?"

Both men squared off. They stood in the hallway outside the court. Christine was just about on her way into the courtroom.

Harris stepped back, got on his cell, and called his boss.

"Look, whatever you guys do, when the judge is finished with her, do *not* allow them to put her back into a San Antonio jail. You grab her and you go. Got it?"

McCorvey was explaining to the San Antonio officer, who had made it clear that things needed to be done by the book, that all they wanted to do was take her back to Houston and get her out of San Antonio's hair. But the guy, an old Texan lawman who appreciated jurisdiction values and apparently busting the chops of outside departments, wasn't going to allow it until the proper warrant was signed.

Harris told McCorvey what their boss had said.

Meanwhile, the officer McCorvey was going head-to-head with realized that McCorvey, who is quite a bit bigger than most men, was not someone you necessarily wanted to aggravate to the point of boiling over. Thinking more about it, the officer said, "You know what. That's fine. Y'all are on your own here, though."

Harris needed directions to the small airstrip where a state police plane was supposed to be meeting them. They had no idea how to get there.

"On your own" meant exactly that: San Antonio was not going to lift a finger.

Thus, as soon as the judge finished, Harris and McCorvey, along with Breck McDaniel, grabbed Christine and got her into a waiting car, where they proceeded to inch their way to the airstrip with directions from the state police.

McDaniel drove the car back to Houston. The flight for Harris, McCorvey, and Christine was long, hot, and bumpy. They were flying into a wind so powerful the entire way home, Harris said, they could have gotten there sooner if they had driven.

Harris sat on one side of the small cabin; Christine cuddled up next to him. McCorvey was perched on the opposite side, facing them. It was cramped, the size of a small closet. Christine thought the ride was "neat" at first, looking out the windows like a kid, smiling, saying, "Wow, look at that . . ." Then she sat back and fell asleep as the plane leveled off, her head falling on Harris's shoulder.

McCorvey looked at the two of them and laughed. "Y'all make a cute couple."

Harris rolled his eyes. "Yeah, right."

"Love that drool running down her mouth and onto your shoulder."

"What?" Harris said, looking at the wet spot growing on his shirt. "Son of a bitch."

CHAPTER 55

BACK IN HOUSTON, the team felt a bit more comfortable and confident that Christine, now near her mother, would open up. On Thursday, July 20, 2006, Breck McDaniel drove to the Harris County Jail, where Christine was being held, and signed her out.

Christine was brought to the courtroom of municipal judge Gordon Marcu, who officially read Christine her rights and let her know that she was being held for an additional thirty-six hours. If the DA did not charge her by the end of that time, there was the chance that she could be set free.

After that, McDaniel drove Christine to HPD headquarters, but first, per her request, stopped at McDonald's so she could get, of all things, a Happy Meal.

"Sit in there and eat," McDaniel said while walking Christine into the box. He mentioned he'd be back to speak with her after she was finished.

"Can I smoke when I'm done?"

"Yes."

As Christine ate her Happy Meal and thought about what she was going to say, the idea that Chris Snider was the master manipulator behind the murders became the focal point. In going down this road, she was making Snider out to be perhaps smarter than he actually was, thus creating a bit of a quandary for herself. Christine didn't know it, obviously, but she was about to bury herself with her latest round of innuendo and weak accusations. Number one, she had wanted nothing more than to be as close to Chris as possible when she was with him. The evidence would prove that she often used family members to get there. She had never even hinted at the idea that Chris was some sort of rough, abusive, controlling maniac, who was driving the relationship, several of Snider's relatives later said. In fact, from the outside looking in, things appeared quite the contrary.

"Christine realized how close Chris and I were," Brandee Snider later said, "and she would routinely try to be my best friend. She made me collages of Courtney Love and Bettie Page on her computer. . . . She always came over to the house with little gifts for me."

It was Christine's way of staying as close as she could to Chris, watching his every move. If she got in good with the sister, she was certain to be loved by him.

More than that, Chris Snider hadn't always been a dark, twisted, wounded soul, out drifting aimlessly in a world of violence and drugs. ("Look, I know Chris wasn't even close to perfect," Brandee recalled. Still, her brother did have moments of humanity and humor.) When Brandee was a high-school freshman involved in the drama club at Clear Lake High and her class had been assigned the task of making a music video, Chris offered to help. There were four girls at her house one afternoon doing the Spice Girls, hamming it up for the camera. "It was so funny," Brandee said. "I asked Chris to join us. My class ended up enjoying him the most because he had makeup on and was eating a corn dog throughout the whole video."

This was the goofy, happy-go-lucky side of Chris Snider. His sister started playing guitar when she was fourteen. She and Chris cowrote a song called "Doggie Food."

"We had a lot of fun when we did hang out. It sucks to remember good memories—those hurt more than the bad ones."

Now, after finishing her hamburger and fries, Christine Paolilla was ready to talk about what she warned was a far different side of Chris Snider, a man, she would soon assert, who would have killed her if she had not participated in that violent quadruple murder three years ago.

CHAPTER 56

THERE WAS A bump in the road on the way to getting Christine to open up about the murders. It was 11:38 P.M. before Breck Mc-Daniel sat down with Christine to interview her for what was now the third time (HPD interviewed her briefly in the hospital). By this point Christine was nowhere near out of the woods as far as her addiction. She had spent a better part of the night (after vomiting and suffering through the shakes and shivers) at the hospital ER engaged in withdrawal symptoms. But after nurses provided her with the proper meds, she said she was fine, and the hospital discharged her.

Back at HPD, near midnight, Christine was "lucid," Breck Mc-Daniel noted in his report. He observed that she "understood her rights" and she didn't display any signs of "health problems" or "discomfort" as the interview got under way. She was not going through withdrawal symptoms. Christine was, instead, able and quite willing to talk. McDaniel had gotten out of her earlier in the night that she was ready to begin talking about what *truly* had taken place inside the Millbridge Drive house. No more BS. No more dancing around the truth. She wanted to explain her role.

Sitting on a chair in the box, her legs crisscrossed underneath her butt, staring at the floor, Christine began by framing Chris Snider as an angry monster of a human being whom she had been tied to at the hip and could not manage to wiggle away from.

"There were times when, um, he was almost satanic when talking about people, like, 'I wonder what it would be like to kill someone,' or 'I wonder what it'd be like to die.' "

She called it a "love-hate relationship," placing the liability of what was certainly to be a death penalty murder case entirely on her lover's shoulders. By now Christine was under the impression that Chris was in custody and talking about her, telling HPD everything. She had no idea HPD was, as she sat telling her version of the events, scrambling to find him.

Christine tried to play off the idea that Chris Snider had taken over the role of a father figure in her life (though he was only two years her senior) and filled a void she felt from not having a disciplinarian to teach her the value of right and wrong. The way she outlined it, Snider had poisoned her sense of morals and taught her how to be bad, how to hate. She claimed he became the "dominant male" in her life. She said he was able to influence every decision she made. She went on dissing Snider so brazenly and repeatedly that Detective McDaniel had to ask her to move on and begin talking about what happened. The more she downplayed her role in the relationship and tried to portray Snider as an evil, violent boyfriend who would stop at nothing to keep her, the more her argument came across as transparent. Truly, you could only trash a person so much before it became a mishmash of words and accusations that sounded weaker with each new allegation that was piled on.

"Can we move forward?" McDaniel encouraged.

After settling down, Christine told the same story of asking Snider to stop smoking weed at her parents' house on that July 18, 2003, afternoon—and her falling and hitting her head on the marble outside after he shoved her.

She described what she wore. (Walgreens made her wear "black pants and a dark blouse and black boots.")

She explained what he looked like, and what color shirt he had on that day (black).

After a few more minutes of the same reasons she had given Brian Harris for ditching a Seabrook drug connection in lieu of going to the house of her "homeboys" to buy some drugs, Christine said they went to Tiffany's, but she "didn't feel like going in." So she told Chris to go get the stuff and meet her outside. She assumed he was going in to purchase the drugs, not rob them.

When he came out "ten minutes later," Christine explained, he was stoked and running on adrenaline, having just stolen "a sandwich-sized bag of X." There had been no shots fired. No dead people. No scrambling to get away from the scene.

Not at that time, she claimed.

The story up to this point was nearly identical to what she had told Harris, save for a few new details. When Snider admitted to her inside the car that he had robbed Marcus's pills, she felt like running into the house to "tell Rachael"—who she said in a previous interview did not live there at the time—"I had nothing to do with it. . . ."

The question McDaniel asked himself as she talked was what many would later wonder: *How would she know Rachael was inside the house?* She had given part of herself away here by mentioning that small fact of Rachael being *inside* the house. She could have never known that, unless she had been inside the house herself.

McDaniel made a note of that in his head and told her to move on.

After arguing with Snider about stealing from her friends, she said she convinced him to walk back up to the house with her, go in, and talk about what he had done. Maybe he could apologize and it would all be forgotten.

Christine knocked on the door and Rachael answered. Snider hadn't, by then, killed anyone. According to this new version, all he had done while inside was brandish his weapon and take the drugs. Christine claimed that she was under the impression they were going back to return the drugs and say how sorry she was for what he had done.

Rachael was upset because of what Snider had done. She opened the door, saw them, but then turned and walked away, almost as a diss.

Snider walked in, Christine said. She followed. She was nervous. She didn't want to make any problems with her friends. She knew how pissed Marcus was going to be; he and Adelbert would want to retaliate. This was going to be her chance to make it all right again.

"I was so scared, you know, I thought—I thought that, you know, like he (Snider) was gonna shoot me."

She explained that Marcus was sitting on the couch when they walked in. "Like, you know, all mad."

Rachael took off, out of the room. Tiffany walked into the living room from down the hall and said, "Hi, Christine."

Christine didn't say anything because she was ashamed of what Chris had done.

But then Snider, she claimed, without warning (or telling her), pulled out his gun and waved it around. As he did this, Christine said, she was not the least bit scared for her friends. She didn't think at this time that he was wielding the weapon for their sake—but for hers.

"I thought he was going to do something to *me* with the gun. . . ."

Instead, Chris initiated an argument with Marcus, saying, "Where's your money?"

And that's when Christine knew he was going to rob them again.

"I don't got no money," Marcus answered. "I just deposited it in the bank."

"You better go get that money," Chris ordered. "You better go *right* now and get that money."

Christine said that by this point she had worked her way away from Snider's side and was "crying in the corner," thinking he was going to kill her, along with the others. She believed he had effectively *snapped* and was under some sort of crazy spell.

When Marcus didn't come up with any money, Snider told him again that he had better get his money and the rest of his drugs—or else. As he spoke, Christine said, Chris pulled out a second gun and held both weapons out in front of himself, hip high, like John Wayne. He stood, facing all of them. Christine's knees buckled underneath her small body as her nerves exploded.

Without warning, Marcus got up and walked toward the back of the house, apparently beckoning Chris to follow him.

Snider yelled: "Are you stupid? You know, what the hell are you thinking? Turn your ass around, you big baby. Don't let me . . . walk back there!"

When Marcus stopped, Chris called on his girl for help. Christine said she was heading toward the back of the house herself, when she heard Chris say, "Get . . . back here."

Near him once again, Christine said, he pulled her close to his body, grabbing at her, his teeth grinding in anger. "It was like, 'You better take this'—the weapon—and I didn't think it was loaded or anything. You know, he was like, 'Just take this. Just take this, come on.' Just, like, pushed it on me."

An important point that no one—not the police or the prosecutors—later made was that Chris Snider had two guns on him. He had taken the weapons from his mother and father's house. If he had planned on doing "the job" by himself the entire time, he would have taken only one weapon. But he grabbed both. Why?

One for him, and one for his lady.

CHAPTER 57

THE IMAGE CHRISTINE was trying to paint as she told the story was of a scared teenage girl, her boyfriend's prisoner, who was now being forced to become an enforcer. She claimed Chris Snider made her take the second gun and point it at the four, all of whom were gathered in the living room. (The crime scene evidence left behind, though, disputes this claim. It is clear from the way in which the bodies were found that Marcus was walking away from his murderer and Rachael had her back to her murderer.)

Christine grabbed the gun. "I just felt like, 'Oh, my God, I am going to die. . . . I am going to die if I don't follow his directions.' "

She watched Snider take Marcus and walk out of the living room. Both of them walked into a bedroom, where Marcus, under Snider's watchful eye, shuffled through drawers, looking for his money and any additional drugs. As they did this (out of sight from the others), Christine essentially held Tiffany, Rachael, and Adelbert at bay with the second weapon—that is, instead of running out of the house with them (after all, she was armed), or handing the weapon to Adelbert, who was sitting on the couch.

Christine next described a strange circumstance. She said she tried to hide. She was crying and kneeling and standing behind a wall in the kitchen. She felt as if there was going to be, "Like, you know, like," this big fight. She heard "Marcus . . . talking [stuff] . . . you know, like, real bad [stuff] to Chris."

The two of them were getting louder and louder, and then Snider yelled, "Are you getting scared? Are you getting scared?" The girls broke out into fits of tears. "I just started praying," Christine explained, "you know, like, 'God, please, please, please,' you know, just 'God,' that's all I could say in my head . . . and that's when I heard the first gunshot, and I don't think it hit anybody."

By now Chris and Marcus had walked back into the living room.

Then a second shot rang out.

The girls "started screaming."

"Shut up. . . . Shut up. . . . Shut . . . up," Snider screamed. "I'll get you, too. . . . I'll get you! You better *shut* up."

After that, Snider turned to Christine: "You, bitch. Get out here." She was standing behind that wall in the kitchen.

"What was, like, going through my head, you know, just out the other ear, and then—and then, uh, when I heard the . . . shot . . . I heard, like, you know, Marcus and the other guy, um, was just like, '[Damn] . . .' you know, like that. Then I heard the other gunshot and then that's when, like, the girls, like, they started, like, you know, like, not screaming, screaming, but like, 'Oh, my God' . . . and then . . . I—I keep hearing, you know, kind of like, you know, the bubble wrap stuff, like *pop, pop, pop.* Like that."

She claimed Chris walked over to her after those first shots shattered the silence of the room, pointed his gun in her face, and said, "You get out here. Get out here . . . you bitch, you bitch."

"Well," a source close to Chris Snider later said, "I certainly don't think he would have pointed a gun at her. . . . If he would have, he wouldn't have had any problem shooting her, too, so as to have *no* witnesses. Secondly, he wouldn't have spoken to her that way. He was forever teetering on the fine line of her bipolar moods, and calling her a bitch would have inflamed Christine quite a bit."

Christine said Snider broke into a diatribe whereby he had made her feel "like a piece of [crap]." She wanted to leave, but "I was glued down to the spot where I was at," she said.

Frozen.

Snider said he wanted her gun if she wasn't going to use it. "[Hey], give me the gun," she claimed he said. Then he called her the *B*-word several times. He said it "over and over—that's all I kept hearing in my head. Then he took the gun and he ran into the room [where everyone else was] for something, I don't know what, but I heard like a *pop* noise . . . and he ran back up, and he was like,

'Come on. You're . . . getting me out of this place. You're getting me out.' "

Christine said he helped her stand up, but her "body felt very weak . . . like, you know, like I was passing out or something, and kind of like, you know, when you, like, run out of breath. . . . And he kept yanking me up, yanking me up, and then he made, like, another . . . and my eyes were closed . . . [but] I could hear [additional shots being fired]."

She was now by the doorway in the foyer. She heard voices (some of them her own). Crying. Pleading. *Stop. Stop. Stop it.* She claimed she couldn't see anyone because she kept her eyes closed.

As Snider stood there, his gun going off, the four of his victims screaming, Christine said she fell into him and grabbed at his shirt, pulling, yelling, and begging for him to stop.

" 'Stop, stop, stop,' that's what I was saying in my head, but I couldn't, like, nothing could come out, but just tears, whatever, and then—and then he took—he took my gun, and he was trying to put it in my hand, and I had it in my hand and then . . ."

"One, two, three," Snider said, over and over, counting down. "One, two, three . . ."

She felt as if he was forcing her to shoot one of them. Demanding that she take the gun and become part of this massacre.

"I just shot, but I didn't shoot anybody, 'cause I, like, I was . . . at the time I remember I was, like, you know, I was trying to, like, move and, you know, it was, like, toward, uh, I think it was just the back of the room or something, I don't know. But then he kept, like, you know, he had my hand, like, like, on the, oh, the handle of it. And he was just . . . God, I can't. Please, can I take another break? I'm sorry. . . ."

She was out of the moment.

Breck McDaniel allowed a break.

"I'm sorry I'm freaking out."

"Okay."

"Like—"

"But you know we need to get to this. This is an important part, okay?"

They talked about various brands of cigarettes. But when McDaniel asked Christine to get back into the narrative of what had happened, Christine said, "I feel like I am going to throw up."

Then she started again. "He was on to it, too (the gun)."

"Okay, like on the top of your hand, or something?"

"Yes!"

Christine Paolilla was saying that Chris Snider had placed the gun in her hand, put his hands over hers, and was effectively forcing her to pull the trigger.

"I was scared and I was crying, and then I, uh, I had made the gun go off—not purposely, though"—of course not!—"but, like, it went to the back room 'cause I was just, like, screaming, just, like, shaking."

"So somehow," McDaniel asked, "*you* pulled the trigger?"

"Yes."

There it was: the admission. All they needed.

Christine claimed Chris noticed how awkwardly she was handling the weapon. "You bitch," he allegedly said, "what are you doing? You bitch. You bitch. You bitch." Then he "jerked" her toward him.

McDaniel stopped her there, asking, "How many times do you think it went off in your hand?"

"A million times."

This was a confession of murder.

"So you were pulling the trigger somehow?" McDaniel asked.

She stopped him: "No, no. Like"—she was trying to explain with her hands—"it's like he has his hand, my hand was like, I can't even tell you how, like, it was, it was—"

"Okay."

"But it was his force that was making—"

"Making it go off?" the detective offered.

"Yes!"

"Okay. Were you hitting anyone?" McDaniel asked.

"I don't—I don't know. I, anyway . . ."

According to her, Snider put the gun in her hand, placed his fingers over hers, and pulled the trigger. The question that might have broken Christine needed to be asked: *What were the four victims doing at this time?* If Snider and Christine were struggling with each other to point the gun, pull the trigger, jerking back and forth, why didn't one of the boys or girls run up and confront the situation? Christine hadn't made the claim that they were all dead by then. The only claim she made was that this entire scenario with Snider forcing her to fire the gun took place in a matter of seconds. She even described the moment as a "blackout," but somehow she had no problem recalling that he had made her fire that weapon.

"You know, hypnotized, kind of like . . . all I can remember was just, like, you know, I was screaming and . . . I kept trying to . . . pull, pull away, but . . . I couldn't 'cause, like, I felt like spaghetti almost."

She heard shots throughout this entire time. "But it wasn't from my gun. . . ."

How could she know that?

Then, after a short time, "everything got, you know, like, quiet, like . . . in the movie *Saving Private Ryan.*"

The slaughter had come to an end. Each of the four bloodied and bullet-ridden victims lay dead in front of them.

CHAPTER 58

AS SHE DESCRIBED these bloody scenes, Christine recalled, "I'm still hearing [Chris's] voice and seeing his face, in my head, every time I speak to you."

Then she followed this statement with a blatant lie, which was later disproved by phone records.

McDaniel asked Christine when she had spoken to Chris Snider last: "He called, um, it was while me and my husband, we were engaged, and he called and acted like, you know, nothing ever happened, you know, 'cause I swore I'd . . . have nothing to do with him after that."

She *swore* that she would have nothing to do with him after they had committed murder together—that she wanted to be as far away from him as possible. But between July 22, 2003, and August 2, 2003, a mere eleven days, the phone where Christine lived at the time (her mother's house) called Chris Snider's home eighty-four times for a total of 454 minutes of conversation—and that's not counting the dozens upon dozens of times Snider's phone called Lori Paolilla's phone. In fact, Lori Paolilla's phone had called Snider's house obsessively between July and December, thousands of times, logging thousands of minutes. The calls ranged from one minute to over sixty minutes. Now, we have to assume that Lori Paolilla was not calling Chris Snider, or vice versa. If it was Christine calling Chris, how could one believe that she was scared of this guy? There were times when she would call him ten times within a half hour. Twenty times per day, even. Was this a frightened girl who had been forced to shoot her friends?

"You never saw him again after that?" McDaniel asked Christine.

"No."

("She drove over to our house," a Snider family member later said, "after the murders—an hour away, mind you—every chance she got.")

"Did you talk to him after that?"

"Just, he was just, like, you know, 'What are you doing? What's up?' "

From there, perhaps to break McDaniel's momentum, Christine went into one of her classic "like, you know, like, yeah, um," stumbling, ranting, raving, stammering speeches about how she and Snider had never spoken after the crime, but he had maybe called her a *few* times, and that she had felt safe then because she was engaged and Justin Rott was now protecting her.

Back into the narrative of what had happened, Christine explained how she ran out of the house after the shooting spree came to an end, bolting for her car. "I still had the gun in my hands." She said she wanted to "throw it," but "it was, like, glued to my hands."

She sat in the car, asking herself: *Oh, my God, what just happened in there?* ("I wasn't even crying anymore.")

Snider jumped into the car, pushed her aside, started the vehicle, and sped off. As he drove, according to Christine, Snider said, "Those [M-F-ers]" over and over, mocking Marcus and Adelbert.

She started screaming, calling Snider the *MF*-word and adding other obscenities.

"It's me and you now, baby. It's me and you."

"Everybody's dead?" she asked, wanting to know if the barrage of bullets had actually killed everyone.

According to Christine, Chris answered, "Yeah . . . I beat 'em up to make sure."

He drove off, "going all these different ways and stuff, and we just, like, parked, and then [I] started crying, and then, um, like this time, I, like, I, uh, I wasn't holding on to the gun when I got into the car, I just, like, put it down. . . ."

Chris picked up the gun then. "I'm not getting caught for that, you know," he said. "You just better not say [anything] or I'll do to you what, you know, like what happened inside. . . . You'll regret it if you say anything. Anyway, I'm your man! I'm your man. I take charge. I take charge! You're my girl."

"No, no, no. . . . I hate you. I hate you. I hate you!"

"You're gonna go to work now, and you're not gonna say anything. You got me?"

"I just want to go home. . . . I can't go to work. Take me home."

"You are *not* going home. You're with me now. You're not doing anything. You're my girl."

He kept saying that—"You're my girl!"—over and over, Christine claimed.

She said Chris drove toward Red Bluff. This was an odd choice of destinations, out and away from Clear Lake by 113 miles, a near two-and-a-half-hour drive. Christine's time card at Walgreens showed that she was at work by 4:23 P.M., not even an hour after the murders. Why would she say they drove toward Red Bluff? Why not downtown Houston, Sugar Land, Missouri City, even Wharton?

As Snider drove, Christine stared out the window while at first silently praying to God: *Please help me, God. . . . Please help me.* As she became more absorbed in these pious words, she began to say them out loud, which enlivened Snider's atheistic views.

"You know, God can't help you," he said.

Ignoring him: "Help me, God. Please help me."

"God won't help you."

He grabbed her, she said. Yanked at her. Told her to stop it. Shut the hell up. "Get your [stuff] together!"

"Somebody's gonna know," Christine said.

"You're going to work."

McDaniel stopped her. Then he posed an important question: "When you were praying to God, I mean for yourself . . . were you worried about the people, if they were hurt?"

"Oh, of course."

"You were?"

"Of course. Rachael and, you know, Tiffany, they were my good friends."

CHAPTER 59

CHRISTINE PAOLILLA AND Chris Snider began to argue, she claimed, while sitting in her car, parked somewhere between the murder scene and Walgreens. She didn't want to go to work. Chris wanted her to carry on as though nothing had happened. What became obvious throughout this part of the interview was Christine's hubristic sense of self and what was going to happen to *her*. Breck McDaniel was a master of subtly pointing out the fact that here was a girl who had just seen her two "best friends" murdered in a hail of gunfire (an evil of which she had, according to her, unwillingly participated in), and yet she was more concerned about getting caught than if her friends back at the house were dead or alive. According to her account, neither Christine nor Chris knew for certain that the four were dead.

The idea that her friends were dead didn't stop Christine Paolilla from going to work at Walgreens. Nor had she even attempted to call the police while at work and away from Snider all night long.

"I put on my best" was how Christine described her demeanor during those hours just after she watched two friends being shot to death. Not only did she put on her best, but she waited on customers and smoked cigarettes outside the building during her break.

She said Snider waited in the parking lot for her, and whenever she went outside for a smoke, there he was, staring at her from the front seat of her car, dangling the keys, as if to say, *You aren't going anywhere*.

And yet, at some point that night, she explained, Chris gave her the keys back and took a cab home.

McDaniel explained to Christine as the interview wound down that he needed to ask her several "hard" questions. Some things were not adding up.

She looked at him, startled.

The detective started by asking if she remembered whether those shots that she had fired had hit anyone?

She said she didn't know.

"Did you hit anyone with your fists?"

"No."

"Did you hit anyone with the guns?"

"No."

"Like hit 'em in the head?"

"No."

"Are you sure?"

"I'm sure."

"Did you get anybody's blood on you?"

She paused, and thought about it. "Um, I felt like there was some, like, on my hand, but I . . ."

"There was blood on your hand?"

"Yeah."

"Whose blood?"

"I don't know."

"When did you realize there was blood on your hand?"

"I think it was toward my break. . . ."

"At work?"

"At work."

They discussed this blood in detail. Christine called it "one or two spots."

McDaniel asked where her clothes had been placed from that night.

She didn't know.

The other interesting lie she told here was that she and Chris Snider never saw each other again after the murders, which went against what several other witnesses had said. She also claimed that she pleaded with Snider to go to the police and admit what they'd done, and his response to that came as: "You're kidding me. You're *not* backing down."

McDaniel asked if the cops had ever been summoned because of a fight between them.

There was one time, she admitted, when they fought on the side of the road. "He was starting to, like, you know, kind of like, you know . . . punch me."

She said that she had told only one person—a guy she met in rehab whom everyone called "Waco"—about the murders.

Why had she spilled the beans to this Waco person?

"I had to get it out of my head."

It was one thirty-five, the morning of July 21, 2006, by the time the interview concluded.

After being prompted, Christine Paolilla said she had lied in previous days because she was scared that Chris Snider would get to her or her family.

CHAPTER 60

HPD CAPTAIN DALE Brown released a statement on July 21, 2006, detailing Christine Paolilla's arrest on first-degree capital murder charges: *"Our investigators have a deep commitment to bringing these people to justice because one, they are accountable, and two, for the families. So much of what we do is for families, to bring as much closure as we can. But it's not over until we get this second person arrested and in jail."*

This second person, Chris Snider, was on the run, it could be safely said. Snider was allergic to Soma, a muscle relaxant used to relieve pain and discomfort caused by strains, sprains, and other physical injuries. This was something he knew, of course. Yet Snider had taken all of Haley Dawkins's Soma pills, along with prescription bottles full of Lortab (a pain med) and Xanax (anxiety smasher), culminating in some two hundred pills.

Grabbing these pills and taking off was the start of a story. What Snider didn't take, however—when he left Haley's house in Greenville, South Carolina—concluded that tale: the cash he had, his wallet, or his phone.

Chris Snider did not plan on returning.

When cops reached Haley's house and asked her to describe Snider, she said, "Useless. He had even gotten lost while walking a few times since he'd been living with me." She further elaborated, "After he left, I called his sister, who told me that this was all about a murder. She told me that he expressed to her the last time they spoke, 'They will find me dead somewhere.' As a matter of fact," Haley added, "he liked to talk about death and suicide. We were arguing before he took off. He told me the cops were looking for him because of a probation violation."

The area around Haley's house—the region of Wade Hampton Boulevard and Chuck Springs Road—was a densely populated suburban section of the town, with streets crisscrossing and wrapping around one another as tangled as veins. There were several thickly wooded areas spread out among the denizens of this rural, middle-class American town, though. And for a man who supposedly got lost walking into the next room, on top of running from having murdered four people, finding him—or his corpse—was going to take some serious effort. Maybe even a few bloodhounds.

Which was where problems between HPD—those good ol' boys from Texas—and the tried-and-true Southern cops in South Carolina began. The main issue, according to some of the HPD detectives now having to deal with them, was that South Carolina lawmen liked to do things their own way. They did not like being told how to run a search party.

Brian Harris and Tom McCorvey had been traveling for most of this period; they didn't yet know the status of Snider. They had gone home that night to get what turned out to be three hours' worth of sleep. When they got up early the next morning, as Christine slept off her Happy Meal and confession, Harris and McCorvey drove straight to the airport and flew to Kentucky.

After they landed in Louisville, all set to head over to Snider's parents' house to get a handle on what was going on there, they were told via radio that the guns had been recovered, but Snider was nowhere in sight. Then they were brought up to speed on everything that had taken place in South Carolina. In lieu of not getting anything additional at Snider's parents' house, Harris and McCorvey drove to the Louisville police station, where they sat and went over all of the evidence they had, up to that point.

Harris turned to McCorvey and said, "You know, we're no good here. Let's head back to Houston and work this thing from there."

It was 5:45 P.M. The last flight of the day, Harris soon found out, left Louisville at six o'clock.

"Damn, we're stuck."

The next morning, as Harris and McCorvey killed some time during a layover in St. Louis, they figured the best place for them would be in South Carolina. Why not help the locals out?

So, after discussing it with U.S. Marshals Service, who had an outstanding warrant for Snider, Harris decided that he and McCorvey would fly to Greenville. The U.S. Marshals were already set up on Haley's house ("Actually," Harris said later, "it was one U.S. Marshal—the locals would not help.") When Harris and McCorvey got there later that same day, July 22, a Saturday, law enforcement "took the house," sat Haley down, and interviewed her for a second time.

Harris knew Snider was dead by listening to Haley talk through the circumstances surrounding Snider's departure from the home. Chris Snider was likely on his way to never-never land. Harris didn't need any more evidence than seeing Snider's wallet, keys, and cash left on the counter. No man in Snider's position would leave without those items.

"We need to get dogs in here," Harris suggested.

By now the Greenville Police Department was at Haley's house, along with the U.S. Marshals Service. One of Greenville's officers, a rank-and-file supervisor, explained to Harris, "Hell, I don't know who we would call to get y'all some dogs."

They decided that Greenville officers would conduct a cursory search of the area to see if they could locate Snider or his corpse. There was no need for dogs yet, the Greenville officer told Harris. Plus, it was a Saturday. No one knew where to begin looking for "dog people," as they were described, during the week; better yet, on the weekend.

"They had no idea how to conduct a search with dogs," said one officer. "And the funny thing is, the State Police Dog Unit was housed in the same building as the Greenville Police Department."

As they were out in the neighborhood helping to search, Harris pulled McCorvey aside. Frustrated, he said, "We need to get cadaver dogs out here. The sun is setting. It's getting dark."

They stood on the top of a hill in the Westview area of Greenville, looking around. They were perched on the foothills of the Blue Ridge Mountains, across the street from Haley's house, on a hillside by a creek, in a heavily wooded area. At any other time Harris might have looked out and took a moment to appreciate what was, truly, God's country: a thin sheen of fog, green trees as far as the eye could see, the magical transcendence and curvature, jagged and perfect, of the mountain range off in the distance. But today they were in search of a quadruple murderer, a case that was so close to the finish line that Harris could see it coming together—and finishing here—without any additional pain for the victims' families.

Harris pulled out his cell. He dialed.

"Tom," Harris said, "it's Harris." The one guy Harris wanted to give this information to was Tom Ladd. The guy had worked doggedly on the case. Harris wanted to assure him that, as Ladd had suspected long ago, Harris had finished the job. "We got 'em!" Harris said.

"Son of a bitch," Tom Ladd said, realizing he hadn't a clue as to who these two murderers were.

There was a house, someone's backyard, near the small hill Harris and McCorvey stood on, which led down into a ravine and densely wooded area, a welcome mat into Blue Ridge territory.

"That son of a bitch is in there somewhere," Harris told McCorvey, staring into the thickly settled woods.

McCorvey nodded, agreeing.

The region was perfect. It was close enough to Haley's house. You could hide, Harris noted, in this small area and not be found but for a dog sniffing you out.

Finding someone from the Greenville PD who was in charge, Harris asked again about getting a couple of dogs out there. Maybe a cadaver dog or two to search the area where his gut told him Chris Snider was.

"Yeah, sure," the cop said, according to Harris. "But, you know, how do y'all go about getting one?"

Are you kidding me? Harris looked at McCorvey.

"Call Search and Rescue," Harris suggested. "They would probably have a cadaver dog or two."

"Ah, okay. Yes. We'll take care of it."

"You sure?" Harris asked. He had a feeling he was being stonewalled and patronized.

"Yeah. Yeah. No problem."

Harris and McCorvey flew back to Houston the following morning. They were no good to anyone in South Carolina. Finally able to get some rest, both men went back into the office on that Monday,

July 24, still certain Chris Snider was dead, and in those woods. Nothing had happened over the weekend since they'd left Greenville. They had been told by the Greenville Police Department that a few dogs would be brought in and a search would be conducted. One cadaver dog, Harris knew, could run into that brush and sniff out a dead man within ten minutes.

But no dogs had been brought in.

Harris was livid.

Then another problem arose. One of the powers-that-be inside the Greenville Police Department had called an HPD white shirt and complained that the Texans were "trying to ride roughshod" over the local Greenville police. His boys in South Carolina were not going to have any of it. The idea was that Harris and McCorvey had ridden into town on their horses and barked orders at the local yokels.

"You need to call the Greenville police chief and straighten this mess out," Harris was told.

The two men spoke cordially.

"Listen," the chief told Harris, "I'll provide you with *one* detective, but you are going to have to find your own cadaver dogs and find this guy yourselves. Unless there's evidence of a body, we're not getting involved."

To the Greenville authorities, Chris Snider did not exist. They had no record of him being in their town. Why should they use town resources to help locate him?

I wouldn't need a cadaver dog, Harris thought, *if I had evidence of a body.* But he kept his mouth shut.

HPD was on its own.

Harris spent a better part of that week—July 24, Monday, through Friday, July 28—searching for the right person to locate Chris Snider.

By July 26, Wednesday, Harris found the South Carolina Search and Rescue Dog Association, Inc. (SCSARDA). Snider had not been seen for six days. SCSARDA contacted the Greenville Police Department and were told they had searched Dumpsters and the periphery of the woods around Haley's house, but they had come up with nothing. The SCSARDA supervisor decided from there that, yes, the dogs were needed. But they were not going to be able to get the dogs out there until that coming weekend.

"It's volunteer," the woman explained to Harris. "They can only work on weekends."

"Okay."

Harris called the Greenville Police Department, which told him, "No, no, no. They can only search during the week when our detectives are on duty."

What the heck?

Harris thought he was going to have to fly back out to Greenville.

The plan Harris suggested was to use the four dogs the woman from SCSARDA suggested for the job and spread out across that area Harris had pointed out on day one.

The Greenville Police Department, however, decided that Chris Snider was somewhere else and sent SCSARDA to the town park.

CHAPTER 61

WHILE THE SPECIFICS of the search for Snider were sketched out, the tip line received a call from someone who again shared information about Christine Paolilla that backed up what had been reported earlier. This time, though, the caller had claimed that Christine told her she and Snider had used a "forty-five and a nine millimeter" (either Christine or the caller was wrong about the .45—it was a .38) during the murders, something Christine had said she knew nothing about. The only other important piece of new information from the caller was that Christine had run out of the house *with* Chris Snider, who then convinced her to go back in and "open fire" on all of them to make certain they were dead. But that once she got back inside the house and realized she was out of bullets, seeing Rachael "crawling on the floor," Christine beat her to death with the pistol.

Here was a third party now telling that same story.

Harris hoped another piece of the puzzle was uncovered when he heard that the lab had finished its examination of Christine's computers. HPD's Digital Forensic Laboratory reported that three computers and an external hard drive taken from Christine's residence and the hotel room, where she and Justin were holed up, contained evidence. There was no smoking gun, just a bit of additional proof corroborating what witnesses were saying.

For one, Christine had utilized a program called "Registry Mechanic," which cleansed and destroyed traces of any computer activity. "While the program," Harris was told, "is somewhat of an 'antiforensic' tool, it did leave some traces."

The lab could not find any communication between the tipster Waco and another guy Christine had opened up to: "Dave." But it did uncover that Christine was registered on a porn site and that she had downloaded several hard-core porn photographs.

Beyond any normal computer activity, "Nothing of relevance to this investigation," the lab concluded, "was discovered."

CHAPTER 62

DURING THE EARLY-MORNING hours of August 5, 2006, the team in Greenville searched the town park and found nothing. The SCSARDA supervisor called Brian Harris, who ended up staying in Houston, despite an eagerness to be back in Greenville, overseeing the search. She explained what had happened at the park.

"You need to go to that area I pointed to on the maps," Harris explained. It was that wooded section near Haley's home where Harris and McCorvey had stood while out there the previous week.

"We'll head out there now," she said.

Harris waited.

Within ten minutes of the dogs searching that area, they found Chris Snider's bloated and badly decomposed remains.

"A lot of bones," said one source. "Bloated and nasty. A lot of animals had come up to him during those two weeks and nibbled at him."

Snider had burrowed into a deeply settled area of brush, "under a canopy of kudzu vegetation, approximately twenty feet from a creek that ran through the center of a wooded area." He had gotten himself comfortable. There was a two-liter bottle of Coke nearby and, of course, several empty pill bottles scattered around him.

Greenville wanted DNA confirmation.

Harris sent Snider's dental records.

It was Chris Snider, all right.

At 2:43 P.M., Saturday, August 5, 2006, the Greenville City Police Department issued a media release, basically saying that *while acting on a lead developed by Houston Police investigators, cadaver K-9s were utilized ... [and] did locate a male decomposed body meeting the same physical description as [Chris] Snider under kudzu in a deep wooded area behind Westview Avenue.*

That part of the saga was over.

CHAPTER 63

CHRISTINE PAOLILLA WAS denied bond. Yet for Christine, if she was going to be using the "he made me do it" defense, Snider's death was going to help her perhaps win that argument in court. A dead man could not defend himself. Nor could he laugh when his girlfriend made the claim that he placed her hand over the trigger of a gun and made her fire the rounds that killed four people.

Months went by as both sides prepared for Christine's trial.

On April 20, 2007, Christine filed a writ of habeas corpus with the Fourteenth Court of Appeals requesting bail, spelling out for the court why she had been denied back in July (2006) was a mistake.

On May 9, 2007, the court set a $500,000 bail for the accused multiple murderer.

Christine argued it was too high. She claimed $150,000 was a figure she could handle.

The only witness Christine's defense team called at the hearing to discuss her bail being lowered was Tom Dick, Christine's stepfather, a man who had walked into Lori and Christine's lives one day and had dealt with nothing but a troubled kid ever since.

Tom Dick said Christine would "reside with" him and Lori if she was set free on a lowered bond. He explained that he had visited Christine at least fifty times since she had been incarcerated; Lori at least 150 times (all within just ten months). Christine was currently on a cocktail of meds: Adderall, Trileptal, Trazodone, and Zoloft. This was the favored concoction of recovering heroin addicts.

Beyond the fairly routine (boring) court-inspired arguments that both sides presented, the most interesting facts to come out of the hearing related to Christine's finances. All that cash her dead dad had left her by osmosis (the peerless trust-fund baby that she was) was gone, according to Tom Dick, who claimed it was $400,000, not $360,000, which Christine had been telling everyone. At the time of Christine's arrest, Dick said during the hearing, Christine had $140,000 left in her trust, which was turned over to her attorneys for legal fees. Christine owned a condo, which Dick said he bought from her for $80,000, more money that went to legal fees.

Dick told the court that the most he and Lori could hand over for bond was $75,000. Prior to the hearing, however, he had filed paperwork indicating they could afford $150,000.

"The affidavit was based on paying ten percent of the bond," Dick clarified.

There was still no indication whether the state would seek the death penalty; although, it was known by now that if Christine was convicted of capital murder, she would automatically receive a life sentence, simply because a U.S. Supreme Court ruling forbade capital punishment for anyone aged seventeen and under at the time of the crime. This was a category that Christine, luckily, had fallen into. Unless, that is, the prosecutor was able to find a way around it.

Citing the fact that there was no doubt Christine was a flight risk—if not for the severity of the murders alone, the fact of her own addiction to heroin and cocaine—the appeals court denied her request.

Christine was going to stay in jail while the courts decided when and where to try her on four counts of capital murder.

PART FIVE

THE NORMAL WE KNEW WILL NEVER BE

CHAPTER 64

AFTER A YEAR and several months of motions, hearings, and filings by both sides, Christine Paolilla's trial was finally set to begin in early September 2008. It had been over five years since the kids were murdered; yet the pain and loss experienced by family members was as raw and nerve-shattering as it had been back on July 18, 2003, when they got the call that had changed their lives forever.

Christine Paolilla was now a twenty-two-year-old woman, with a few years of living behind bars under her belt. Several sources reported that Christine had fallen into prison life and taken to the new lifestyle rather congenially, even scoring herself a very large and aptly named girlfriend, "Big Momma," whom Christine was seen having lesbian sex with out in the open on several occasions. She had gained some weight—not too much—and looked healthier than she ever had. When in court Christine was able to fix herself up nice with makeup and a wig, obviously with the hope of coming across as sweet and demure. One lawyer later described her as "a babe in the woods, like they tried to portray her. They dressed her up in those cute little pink outfits . . . and, you know, the jury [was going] to see right through it." The idea was to make Christine look like the child she supposedly was when the crimes had been committed—a child, as it were, under the wielding and abusive hand of Chris Snider, the true villain in this tragedy. Some tears would work to her advantage; although there was a fine line between how much emotion she could project believably. A bit of temerity, too, might help. She shouldn't sit stoically, as if the proceedings were merely a "day in the life." She should show interest. She should sit up straight. She should stick to her story of being intimidated and controlled by Chris Snider.

Harris County District Court judge Mark Kent Ellis ran a tight courtroom. Ellis wasn't a judge who sat back and waited for something to happen; he spent a lot of time watching, making sure that things went accordingly, in the eyes of the law. Formerly with the district attorney's office, Judge Ellis, a Republican, had cofounded the Harris County Mental Health Court, which helped mentally ill criminals complete probation and continue treatment after the dues of their crimes had been paid. Ellis wore glasses underneath straight black hair, graying slightly on both sides. He had been an assistant district attorney (ADA) and had a private practice at one time. If the people of Houston, Texas, wanted neutrality and fairness, this judge was the one who could give it to them without condition.

One of the two lawyers in charge of prosecuting Christine, Assistant District Attorney (ADA) Rob Freyer (pronounced "frair") was a man who held little back when speaking in terms of those he saw on the wrong side of the law. As any great prosecutor should, Freyer had a reputation for going forcefully after criminals—however big or small—with an iron fist he did not mind smashing on the table when speaking of them in open court. Some defense attorneys called him "Ag Rob," a play on his name and the crime of aggravated robbery because he did not like to cut deals. Freyer was fit, trim, healthy-looking. He sported closely cropped black hair and dressed sharply. The much-liked prosecutor had taken on the case only after a colleague, who had parked her car one morning in the garage, stepped out and then dropped dead of a heart attack. Freyer had been in the DA's office since 1995, beginning his career as an ADA in 1997. Leading up to the Paolilla case, he had handled some one hundred felony jury trials.

Freyer's biggest worry heading into trial was not convicting Christine Paolilla; he was confident about doing that. It was getting the case in before he left the office; his departure slated for that December.

"I wanted to make sure that the voices of the victims' families were heard," Freyer later said. "Through [ADA] Mr. Tom Goodhart [his co-counsel] and myself . . . I wanted to make sure that we could at least get some satisfaction under the law that she was held responsible for what she did."

To Freyer's way of thinking, there was never a doubt that Christine Paolilla walked into the Rowell house on that day with the intention to kill. She was evil personified. A dark and twisted human being who had killed four innocent kids.

"Her explanation of this crime was insulting," Freyer said, ". . . to anybody's intelligence."

Jury selection began back on September 8, but then something out of everyone's hands happened, pushing the the trial (once again) two-plus weeks out, or the end of September.

Mother Nature.

Hurricane Ike had made landfall near Galveston on September 13, 2008, as a Category 2 storm, with a Category 5 equivalent storm surge. Hurricane-force winds from Ike extended some 120 miles inland. It was one of the most significant hurricanes to hit land in Texas, ever. With the Ike forecast, the court postponed the trial. As the judge explained on September 30, when opening arguments were (re)set to begin, Ike had closed down the courthouse during the week of the thirteenth, but set the trial back another two weeks until the week of the twenty-eighth because of scheduling conflicts.

Nonetheless, here it was, time to begin, with a jury selected back on September 9.

"So," Judge Ellis explained, "we've had communication about the jury since the time the case was delayed. We actually brought them in on the eleventh and told them—I told them in person—that we were going to delay the trial. And at that point, we weren't sure how long, but we wanted to let the storm play itself out. The communication with the jury in the time between now and then has either been by way of the coordinator or the bailiff, and, basically, just to apprise them of what the court settings would be."

The judge concluded that he'd had no "personal contact" with any of the jurors. Then he spoke about a letter he had received, excusing one juror, who was quickly replaced. Christine Paolilla's attorneys had filed a motion for a mistrial on the grounds of the jury having all this time between being picked and the start of the trial. Defense attorneys loved to do this: hold things up even more. The fact of the matter remained: it was time to put the gloves on and get it on. The trial had been pushed back and delayed long enough.

Ellis had the jury settled in the courtroom, where he could question each of them to see if there had been any problems during the break. He made a point to say how every person in the room had "suffered" because of the hurricane, "some more than others, and that certainly has been stressful to me, I'll say honestly, and to other people involved in this case. I'm sure it had been stressful to y'all."

The jury was ready to move forward.

The state asked the judge to dismiss the motion for mistrial.

"The motion is denied."

Christine sat transfixed. She wore what would become a trademark scarf over the top of her wig, Mary Tyler Moore–like. The court read the charges a grand jury had agreed with, and then asked, "Miss Paolilla, to the charge of capital murder, how do you plead, guilty or not guilty?"

"Not guilty," she said without hesitation, and then sat down to the judge's order.

Rob Freyer took a nod from the judge, indicating that it was his turn to stand and deliver the state's opening argument. As any good ADA knew, the object with the opening was to keep it short and to the point. If you made big claims, you had better provide that evidence during trial to back them up, or you'd be taken to task. Brevity, Freyer was well aware, could carry his argument a long way.

"What the evidence is going to show in this case," Freyer began, "a long and very twisted tale, is a different form of wreckage, a different form of suffering, and a different form of pain."

Mike DeGeurin, Christine's attorney, objected.

"Overruled."

"And if in the course of my attempting, or trying to attempt, to summarize all the facts," Freyer continued, "if for some reason they are out of place or jumbled up in some way, I apologize for that. Because I did not author this scene! I did not *write* this script. The evidence will show *she* did."

He walked over and pointed at Christine Paolilla, nearly close enough to put his finger in her face. She sat with a look of total embarrassment and hatred for him on her pinched face. There was so much drama surrounding the move on Freyer's part that defense attorney Mike DeGeurin walked in back of his client, put his arms on his hips, and objected.

"The evidence will show," Freyer continued, walking away from the defendant, "that she and Christopher Snider did these horrible things—"

"Again, Your Honor," DeGeurin, said, "argument and not an opening statement. I *object* to it."

"Overruled."

"The evidence will show that on July 18, 2003, she and a guy named Christopher Snider—his name will come up quite a bit in this case. You will learn a lot about Christopher Snider. They were dating. They decided to take it upon themselves to drive from her house in Friendswood, thirty-five miles, to Christopher Snider's house in Crosby, Texas. Now, she later told the police after she was arrested, three years later, that she didn't know why they were going there. She later told the police she thought they were going there so he could get his fix on more drugs. She also didn't expect that as the events played out, that the guns that [would be] used to kill Rachael Koloroutis, Marcus Precella, Adelbert Sánchez, and Tiffany Rowell were found three years later. So, they drive from his house in Crosby, Texas, Christine and her boyfriend, nobody else. She's driving in her car. They go to a house in Clear Lake. The evidence will show—and by her own admission—she knew Rachael and Tiffany. She, in her *own* words, called them her, quote, 'best friends.' She had their confidence. She had their trust. She had their admiration. And they walked up to this house [on] Millbridge, Rachael Koloroutis opened the door, and they started shooting. They started shooting a lot. They started shooting with fury, the evidence will show. . . . We know for a fact that over twenty-one rounds were shot inside that house."

It was damaging for Christine to hear how the crime was being played out, right here in front of her peers, in such a dramatic way. She was going to be crawling uphill throughout the trial. How could she explain that she was *forced* into pulling the trigger on one of the weapons that killed four people? It seemed an impossible task and an unbelievable scenario.

Freyer went on about the facts the state would present as Christine's attorney objected at random intervals. The judge sustained one objection after Freyer went a bit too far, telling the jury he was going to explain what was going on inside the defendant's mind at the time she fired the weapon.

But then, to put a bit more of a motive into play, Freyer talked about the fact that Tiffany Rowell *wasn't* pistol-whipped on that night. Tiffany had been, instead, shot in the face, twice.

"The evidence will show . . . that Tiffany was shot *three* times with a thirty-eight revolver and at least three or four times with a nine millimeter. Marcus Precella was shot twice with a thirty-eight and at least three times from a nine millimeter."

The jury sat and pictured a bloodbath: four teens going down in a hail of gunfire, with no chance to react.

"They started shooting the moment Rachael Koloroutis opened that door," Freyer pointed out. "Look at all the shell casings in the foyer!"

Freyer made another important suggestion. Forget about "how pretty she looks," he said, again pointing fiercely at Christine. He wanted jurors not to focus on how Christine *looked*—all *purty* and done up good—or how young she was at the time of the crime. No! Look at the brutality and the end result of what the crime scene showed investigators. The ADA seemed to imply with his tone and demeanor and word choice that a vicious sociopath had showed a total disregard for human life, toward two girls she had bequeathed her undivided love and friendship upon. It was even "unfair," Freyer noted, to refer to the house as a crime scene, because it "was outright carnage."

Carnage would become a popular word for law enforcement, a sort of mantra referred to throughout the trial.

From there the ADA went through the timeline of his evidence: the Lackners, those neighbors who spotted two people and were able to produce a drawing; Nancy Vernau; and then how it all tied together with what Christine Paolilla later admitted to Justin Rott, a man who could not have known several facts unless she had told him.

Freyer's bottom line came next. When you are offered the opportunity in life to get away with something, and that something is quadruple murder, what do you do? You use the "age-old and most convenient excuse—that is, you *blame* the person that's not here."

Chris Snider, after all, could not speak from the grave.

" 'He made me do it,' " Freyer mocked Christine. "You will know based upon evidence, and applying your common sense, that there is no way whatsoever that one person did all of this."

If there was one thing Christine's attorneys could not accuse the state of, it was not being thorough enough, as Freyer made clear by his next statement: "They (HPD) chased down an investigation that lasted *three* years and involved no fewer than two hundred to three hundred interviews from witnesses in South Texas, Bastrop, Texas, Beaumont, Texas, Boston, Massachusetts, Nashville, Tennessee, Louisville, Kentucky, [and] Jacksonville, Florida. They went all over the place to seek justice for those four kids. What's ironic—and there's no way they could have known this at the time—is that the answer was right there in front of them the entire time, through no fault of their own. Because when Rachael Koloroutis died, the *evidence* will show, guess whose picture was in her wallet?"

He pointed at the defendant. "Got it. Hers!" He paused. "She goes on with her life. The evidence will show."

CHAPTER 65

MIKE DEGEURIN WAS not some sort of nimble ambulance chaser, pimping himself on late-night local television, dabbling in felonious criminal waters from time to time. Christine Paolilla had spared no expense in hiring DeGeurin, and the man's résumé proved that she had chosen herself a class act all the way. Since joining the Percy Foreman firm in 1977—Foreman being an iconic Texan criminal defense attorney—DeGeurin had earned, according to the now Foreman/DeGeurin/Nugent firm's website: *international acclaim by proving Clarence Brandley's innocence, freeing him from ten years on Texas Death Row.*

DeGeurin had also successfully defended Paul Fatta against murder charges arising from the government raid on Waco's Branch Davidians; and, in a case featured on *60 Minutes,* he had exonerated Kelley Koch from murder charges by proving that her confession was "false and coerced."

The guy had some notoriety and certainly several successes behind him. He was no stoolie who was in the courtroom just collecting a paycheck. Mike DeGeurin, with his wispy white-blond hair and serious gaze, was a fighter.

"Mike was a very formidable opponent," Rob Freyer later said. "His hands were tied in a way because his client had confessed and put herself at the scene. Her doing that really limited his options of putting on a defense."

This was the first time Freyer and DeGeurin had met inside a courtroom.

DeGeurin started his opening argument by thanking the jury for

sitting on the case. Jury service alone was hard enough, he com-
mended. With a trial expected to go a month, and the horror that
jurors would have to see and listen to vis-à-vis crime scene photos,
videotape, and testimony, DeGeurin made a point to say how grateful he and his partner, Paul Nugent, the younger of the two, were for
each juror's service.

It did not take the veteran defense attorney long to play what was,
essentially, his only card: the sympathy argument. Within minutes of
beginning, DeGeurin said, "You might imagine that there's another
view of what happened. And it's stark reality that you're going to be
faced with throughout this trial. That's not easy. You like to think that
awful things *don't* happen. If they do, they happen to someone else.
We like to think that way. It's easier to live. But terrible things happen. And there are *bad* people out there. [But] what the evidence is
going to show is that . . . when [Christine] was about two and a half
years old, going on three . . . her dad was killed in an accident. . . ."

Setting that idea in motion, he then talked about how a court had
awarded custody of Christine and her brother—whom DeGeurin
misnamed and Christine had to openly, quite embarrassingly, correct
him—to her grandparents. But they persevered and became a family.

Next he ladled on the poor-me tale of Christine having been diagnosed with alopecia on top of being fatherless at such a young age.

Then he talked about the "special classes" she had to take in school.

All the teasing she had endured.

How she wanted nothing more than to be "normal."

He spoke of Lori Paolilla getting custody of Christine and her
brother and heading off to Texas.

And then, after all that, here was Christine, a fragile and broken
youth, who just happened to run into a monster.

"And that's what happened here. At age fifteen, maybe around sixteen, she runs into a guy out there named Chris Snider. Snider is described by the police in their psychological unit, or however they get
their information together, as a ward psychopathic killer. Weirdo.
Predator. That's the way they describe him. And satanic! This is the—
this *is* Chris Snider. . . ."

Nobody was denying those opinions. Yet, ADA Freyer interrupted
the defense attorney: "I respectfully object to him referring to something that is *not* in evidence."

"Sustained."

"It *is* evidence, Your Honor," DeGeurin argued.

"I sustained the objection."

DeGeurin wouldn't let up. He pushed.

The judge unleashed on him: "Mr. DeGeurin, I sustained the objection. That means you're *not* going to talk about it during opening statement. Is that clear?" Ellis gave DeGeurin what would become one of his trademark stares that he would project whenever he became frustrated and impatient with the lawyers.

"Yes, Your Honor." DeGeurin paused and collected his thoughts. Then he carried on, adding, "So, you have a *predator* coming into her life. And the parents see it and they try to prevent it. . . . He wanted her under his control and the parents tried to *prevent* it. They called the cops on him. The cops arrested him out in front of their house because he wasn't supposed to be there, wasn't supposed to be around their daughter."

This was Christine's one and only way to paint a picture of Chris Snider in the jury's mind, and then use the trial to build on that image. DeGeurin had to make sure the jury came out of the trial thinking that Snider was the bad guy here all the way, and Christine was simply too young, naïve, and delicate to make up her own mind, not to mention too weak to disobey him.

And so, on that note, DeGeurin continued bashing Snider.

After explaining how Christine and Snider lost touch for a while, DeGeurin worked in the friendship Christine began with Tiffany and Rachael.

"In this interim she had become friends with—through, I think, a church group and school—Tiffany Rowell and Rachael Koloroutis. They were her friends."

Not true.

He talked about how important her job at Walgreens was to Christine because it had taught her about cosmetics, which helped bolster her self-esteem and allow her to make herself look pretty—something Tiffany and Rachael had helped her get started with.

He mentioned how great Christine's life was going, with friends like Rachael and Tiffany by her side.

How Christine was excelling in school.

How her social life was on fire at one time.

But then that one-eyed monster returned—and things began to change.

"So," DeGeurin said, "Snider comes back and there is a party at Rachael's and Tiffany's house. There were teenagers there. It was a nice—I mean, it was a party of friends. And Christine takes Chris Snider to that party. They're not there long because Chris Snider doesn't know any of these people, didn't like her having friends, doesn't like those people, but Chris Snider learns that Marcus is living there and maybe Adelbert can hook him up with drugs."

From there, DeGeurin told the jury the same story Christine had tried to snowball Detective Breck McDaniel with on that night she ate a Happy Meal. Chris Snider killed these people on his own and made her a part of his crimes, forcing her to participate.

DeGeurin's next hurdle was Justin Rott. How was he going to explain away Rott's damaging testimony, which placed his wife at the scene of the crime, and had actually put a pistol in her hand as she beat Rachael Koloroutis to death?

The only way to accomplish this was to call Justin Rott a predator, too, adding how he sought Christine out and married her for all that money she would be coming into.

"So, Justin Rott marries her. They elope, contrary—against the wishes of Christine's parents—because it's her money, her life. She apparently loves this guy and they elope. She immediately buys a condo for him, a car . . . [a] big-screen TV. All with *her* money. And for a little while . . . she starts using heavy drugs."

He failed to say that her drug use was an escalation. She had started to dabble in hard drugs long before meeting Justin Rott.

DeGeurin next keyed on the fact that Christine was suffering from withdrawal during that time frame when she was interrogated, and was no less than bullied by the police and not given proper medical treatment. So, of course, she was going to admit to anything to get out of there. He went as far as to say that her statements to police were not given voluntarily.

Finally, after carrying on too long, DeGeurin concluded, saying, "So, I think I've given you enough information that I expect the evidence to show. You've been sitting here quite a long time. I appreciate that. As you can see, this is not going to be an easy case. It's going to be a very difficult case. I have great sympathy for some of the people here that are relatives of the people that were killed, but I also have a great interest and a great desire to protect Christine Paolilla from a *rush* to judgment and for something that she *never* intended—she never intended and thought would happen. Thank you very much for your attention."

CHAPTER 66

ROB FREYER CALLED his first witness not long after Mike DeGeurin finished his opening statement. Sergeant Richard Pitts was the first responder on the scene.

Pitts laid the crime scene out in graphic detail. When asked what he saw inside the house when he arrived, Pitts uttered that familiar mantra: "Carnage."

"All right," Freyer said.

"Death," Pitts added, and then spoke of what the inside of the Rowell "house of horrors" looked like.

DeGeurin didn't have much for the officer.

The idea was for Pitts to set the scene for the man, Freyer said later, who was his most important witness.

Andrew Taravella had been with HPD for sixteen years. The officer, a member of the Homicide Division Crime Scene Unit, talked about what he saw when he arrived. For Freyer, this was going to be the most damaging testimony for the defendant because Taravella had been in charge of deconstructing and documenting the crime scene. He had spent upward of eight hours at the house.

"It was a bloodbath," Freyer said later. "And Andrew's job was to make some sense out of it all. It took the concept of a crime scene to levels where it had never been before—at least in my experience. . . . It showed that the minute they walked into that house, they started shooting."

More than all of that, Taravella introduced the all-important crime scene photographs. The public viewing of these photos was going to put the trial into perspective, showing graphically and horrifically just how violent the deaths of these kids had been. The photos were so striking, in fact, that many of them were shown only on the jury's monitors and not on the overhead courtroom video screens, for fear that family members would cry out, or maybe run out of the courtroom. If that happened, Freyer knew, it could be grounds for a mistrial.

Taravella talked the jury through one horrendous photo after the next, almost one hundred in total. Whenever they got to a photo that had been significant to the evidence of tracking the killers, Taravella explained it in detail, keying in on why he and the ADA believed the photo was important to uncovering the killers' identities.

Taravella's comments over the display of photos was gruesome. In fact, a friend of George Koloroutis's had been at the trial since it started, supporting his friend. As the photos were shown inside the courtroom, the guy stood, walked out, and then collapsed in the hallway. Meanwhile, Christine Paolilla stared at each of the exhibits intently as they passed over the monitors.

"She did not gasp, she didn't cry, she didn't look away," a source in the courtroom sitting in back of Christine said. "She stared at those images like, 'Yeah, this is what I did.'"

Taravella continued, and didn't miss a beat. He talked jurors through the house.

Room by room.

He talked about where the bodies had been found, spending time on each of the four.

He focused on where the shell casings had been uncovered.

The type of weapons used in the murders.

Blood spatter.

Muscle tissue.

How each body at the scene "entails an extensive, detailed investigation of its own."

Fingerprints.

Ballistics tests.

Bullet fragments.

Drug paraphernalia.

The "small amount of money" they found in one of the bedrooms.

The fact that the photos—and ADA Rob Freyer brought each one up as Taravella talked about it—showed how Tiffany Rowell was "caught off guard" and "shot multiple times" as she sat next to Adelbert "watching television."

The terrible reality of this crime went on and on. The bottom line was that Andrew Taravella was there at the murder scene. It would have been nearly impossible for Chris Snider to have walked in and surprised those kids by himself. Marcus and Rachael "were in motion" at the time they were murdered, Taravella said.

"All right," Freyer asked, "what kind of injuries do you note here on State's Exhibit Number forty-nine (a photo of Marcus's body)?"

"In addition to gunshot wounds, Mr. Precella also had blunt-force trauma to the head and to the face. Now, looking at State's Exhibit Number fifty-one, you notice some dots and other items over here, by the back of the center of Mr. Precella's head."

"What do you draw from that?"

"Again, those are just—it's blood spatter that was fed by gravity. Those are drops that impacted the carpet in what appeared to be ninety degrees. Likely just dripped from his head, from his hair onto the carpet."

"Could it be consistent with somebody standing over him holding an object that's dripping blood?"

"It could be."

Marcus Precella, ADA Freyer suggested with his questioning, had been beaten and shot.

Well into the morning, Freyer was up to State's Exhibit Number 269.

Freyer had Taravella describe Rachael's body and how she was found. The phone next to her head. Her arm reaching for it. And the fact that a lock of hair found at the scene in Rachael's hand was different from hers.

"It actually appeared to us to be a different color," Taravella explained. "It had some blood in it. We didn't think at the time that it was her *own* hair. We suspected at that time it was possibly pulled from a suspect during a struggle, and that was the reason for that photograph and the collection of that hair."

As Taravella gave the jury a tutorial focused on "castoff," or the blood spatter on the walls up toward the ceiling above Rachael's body, it became clear that two of the victims were not dead upon being shot. Someone had gone back into the house to finish the job, and that someone, Freyer would argue with additional witnesses, was Christine Paolilla.

Taravella testified all day long. By the time Freyer "passed the witness" off to DeGeurin, Judge Ellis closed out proceedings for the day.

CHAPTER 67

THE **PAOLILLA TRIAL** was front-page news for the *Houston Chronicle,* the lead story on all the local television news stations. In Houston, there was no getting away from the case. GRIM CLEAR LAKE CASE BEGINS, said one headline. The accompanying article in the *Chronicle* spared no details depicting the reality that Christine faced, calling the crime scene "grisly," adding that the *allegations that a former Clear Lake High School student helped kill four friends* were at the forefront of the trial, and prosecutors had argued during the first few days of the case that Christine had returned *to the murder scene to ensure they were all dead. Prosecutors allege that after [she] shot her best friend, she went back and pistol-whipped her as the girl crawled to the phone to call 911.*

This was not the type of press you wanted as a defendant in a quadruple murder trial.

The second day of testimony began first thing on Wednesday, October 1, 2008. Andrew Taravella finished under a cloud of some rather heated discussion between the judge, Rob Freyer, and Mike DeGeurin, as DeGeurin picked up on his cross-examination.

There was a fine line to walk with Taravella for DeGeurin; he couldn't let the guy slide without questioning, but then he couldn't necessarily come out of the box and attack him, either.

DeGeurin stuck to the facts he believed he could go after without coming across as too far reaching. Bullet fragments. Reports. Where certain pieces of evidence were found as opposed to what a specific report might have said. DeGeurin focused his argument on a single bullet fragment and why Taravella had never written about it in one of his reports. It was inconsequential, truly, to the scope of the accusations against Christine, but then maybe DeGeurin wanted to point out to the jury that nobody is infallible and that even law enforcement made mistakes.

After a brief back-and-forth between them about bullet fragments and where the *shooter* was standing at any given time, DeGeurin moved on to trashing the victims, saying, "I noticed that you found multiple discount cards from Club Exotica—you pointed that out—in different areas of the house and stacks of them, is that correct?"

"Yes, sir. They . . . were, like, five-dollar-off admission into the club and they had a place to write someone's name on them. And there were some that had Rachael's name on them, some that had Tiffany's name on them, and there were stacks around the house."

This was a good way to get into the record that Tiffany and Rachael had worked for a strip joint.

"You also pointed out some cards from Heart Breakers. Do you remember that?"

"I believe so. Yes, sir."

"What *is* Heart Breakers?"

"I don't know. I assume it's another adult nightclub."

"It's not something that you followed up on? That would be something that the detectives would have followed up on, is that correct?"

"Yes, sir."

"Thank you, Officer."

"Pass the witness."

Before Taravella stepped down, some bickering about a report and what was in the report started between DeGeurin and Freyer, the judge getting involved soon after.

Taravella then endured a recross and was dismissed. DeGeurin and the judge got into a debate over the report. By Freyer's estimation, DeGeurin had insinuated—while the jury was present—that Freyer, when he got back the report DeGeurin had used to cross-examine Taravella with, would "hide" something within the report, or even add something that had not been there.

This infuriated Freyer, who kept his composure despite the outright attack.

"I have never seen anybody be so insistent," DeGeurin said at one point during the conversation—the jury out of the room—"that immediately upon me looking at something . . . and taking rough notes, just to take them back."

"I've been down here twenty-two years," Judge Ellis said. "I've seen it (the exchanging of documents between lawyers) happen every single trial I ever tried. So, I don't know where you have been, but I don't care if you get it marked, that's fine. You only get it for cross-examination. You know that. It is the work product and part of the district attorney's file. They always do that in every single case, so—"

DeGeurin interrupted, saying, "Well, that's not been my experience, Judge."

"Well, whatever," the judge snapped.

"Out of respect to the court, just for the record, I resent any personal insinuation that I would—or Mr. Goodhart or I would—ever hide anything," Freyer said with a bit of discontent in his voice, obviously upset that DeGeurin would accuse him of such a thing. "And I think that . . . in the hundred-plus felony cases I've tried, and in the cases that I've tried in this court in front of you, Judge, I don't think we've *ever* been any more accommodating to the defense when it comes to—and, you know, Mike, if you're going to make those allegations against me, then don't do it in front of the jury. I resent it."

DeGeurin continued bantering about his desire to have the documents marked as exhibits, again insinuating that something might mysteriously appear in them that had not been there when he had used the documents to question Officer Taravella. He went on and on.

The judge explained to DeGeurin that he could mark down any page numbers of documents he wanted to, and then check them against the record posttrial, but he wasn't going to go through this nonsense anymore, and certainly not after each witness. Concluding with a smidgen of *You had better!* in his frustrated tone, Ellis asked, "Do you understand that?"

"Yes, Judge," DeGeurin said.

The judge brought in the jury, sat them, and then Tom Ladd entered the witness stand. Tom had been retired for more than four years. He looked better, healthier, although he walked with a limp because of those bad football knees catching up with him and the sad fact that arthritis had been kicking his ass these days.

Ladd spoke about his career for just a moment and quickly got into how he had arrived at the Clear Lake crime scene "sometime after seven" and ended up staying until "three, four o'clock in the morning, maybe longer."

The retired detective established many facts for ADA Tom Goodhart. Among those at the scene, Ladd explained, was the notion that a robbery might have occurred. But looking further, he said none of the drawers had been opened and pulled out.

"Did you find any drugs in that house?"

"No, I did not."

"Did somebody find some drugs in that house?"

"Yes."

"Who was that?"

"I don't recall who it was."

"Did you ever go look at the drugs?"

"No. Yochum, you know, handled that part. He just advised me of it."

"But it was small amounts of marijuana?"

Ladd spoke of how he came to the conclusion that Marcus and Adelbert had "sold drugs" for a living.

"People came up and started telling us that."

After discussing the drug scene in Seabrook, Ladd talked about all the Crime Stoppers tips HPD had received and how they had to check each and every one.

When Goodhart asked Ladd who he believed had killed the kids, Ladd did not hesitate, saying, "Dopers!" Dope and dope dealing was, in fact, the definite focus of the investigation in 2003 and even into 2004. He mentioned Jason Uolla by name. He talked about others he interviewed. Once Ladd said he made up his mind about it being a drug-related crime, there was no turning back. He never wavered.

Why?

Because the evidence had pointed to it, time and again.

DeGeurin took his crack at Tom Ladd and could not get the man to admit anything other than the truth as he had uncovered it.

In the end Tom Ladd had been right—the murders, if you believed Christine Paolilla and her version, were the result of a man who set out to steal drugs from a pair of dope dealers.

Next on the witness stand was another officer who was present at the Millbridge Drive scene. He walked in and told his stories, which included more of the same gory and graphic detail.

Then Brian Harris took the stand and related how he had become involved and how the hierarchy of assigning a murder case to the unit operated inside HPD. After that, Harris mentioned how, when he became involved months into the case, he took some time and read through every piece of paper connected to the case in order to get acquainted. And when Tom Ladd retired the following year, Harris said, he took the lead in the case.

Then Katrina happened.

There was a lull. But the case was always in his mind, tugging at him.

Then came the tip.

For some time—perhaps longer than he needed—Harris talked about how large the case was as a report itself, and how much information had been collected throughout the entire length of the investigation.

As DeGeurin kept objecting, citing relevance, Freyer had Harris move on to Crime Stoppers and how important it was to the success of the program for callers to maintain their anonymity if they chose so.

Then they talked about how much media coverage the case had received, and because of all the news stories, several policies had to be changed as it pertained to the way HPD gave out information to the press regarding unsolved crimes.

Harris explained all the red herrings he had chased down throughout the years.

He mentioned that several of the tips late into the investigation he followed up on contained information that had never been reported by the media, including where Christine worked. Or that Snider had moved from Crosby, Texas, to Louisville, Kentucky. Or that Snider was incarcerated. Or that the guns used in the murders could be found inside the safe in Snider's parents' house.

Nobody, Harris insisted, but the killers could have known those facts.

And just like that, Harris had given Justin Rott the credibility he would soon need to carry him through what was surely going to be a rough time on the stand. No matter what DeGeurin asked, what Christine said about him, or how many times the guy had been arrested or in rehab, no *one* and no *thing* could change the fact that Justin Rott could have never known the facts Harris described without them being passed on to him by his wife.

Then came an important part of Harris's testimony. His questioning of Christine on that first night she was taken into custody in San Antonio. Harris had to make sure the jury knew that he was well aware of her "condition" and that he'd had experience with questioning "intoxicated" and/or "high" suspects. He knew when the right and wrong time was to question a suspect and made several good points to the jury in answering Freyer's tough questions.

"Would you expect to be able to successfully or—interview someone who was unable to process in what you were telling them or asking them and then process it and then give an answer, too? If that person was unable to do that, would you interview that person?"

"No. Because my interviews are very complex. Very detailed."

"Okay. And just jumping ahead before we talk about a couple of other things, did you later perform two interviews of this defendant that you've identified here in court?"

"Yes."

"And without getting into the contents of them right now, did you believe that in doing so that she was unable to understand your questions, or that she was intoxicated and that she could not be interviewed?"

"No. There were numerous occasions throughout the interview I was quite impressed with her coherency and her ability to reason."

"And when she was arrested, did you see with your own eyes a large amount of evidence in this hotel room of previous drug usage?"

"Yes."

"And what was that in the form of?"

"Hundreds of needles, blood on the wall, the stench of unclean clothes, and just—it was—"

"Nasty?"

"—filthy. It was almost indescribable."

"All right. Now, regarding your training in intoxication and observing intoxicated people, I mean, when you're out on the street doing murder cases, do you often come in contact with people that are high, intoxicated?"

"Yes."

All a juror who might not have believed Harris needed to do was take a look at that videotape of Harris's first interview with Christine and it would become apparent that she knew what she was talking about. Heck, she knew enough to lie. Because she did it, over and over again, knowing where, exactly, to place a mistruth, and where, exactly, to tell the truth. In addition, Christine had not made any major admissions during that first interview.

CHAPTER 68

MIKE DEGEURIN NEEDED to go after Brian Harris. He needed to question the guy's tactics, his skills as an interrogator, his tenacity, his cockiness, and his ability to treat Christine, on that first night she was brought in, not with kid gloves, but with the rough, bare hands of a cop looking to get a confession and close a case that had been cold for years. It was DeGeurin's job to dig, press Harris on the hard issues, and see if he could expose a mistake or two Harris had made.

The way to begin this assault was to go after what was one of the more pejorative pieces of evidence the state had in its arsenal: Michelle and Craig Lackner's interviews and descriptions of those two people outside their window. It was their statements that had led to those now-infamous sketches, and the Lackners picking Snider and Christine out of a photo lineup. If the Lackners had seen sketches of the suspects before looking at the photo lineup, their testimony, which Rob Freyer had planned to bring in last, would register as questionable.

"You had with you the—in your offense report—the description that the Lackners had given back . . . on July 18, 2003, is that correct?" DeGeurin began.

"Yes," Harris said, looking up.

"And when you decided to go to them with a photo array, you had obtained a picture of Christine Paolilla and also one of Mr. Snider, correct?"

"Yes."

It would be stupid to go to them *without* a photo of both suspects. What would have been the purpose?

"Did you call the Lackners up and tell them to come somewhere, or did you go to their house?"

"We went to their office. . . . That address, it's an office complex. We went to their place of employment."

"You say 'we.' Who was with you?"

"Myself and Investigator Tom McCorvey," Harris said.

"Anyone else?"

Where was DeGeurin going with this?

"No."

"And when you went, did you have these two exhibits that we're talking about now—the photo arrays—with you?"

"Yes."

"When you got there, did you tell them," DeGeurin stopped himself and thought a moment. Changing the question, he asked, "First of all, did you tell them on the phone why you were coming by to see them?"

"Yes."

"By the way, was that recorded?"

Why would a cop record such a routine call?

"No."

"Did you make a notation of what you told them on the phone?"

"Yes."

"Okay. You had selected and showed me a few pages that relate to your notes of this happening. Can you show them to me again? Let me look at them?" DeGeurin asked.

"Yes." Harris showed the lawyer what he wanted.

DeGeurin was smart in the sense that he was breaking down the day Harris spoke to the Lackners into single beats, having the detective talk through every step. In there somewhere, perhaps, was a trip.

"Just give me a start [page] . . . stop. It's not too many pages, as I recall."

"Right here," Harris said, pointing to what DeGeurin was looking for.

"Do you mind if I take this over where I can. . . ?" DeGeurin started to ask, but then interrupted himself. "Did you take with you, when you went to meet the Lackners, a copy of the sketch?"

"The case files, yes."

"Which included the sketch?"

"Yes."

"Did you show them the sketch?"

"After the identification . . . we discussed the sketches, showed them the sketches and, basically, reaffirmed their decision."

"Are you saying you did *not* show them the sketches *before* you showed them the photo array?"

"I had them recall what they put on the sketch, what the features were, et cetera."

"And are you saying you did *not* show them the sketch when—"

This time Harris interrupted: "As far as examining the sketch, no, no." He shook his head. "No."

"No, no," DeGeurin clarified, repeating himself, "not *examining*, but just *showing* them the sketch?"

In other words, did you show them the sketches and the photos *together*—did you *help* these people come to a conclusion?

"I don't think I did. I know we talked about the description. I had the sketches there. It's now in the file, but as far as saying, 'Hey, look at this sketch,' no."

"No. But laying there for them to look at, if they wanted to?" (Was the sketch on a table somewhere, maybe in view, so they could compare it to the photo lineup?)

"They could have. I don't know. I don't know if they did or didn't."

"You don't know whether you had . . . the sketches in a spot where they could look at them before they looked at the—"

"Correct," Harris said, not letting him finish.

"You don't remember?"

"Correct."

"But you think they may have looked at them?"

"I don't know."

"You don't know whether you offered it to them? Or you don't know whether they even looked at them?"

"I don't know if they saw it on the desk or a file or something like that."

"If it was on a desk, it would be on *their* desk, right, because you're in their—"

"In their office," Harris interrupted. "It was some kind of office with, like, a round coffee-table type of thing."

"You would have had to take them out of your file and put them on their desk, correct?"

"Much like I'm carrying this now, yes."

"Spread out?"

"Correct."

DeGeurin made a good point, asking pointedly: "For them to look at it if they *wanted* to?"

"I don't know. I don't know if they did."

"You don't know why you had it out on the desk?"

"For the case file! I had them out because of the case file. It's part of a case file. And finding their statements that they had already made, and for reference for ourselves in getting them to recall the descriptions [they had previously given]. Because in an oral interview, both of them recalled the physical descriptions of the people they saw."

"So . . . the sketches were to help them remember what their description was?"

DeGeurin was doing his best to make Harris stumble.

"No. The sketches were as a reference for us as they're describing the descriptions of the two people. It's reaffirmation to me that these were good sketches."

"In other words, you . . . had the sketches there for your own benefit, not for them. Is that what you're saying?"

"Correct. Correct." Harris nodded his head.

They could have gone on forever, back and forth, discussing this subjective topic until jurors fell asleep and became so confused that Harris's testimony meant nothing.

In the end DeGeurin was able to get Harris to admit that he had explained to the Lackners that they now had a few suspects and their help identifying them was going to be crucial to the case.

DeGeurin then began to question Harris about a report he had handed the lawyer during his testimony, asking if that was the actual report he had been referring to during his testimony. They argued about this for several minutes. It was rather inconsequential, actually, seeing that Harris had made his point that the Lackners identified Christine and Chris from a photo lineup and there really wasn't much DeGeurin could do to deny or dispute that simple, detrimental fact of the case.

For the next thirty minutes or so, DeGeurin keyed in on every particular aspect regarding the Lackners' identification of the photo lineups. By the time the witness and the lawyer finished talking about the Lackners, all the jury could do was anticipate the Lackners' testimony even more. In a sense DeGeurin's cross-examination of Harris gave the Lackners more credibility.

Finally Mike DeGeurin passed the witness back to ADA Tom Goodhart.

Goodhart said, "Nothing further."

The judge recessed until the following morning.

CHAPTER 69

IT WOULD HAVE been a mistake for Rob Freyer not to capitalize on Mike DeGeurin's obsession, truthfully, with the Lackners' descriptions of the defendant and Chris Snider. So, on the morning of October 2, 2008, Freyer called Michelle Lackner as his first witness.

The pretty Texan, who had seen two murderers outside her window, walked in and sat down.

Michelle Lackner introduced herself to the judge and jury. She had been at her accounting job thirteen years, married to Craig for ten, and had lived in the Millbridge Drive neighborhood for the past six years.

She then told her tale of seeing two people walk up the driveway toward the Rowell house on July 18, 2003. And beyond all that they would discuss over the next twenty minutes, including how she identified Christine and Chris in a photo lineup, the most important part of Michelle Lackner's testimony came almost right away, after Freyer asked, "Right now . . . when it comes to the people that you observed, do you happen to see one of the two people that you observed, here, sitting here in the courtroom?"

"Yes."

"And for the benefit of Judge Ellis, can you identify her by pointing to something that she's wearing, or a physical trait?"

"A pink headband."

Christine looked down and away.

Michelle Lackner's testimony had the impact of an eyewitness placing Christine at the scene of the crime.

Craig Lackner walked in next and backed up his wife, saying almost the same thing, verbatim.

DeGeurin tried, but could not crack the happy couple. One of the only questionable aspects of the Lackners' testimony came from Craig Lackner, when DeGeurin asked him if Harris and McCorvey had "told them" that their suspects would be in the photo lineup before they looked at the images.

"We were told that—that they were—they were like suspects, but they wanted to show us a lineup. That's all they said."

"I was thinking maybe I didn't ask the question clear enough," DeGeurin pressed. "In your mind, when you were looking at the pictures before you determined which one you recognized, were you of the impression from whatever the officers told you that their suspect was going to be one of those photographs?"

"Yes."

"And do you recall what they told you that led you to that conclusion?"

"They said they had a lineup of people they wanted us to look at. And I think they maybe even said that they had received a tip, I think, and that they had a lineup they wanted us to look at to try to see if we saw the people that we saw."

"In other words, they didn't . . . tell you, 'Our suspect is not even in this group'?"

"They didn't tell us that."

IT WAS OCTOBER 6, 2008, Monday. Brian Harris had been recalled the previous Friday to conclude his testimony. He had walked the jury through every nuance and beat of the case as he saw it. Harris's second round of testimony allowed the state to put into the record several pieces of evidence, as well as scores of additional photographs and witness/suspect statements.

Before the day began, the judge told the jury that the state would be "wrapping its case on Thursday or Friday."

This was a great relief to many.

With that out of the way, Detective Breck McDaniel took the stand and explained how he interviewed Christine two days after she was apprehended in San Antonio, after she had placed herself at the murder scene. It was certainly implicit in McDaniel's testimony that Christine had had some time before this particular interview to think about what she was going to tell police. By then she believed they had evidence placing her at the scene, so she had to come up with some sort of explanation for being there.

The only jabs DeGeurin could take at McDaniel, which turned out to be weak on merit alone, included questions about Christine's medication and how well she was able to answer questions while under the duress of withdrawal.

But Christine had been checked by doctors and nurses at a hospital and allowed to leave. She had been discharged, McDaniel noted.

The day ended after DeGeurin finished his cross and the state passed on any additional questioning. The judge had something else to do that day, but promised they'd work a full eight hours tomorrow.

At the start of the next morning, Craig and Michelle Lackner were recalled to answer a few additional questions.

Then Nancy Vernau told her tale of hearing the gunshots ring throughout that afternoon, somewhere around three-seventeen.

Prosecutors sometimes refer to this portion of a trial as "coasting," whereby Rob Freyer and Tom Goodhart were crossing their *t*'s and dotting their *i*'s, rolling into the station with plenty of fuel in the tank.

An eighteen-year veteran officer, Guillermo "Will" Gonzales, a sergeant in the Homicide Division, sat down next. Will had spoken to Lori Paolilla about Christine during the investigation at the behest of Brian Harris. It was Will Gonzales who tracked Christine and Justin down in San Antonio through bank and credit card records. It was also Will Gonzales and his partner, Detective Richard Martinez, who flew to Louisville to conduct a search for Chris Snider and to look for the weapons used in the murders.

And so now the weapons were entered into evidence.

Next up was DNA specialist Laura Gahn, who had examined most of the DNA in the case.

Quite interesting, Christine's prints or her DNA were not recovered from either of the weapons.

"There was a good reason for that," a source later said. "Chris [Snider] had wiped off the weapons, and he also was caught once in the backyard of [his] home, holding the gun up to his head, ready to kill himself, but was talked out of it. These are good reasons why you'd never find Christine's prints on either of the guns."

What Gahn did make clear was that the guns found at Snider's house were, in fact, the weapons used to commit the murders.

When DeGeurin finished cross-examining Gahn, Freyer passed on further questioning.

With that, the state called Justin Rott.

Rott had some credibility issues; there was no getting around them. The guy was a convicted felon, dope addict, known liar, and convicted thief. And yet, Rob Freyer explained, "The thing that people lose sight of when speaking of Justin Rott's testimony is that he knew details about the crime . . . that had never been released to the public. He knew because *she* told him. We knew she had gone to work at Walgreens after the murders because she had told Rott. The officers followed up on that, and it turned out to be true."

It had been Freyer's job—and what a task it had been—to keep Justin Rott on his toes as the delays before trial turned into months of waiting. For a recovering drug addict, prone to relapse, downtime is the enemy.

"Rott was good and bad for us," said one victim's family member. "For months leading up to trial, we never thought he would make it. The guy OD'd, he was using, he would take off and not be heard from. So Freyer literally had to call Rott every day, visit him, and, basically, take care of him as if he was a child."

But here he was, not looking half bad, ready to do his duty and talk about what his wife had said to him. And that was where the impact of Rott's testimony would strike hardest. Only Christine could have given Justin this information. It was so simple when pared down and looked at objectively. She had confided in her husband, never expecting that he would one day turn around and testify against her.

"The things that he told us in San Antonio," said one law enforcement officer, "all matched up. We would not have known the guns were in a safe, in Kentucky, hundreds of miles away from Texas, if Rott had not told us that fact."

Rott hadn't changed much since he and Christine split up. He still walked with that lanky, wayward shuffle.

Freyer had Rott state his full name: "Stanley Justin Rott," he said, telling the jury where he was from and how long—four years—he had lived in the Houston area.

Christine wore her black overcoat snuggly, as if she was cold. She sat and stared at her husband with a serious gaze that said: *How dare you! We shared secrets.*

Rott didn't mince words when it came time to talk about his problems with drugs. He explained that although he was "in recovery" at the time and a member of NA, Narcotics Anonymous, he had also been going to Cocaine Anonymous meetings, as well. The end of the month of October, he claimed, would mark a year of sobriety for him.

Then Rott talked about his "home group" and his "sponsor" in the drug and alcohol abuse programs he had been attending. He said his sponsor was there, in the courtroom, supporting him.

Freyer asked Rott if drugs had caused him problems in the past.

"Of course, yeah, family problems," he answered, "and all kinds of things."

It was the understatement of the trial. The amount of drugs he and Christine had done would have killed many addicts not accustomed to the potency and sheer bulk. They had lived like animals inside a hotel room, feces and blood all over the place, needles everywhere.

Rott next admitted that he had been arrested for theft and other misdemeanor crimes associated with being a drug addict and having to support his habit. Currently, Rott told jurors, he was on probation for theft and habitation. Five years, in fact. He had been following his probation standards "so well," Rott said, he was a "VIP speaker for the district felony courts in Fort Bend County." He had been asked "to speak to the courts, the drug courts, misdemeanor courts, and speak to families about drug addiction." Thus, as far as recovering drug addicts go, Rott was the poster boy—the man who could speak from the dark end of a tunnel about the evil spewing from the tip of a needle.

Freyer was doing his best to polish the witness.

DeGeurin allowed it to go on for a brief period and then objected. "Relevancy, Your Honor?"

"Sustained."

Rott talked about meeting Christine and falling in love.

He spoke of how their life together was great—in the beginning.

He told how he liked Lori and Tom.

He shared how he proposed marriage to Christine.

And how, during Hurricane Rita, they drove down to San Antonio and began the ultimate drug bender.

Before he knew Christine, he said, he had never heard about the murders in Clear Lake.

One of the most important parts of Rott's testimony included an exchange shortly before Freyer concluded his direct questioning. It had to do with Christine's story of being forced into helping Chris Snider.

"Did she ever indicate to you that she was—in the description that she gave you—that she was ever *forced* to do anything? That anybody else *forced* her to do anything?"

"No."

"Or threatened her?"

"No."

"Pointed a gun at her, or anything like that?"

"No."

Freyer brought up the billboard and how Christine reacted that day she had brought Rott out to see it, telling her then-husband, while pointing to the billboard, "That's the Chris that I said that was with me that day."

Freyer didn't need the Lackners' identification of the sketches. Here was Christine herself doing it for him.

Rott said he didn't leave her and turn her in when he realized she was a murderer because he "loved her."

Then Freyer had Rott tell jurors the version of the murders Christine had given him after he pressed her for details.

"Christine walked in," Rott explained. Jurors listened intensely. This was it, the reason why Rott was on the stand. "Chris followed. They walked in the house. She went around with one of the girls. What she told me was they said they were—they were asking for drugs, and I think one of the girls was taking her to go get some. That's how they got separated, her and Chris, from what she told me. But then she told me she started crying when she was with the girl, with Tiffany."

"What did she say she said to the girl?"

"She said she was sorry. She started crying."

"Did she say why she said that?"

"I guess. I don't know."

"Did she say whether or not this girl that she said she was sorry to had any kind of response?"

"She just asked her, 'What are you talking about?' "

"And what did she say she said in response to that?"

"She just said she was sorry and started crying. And at that time, that's when Chris yelled for Christine to come back in the room."

"And what happened after that?" Freyer asked.

"When she came in the room with Tiffany, Chris already had a gun pulled."

"And what did she say she did after that?"

"That she did?" Rott asked, confused.

"Yes. Not Tiffany, but Christine."

"Chris—she said that Chris told them all to get by the couch, and that's when he did tell her to take out the gun."

"What did she do? What did she say she did in response to that?"

"She took out the gun."

"Did she indicate that she did that voluntarily? Was she scared? Why did she say she took the gun out?"

"She didn't say she was scared. . . ."

Shocking many in the courtroom, Justin Rott talked about what happened when Christine "voluntarily" went back into the house to make sure they were all dead.

"Did she tell you whether or not Rachael said anything to her or asked her any questions?"

"Yeah. She said Rachael . . . just kept asking 'why?' "

"Okay. And did she tell you . . . that—after hearing that—what she did after?"

"She beat her to death."

Gasps could be heard from every corner of the room. The images this exchange conjured were horrifying: a teen girl beating her so-called friend to death, and that girl asking why she was doing it. It was harrowing to listen to, and a few people got up and walked out of the courtroom.

"How?" Freyer asked.

"With the gun."

"Did she tell you that?"

"Yeah. Because she told me that she kept *hitting* her and *hitting* her, and she [Christine] was crying the whole time she was doing it."

"Okay. Did she tell you how many times that she hit Rachael with the gun?"

"No. She just said she . . . When she started hitting her, she just kept hitting her until she was dead."

CHAPTER 70

JUSTIN ROTT CONTINUED to tell the jury his story the following day as Mike DeGeurin did his best to smear Rott's reputation and prove him to be the liar that he was known to be. Still, those snapshots of Christine Paolilla pounding the back of Rachael Koloroutis's head were hard to dismiss.

DeGeurin was able to get Rott to admit that he had met a few women since he and Christine last saw each other. In fact, these were women to whom Rott had lied to, the lawyer said, "for their attention."

Quite shocking, one female Rott had befriended turned out to be Nichole Sánchez, Adelbert's sister. Rott had gotten together with Nichole on several occasions, although both said it was nothing more than a friendship. Nichole wanted answers. Justin had known her brother's killer, Nichole believed. Perhaps he could offer some insight into why Christine had taken Adelbert away from her.

If nothing else, Justin Rott's cross-examination made clear that the guy was unafraid of admitting his faults—be it lying, cheating, stealing, using heroin, or turning other people on to the drug. He was open and honest about everything.

Mike DeGeurin made Justin Rott sound as though he was a predator, out in the world seeking women to turn into drug users with him. According to Rott and several people who knew him, this was totally untrue. Yet the one topic DeGeurin stayed away from was Rott's inside knowledge of the murders.

The state called firearms expert Kim Downs next, who gave additional details about the murder weapons, tying them even closer to the murders.

The next morning, October 9, the state called assistant medical examiner Morna Gonsoulin. The judge warned the gallery before Morna began that there would be gruesome photos coming up and that anyone was welcome to step out now.

Freyer and Goodhart made a classic move here. By concluding their case with the reality and totality of the murders, those photographs of the victims, as they appeared during autopsy, were setting those images in the jury's minds.

When DeGeurin passed the witness back to the state after his cross-examination, Goodhart stood and spoke, "Nothing further, Judge."

"You may step down, Doctor," Ellis told the ME. "What says the state?"

"Judge, at this time, the state of Texas will rest," Goodhart acknowledged.

The judge asked that the jury retire to the jury room.

"YOUR HONOR, NOW that the state has rested," DeGeurin began, "and outside the presence of the jury, I move for an instructed—for the court to instruct the jury to return a verdict of not guilty because the evidence is not sufficient to prove beyond a reasonable doubt, to a reasonable juror, each and every element of the offense, which is set out in the indictment in three separate paragraphs."

Without hesitation the judge said, "That will be denied."

The jury was asked to return.

DeGeurin's first witness was the father of a girl whom Justin Rott had lived with for a brief period of time after he and Christine separated. The guy's daughter was one of the women into whom Rott had supposedly shot bags of heroin. Her father was there to qualify that Rott was a lying thug who took women under his wing and turned them into dopers.

Mike DeGeurin made a strong point with his witness to let the jury know that Justin Rott had not only turned the guy's daughter on to heroin, but had injected her on several occasions and was using dope at a time when Rott had told Freyer—during that lull in the case when Freyer was babysitting him—that he wasn't using.

DeGeurin next brought in the girl in question, and she—guess what?—verified everything that had been said by her dad before her.

As it turned out, the girl knew Rachael, Tiffany, and Christine from high school, and her locker was, incredibly, right next to Christine's.

She said she met Justin Rott in the same place Rott had met most of his women: recovery meetings.

Rott had found out that the girl's mother had committed suicide, so he told her his mother had done the same, in order to build a bond between them. To gain more sympathy, he told her his father had died in a car wreck. Rott had even proposed marriage to the girl, according to her testimony. But the ring he had placed on her finger, when he asked for her hand, had been stolen from another girl's house, she later learned.

After the girl buried Rott, DeGeurin brought in another, who sat and told an almost identical story. Would any of it help Christine Paolilla? That was anybody's guess.

BY FAR, MIKE DeGeurin's most important witness was Dr. George Glass, a "paid," according to Rob Freyer, medical doctor and psychiatrist with decades of experience. Glass talked for the remainder of the day about Christine's state of mind during those days when she gave HPD what amounted to a confession of being at the scene of the crime as it occurred. The topic of addiction came up routinely during Glass's direct testimony, the doctor offering his opinion whether Christine was treated properly when she went to the ER that first night HPD had interviewed her in San Antonio.

"So . . . the hospital people, when they make notations about what they observe, is there some . . . Is there any reason they would write something wrong, or is it . . . when they're writing something in the hospital record, what's it for that they're writing?"

"It's to document what's happening at the time," Glass answered, "as well as to lay the foundation for a treatment plan from there on out. And usually the treatment plan is because, you know, hospital emergency rooms work in shifts, and when the next shift comes in, they need to know, you know, at four o'clock, whenever somebody leaves, what the last person thought and why they did what they did, because they may not have the opportunity to talk with them. So that's why it's written and documented in some detail."

"So, did they give her drugs?"

"Yes, they did."

"What did they give her?"

"They gave her . . . at approximately six-fifteen at night they gave her twenty milligrams of methadone by mouth. Methadone is a long-acting narcotic. Unlike heroin, which has a four- to six-hour half-life, or in that frame, methadone has a, you know, eighteen- to twenty-four-, thirty-six-hour half-life, which means you go through withdrawal much [longer] if you take it. Twenty milligrams of methadone is relatively . . . [for] someone who doesn't normally take any narcotics, that would be enough to, if not put you to sleep, really tranquilize you for a time. An hour later they gave her six milligrams of morphine sulfate in a shot by IV. They had an IV running. The normal dose, if you were to go to the hospital with a heart attack, the first treatment is they give you a shot of morphine sulfate, the normal dose is four to eight milligrams. So, she got approximately what would have been the dose for a fifty-year-old guy with a heart attack—on top of the methadone. And then a couple hours later, before she leaves the hospital at nine o'clock, they give her another twenty milligrams of methadone and they give her another shot of morphine two or three hours later."

The point Glass left out, which would have been critical for jurors to hear, was that for a junkie of Christine's caliber, these narcotics would have brought her to a normal state, calmed her down and leveled her out.

This argument by Glass went on and on. The point he was trying to make was that Christine had not been in her right frame of mind to have been questioned for as long or as vigorously as she had been by police.

He talked about Christine suffering from post-traumatic stress disorder because of her father's death. He mentioned that she had low self-esteem because of her alopecia. She was "susceptible to what are called . . . codependent abusive relationships."

Late into the day, as Tom Goodhart began his cross-examination, DeGeurin needed to leave the room for some reason.

"Doctor," Goodhart began anyway, "we've met once before, correct?"

"Yes."

"May I be excused, Your Honor?" DeGeurin stood and said. "I've got co-counsel—I've got to find out . . ."

"Okay," the judge said.

"Judge, may I approach?" Goodhart asked.

"Yes."

"Considering this is the foundation of their defensive argument, the fact he just left the courtroom, I think, is a bad thing for the record. I trust him completely in his capabilities, but I don't want to take this chance."

"This is ridiculous," the judge said in frustration. He sent the jury out of the room.

Moments later the judge called them back and got the trial going again.

Drama. Every trial had its share.

One of Goodhart's main points was to show the jury that Glass was walking into this situation after the fact, and his comments and opinions should be taken as such. For example, Goodhart questioned whether Christine was addicted to heroin and how the doctor would know if he had not treated her at the time, asking, "Doctor, were there any medical tests run at either hospital to verify the presence of opiate heroin inside of her system?"

"No."

"There were not."

Well into his cross, Goodhart pressed the doctor for his professional opinion of Christine at the time of her arrest.

"Is she a liar?"

Dr. Glass gave the prosecutor a dragged-out version of yes, stating: "She's distorting, as do most addicts. When they go somewhere and they want to get something, to a doctor's office, emergency room, they usually bump up what they're taking when they tell somebody, in the hope that they'll get more rather than less."

"They lie about it, don't they?" Goodhart clarified.

"Yeah. Lie, distort, whatever."

"Addicts are liars—"

"Judge," interrupted DeGeurin, who had not left the room after all, "I'm going to—I can't let that question go. I object to it."

The judge leaned toward the gallery: "Overruled. Answer the question, sir."

"Are you asking me a philosophical question, or are you making a moral statement?" Glass wanted to know.

"No, sir. I'm flat asking you—what you just said a little while ago in your direct testimony—they will do just about *anything* to get more drugs?"

"That's true."

"Okay. That means they're liars, manipulators, fabricators. Would that not be a fair statement?"

"They may do all those things."

"Would you say that's indicative of just about every junkie you've ever known?"

"At different times, yes."

"Sometimes we have to pick the kernels of truth from the lies," Goodhart concluded his point, ". . . when we talk to junkies?"

"Depends on whether they're using or whether they're clean."

The doctor finished earlier than expected. With that, DeGeurin whispered a few words to his co-counsel, said something to Christine, and then addressed the court.

"We'll rest."

Rob Freyer called one more witness, Rachael's sister, Lelah Koloroutis. It took Lelah about thirty seconds to say she recognized Rachael, Tiffany, Adelbert, and Marcus in a photograph that Freyer wanted placed into the record.

Here was a smart prosecutor, once again reminding jurors what the trial was about: the victims.

After that, the day was concluded by the judge, who promised closing arguments from both sides next.

CHAPTER 71

DURING HIS CLOSING argument on Monday, October 13, 2008, ADA Rob Freyer told jurors that Chris Snider "alone, was not to blame" for the murders. He warned jurors about falling for that "tired and pathetic tactic." Christine Paolilla was "just as responsible," Freyer said, imploring each juror to ask him- or herself: "Could this horrible event have happened *without* her?"

He paused.

Then, "Of *course* not!"

Defense attorney Mike DeGeurin suggested to jurors that Christopher Snider was responsible all by himself. He rang that bell at the beginning of his closing, and he continued throughout. It was, after all, the only chance DeGeurin had to save his client.

Yet, none of it did any good.

"Guilty," the judge read into the record after a brief deliberation by the jury.

One of the more interesting aspects of the guilty verdict, which came out later that same day, was a comment made by juror Cliff Sheets, who spoke to reporters outside the Harris County Justice Center, when he said that he had been "among four panelists who had initially voted for acquittal, but who all eventually changed their minds." There were questions, Sheets added, but the answers the jury had come to during deliberations were satisfying enough to send Christine Paolilla to prison.

"There was a lot of contradiction in her stories," Sheets offered, "in the three interviews she gave."

Before she was sentenced, the families had an opportunity to read impact statements. George Koloroutis had written an emotionally charged testimonial that would allow him, for the first time, to face his daughter's murderer and address her actions. George had spent thousands of dollars of his own money and enough emotion to probably strip a few years from his life, while trying to help solve his daughter's murder. This verdict was not a payoff, a triumphant moment of any sort; it was an end to the criminal case.

It was justice.

Nothing more.

The loss. The real pain. The memories. They were all going to be there, waiting every morning for George, same as for the other families. There was no way of getting around the loss, no matter how much Christine suffered. There would be days when, for no apparent reason, after thinking they had come to terms with the loss, when tears would come from nowhere. Or a moment, a memory, a party somewhere, that would send them into a spiral of depression so consuming they had to get away by themselves and recover.

The look on the faces of these families as a video camera panned the room, and the court waited for Christine Paolilla to be brought back in after a break, depicted a group of people who had shed all the tears they had left and were now dredging up an even deeper layer of emotional agony.

Christine, in tears herself, was brought into the courtroom. She wore what had become her standard court attire: pink houndstooth headband to match a collared pink shirt underneath a reddish brown sweater vest. She had gained some weight since her arrest and her face was chubby and heavily made-up. Christine wiped tears and mouthed things to her mother and lawyers, all with a look that spoke of a woman who did not comprehend what she had done or what was happening.

George Koloroutis sat directly behind Christine with a look of absolute seriousness (or maybe disgust), waiting for his turn to speak.

The judge told Christine as she sat down that she didn't need to do anything more than "listen" as the impact statements were read.

Sitting in the witness stand first, facing Christine, Nichole Sánchez read her prepared statement. The tears came almost immediately as

Nichole talked about how much she and her family missed Adelbert. It was the simple things that they cherished the most, Nichole pointed out.

"His smell," she said. "His laugh. . . . My parents will never get the chance to see Adelbert grow up and see what he would have become and done with his life."

Christine wiped tears with a tissue.

Up next was Charlene Gronewold, Marcus's mother, who spoke for both Marcus and Tiffany, two kids in love and ready to take on the world. "Our life is changed forever" was Charlene's opening theme; she said it right away, through a torrent of anguish. Then, perhaps making the most profound statement a parent could make while responding to the death of a child, Charlene Gronewold said, quite emphatically, "The normal we knew will never be. We have to find a new normal. . . . But don't pity me, pity those kids. There's no victory here. Just justice"—and here she paused, dredging up the strength to continue—"because we still leave here *without* our kids, and we forever have to live that nightmare."

Wearing an aqua blue business shirt, unbuttoned at the collar, George walked to the stand, a piece of paper in his hand. George told the story of the evening he found out that his daughter had been murdered, explaining how he, Ann, and Lelah had spent the night in front of Tiffany Rowell's house, waiting for word that Rachael was one of the four.

From there, George talked about how it was that Rachael's little sister, George and Ann's then-nine-year-old daughter, found out that her big sister had been murdered. She had been at a neighbor's house that night, George said. He had walked over the following morning to pick her up, this after not sleeping, watching his other daughter, Lelah, vomit, while his wife curled into a ball and cried as the sun came up.

"Hey, Dad," George's youngest child said as they walked back home. "I know what's going on."

George asked her what she meant.

"I snuck in and saw it on the news . . . four teens got shot."

George told her, "Yeah, that's true." Then, as they approached the house, this broken father added, "Listen, your mom and [Lelah] and I, we need to talk to you."

The little girl asked why.

"Because, you know, one of those teenagers was your sister Rachael."

Five years later, George cried here on the stand, describing this scene, telling the court, "That day will *haunt* me for the rest of my life."

George had become the quasi-public spokesperson for the group of families. Here, on this day, he called Christine—who wiped tears with a Kleenex, looking away and at her attorneys, shaking her head—an "evil" person, "cold, calculated, and heartless." He then gave what was an image of lasting candor, adding, "[Rachael's] picture never ages, while *we* do. . . . Christmas, birthdays . . . college graduation—there's always an absence, a silence that is deafening."

Perhaps one of the more incredible statements made by anyone that day came when George said that regardless of his ill health, both mentally and physically, due to the murder of his daughter, what her killers never realized was that "we would never stop! We worked diligently with HPD. And we give all credit to their heroic efforts—and especially that of Brian Harris. . . . David Gronewold was at my side at all times, as were the Sánchez family in this regard. We never gave up. . . . We take solace in the fact that was it not for our efforts, this killer would have gotten away. . . ."

The judge sent Christine back to her cell and adjourned court, retiring to his chambers from the bench quickly, perhaps in tears himself. As the families filed out of the courtroom, an onslaught of wailing was unleashed from them.

Brian Harris and ADA Rob Freyer stood and watched, both men fighting off tears themselves, staring at the ground, looking up, rolling their tongues around closed mouths, the emotional energy in the room too much to take. It was an ending for these two lawmen, who would go on to other cases and other families. But they knew, deep down, that this moment, the last time they would see Christine Paolilla, would be embedded in the families' minds forever. Although it had been five years since their children had been taken away, it was only the beginning of a lifetime of mourning.

Christine cried as the court bailiff directed her out of the courtroom.

Before bolting from the scene, Judge Ellis had sentenced Christine to serve a mandatory life sentence, which would amount to forty years behind bars before she was even *eligible* for parole.

Outside the courtroom, Mike DeGeurin was asked how Christine reacted behind closed doors.

"She's upset," the veteran defense attorney said. "She totally understands the grief of the families, her friends, the ones who were killed. She only wishes they could understand that she didn't want any of that to happen. But she understands their grief."

TOM MCCORVEY, BRIAN Harris's partner throughout much of the last year investigating and solving the case, walked over to Harris's desk a few days after the verdict.

That cop who had sat next to Harris and had mocked him, from time to time, comparing his efforts to a capable chimp's, was at his own desk doing paperwork.

McCorvey stood over Harris, making sure that the guy could hear him.

"Hey, hotshot!" McCorvey said loudly. "How's it going these days?"

Harris didn't have to reply. The headlines, the newscasts, the appreciation from the grief-stricken families, spoke volumes.

EPILOGUE

I ASKED GEORGE Koloroutis, as we finished up our interviews, if there is closure for him and his family in any of this. It is a word—"closure"—seemingly tossed around at the end of many murder trials, when families are trying to go on with their lives and justice has been (hypothetically speaking) served. "Closure" is something I generally ask all murder victims' family members I write about, if I can. Having experienced the murder of a family member (my sister-in-law, five months pregnant, was murdered many years ago in Hartford, Connecticut: one account has a pillowcase placed over her head and her being strangled by a telephone cord), I could relate on a smaller scale to the families and wanted to know if we were on the same wavelength regarding that strange word.

I look at my nephews, Mark and Tyler Phelps, and my niece, Meranda VanDeventer (all of whom I love dearly). They are all grown now and have families of their own. They seem happy. Yet, the one thing I don't see on their faces or hear in their voices when they talk about their mother is closure. (I should note that their mother's murder remains unsolved to this day, and their father, my brother, Mark Anthony Phelps Sr., died at forty-seven years of age—from what I am *convinced* was a broken heart masked as drug and alcohol addiction.)

George gave me what I believe is the best answer I've heard thus far.

"Closure? There's no closure—and there *never* will be," he said. "My little girl was killed violently. She had the back of her head beaten in. She was going through hell during her last moments, choking on her own blood, while wondering, looking at her friend, *why* a friend of hers would do this. . . . She was scared . . . and I'm sure she was, ah, um"—he began crying, that endless pain deep within his soul emerging—"calling my name out. . . ."

George could not continue the conversation.

Later, when I had a chance to talk to him, he brought it up—because George Koloroutis, if nothing else, is a man who finishes things, no matter what.

"Closure," George went on to conclude, "is *not* something you are seeking."

I FELT COMPELLED to share the following transcript (nearly verbatim) of an interview I conducted with a source near the end of writing this book. I think it's an important concluding (and uplifting) message. In this Q&A with Rachael Koloroutis's sister Lelah, the true spirit of Rachael emerges. I didn't want to incorporate Lelah's answers into the narrative where they belong in relation to a chronological order of the story, simply because some of what Lelah shares is so powerful, if only in its simplicity. It truly shows that the Koloroutis family, same as all the families I write about (and certainly all the families touched by Christine Paolilla and Chris Snider's crimes), is your typical family, going from day to day, unaware that tragedy is about to enter their lives and change them forever. It is also a good example of how I go about the interviewing process, allowing those people involved in the stories to speak on their own behalf by sharing their various memories and anecdotes. My bet is that I could have asked family members of each of the victims in this story the same set of questions and heard the same answers.

> Could you give me one of your fondest memories of your sister?

My senior year of high school, I went to a prom with someone from a private school on a Thursday night. The next morning I was exhausted and wanted to stay home from school but didn't want to be alone so I talked mom into letting Rachael stay home with me. Immediately we threw on our swimsuits and ran out to our pool in the backyard. We played all day. We had these floats and were practicing running and surfing across the pool on them to see who could stay on it the longest. Rachael was pretending to be the surf shop owner and kept doing a "dude" voice that made me laugh so hard I could barely keep standing. Later we built an obstacle course in the pool and made our little sister run courses through when she came back from school. It was a perfect day of sun and pool and popsicles and being young. I have used that day and the image of her standing on the sundeck as a way of meditating before . . . as my happy place. You see, my whole life she was the person I played with, we were imaginative kids, we made up voices and role played, and had elaborate schemes. [We] used to sit in my car outside the grocery store where we worked and make up stories for every person that walked by. We made each other laugh so hard. . . .

What was her dream?

Rachael wanted to help people. She was really interested in criminal justice. When she was a little girl (like 4 through 10) she used to say she was going to be a ballerina or a cop. Later, she wanted to do something with solving crime. She was really interested in James Patterson novels and the idea of profiling because she liked the idea of using psychology to catch criminals and to keep others safe. . . .

What had she told you about Marcus, Tiffany, and Adelbert? What were her thoughts about them?

I can't really speak much to her thoughts on Marcus and Adelbert; she didn't know Adelbert previously and only knew Marcus through Tiffany. Tiffany had also been a friend of mine. She and Rachael were very close because Rachael was one of the only people to really let Tiffany be sad about her mother's loss. When I was a senior and they were juniors we all had lunch together and a sociology class. At lunch, the three of us would go outside the theater area to eat. Tiffany was very involved in theater. She used to say I was her big sister, too. They would write me notes during the day and draw funny pictures. Rachael had an inside joke with her boyfriend . . . about zebras and wallabies so Tiffany and I created a penguin joke. . . . I know that sounds silly but just to let you know that there was so much innocence and playfulness to all of us back then. Tiffany was also interested in psychology and she really wanted to go into therapy or acting. . . .

What had she said to you about Christine?

We hadn't talked a lot about Christine after I had gone off to college. Rachael had introduced me to her while we were all still in high school. I had told Rachael that I felt she was a weird girl, that something was off (mostly because her physical appearance was clownish but I think without realizing it my instincts were kicking in, just not enough to say anything). Rachael told me that she felt sorry for her, that she had a disease and didn't really have a father and that she had really bad self-esteem. Rachael's goal was always to love people, to meet them where they were, and then to show them what to hope in. After we lost Rachael, we went to the school to visit the guidance counselor. The woman said that she'd met with Rachael a couple times when she'd been struggling with her classes but all Rachael could talk about was trying to get the counselor to hope and see that faith in God could help heal her heart (the counselor had lost her daughter to a disease and said she really had a hard time believing but that Rachael was clear that she believed that's what helped the hurting).

For you, personally, what did you think happened (before, obviously, the case was solved)?

Those years were so difficult. My logical brain tried to track the information coming in and to help my parents/investigators with names and faces and anyone I might've known or heard of before I went to college. All the while, I threw myself in my studies just for a break. At night, I had nightmares for years. Dreams about things I'd heard, like a woman on top of her beating her head in. Dreams that she wasn't dead and that the body had been misidentified and she was somewhere waiting for us to find her. I never considered Christine. I hadn't known them to be more than casual friends at school. Oddly, though, the night of the murder I can remember sitting on the curb across the street from the house and thinking about Christine. They told us they couldn't identify the fourth body because she was face down. They said she was very skinny and had long red hair. "That girl, that girl with the wig, mom, maybe it's her." I remember begging one of Rachael's friends to go find her so we could prove she wasn't in there and telling camera people, "oh, it's not us." I didn't have shoes on, only socks, because we'd left the house so fast. Eventually, once the ME arrived and the street had cleared, it was just my parents, the cops, and news cameras. I'll never forget the cop calling us over to the yellow tape. . . . My mom screamed and wailed, falling to the ground, and my dad was shaking and asking over and over "what do I do now, what do I do now." And I just stared at my socks feeling like I was floating above the whole scene. . . .

You knew your sister better than anyone: tell me about her.

Rachael was silly and she loved a practical joke. She hated to wear socks or shoes. She liked whip cream straight out of the can. She had this way of drawing people into her everywhere we went. She was caring but would rather help you smile than cry with you. She always reminded me that we were a team; that we were always on each other's side. She was completely loyal to her family and to her beliefs. She believed that mistakes were used to help teach other people—she told me that so many times. She always had chipped paint on her nails and she could never get to bed on time. She hated to run but loved to dance. And she was so proud of her sisters and she always told us. She made sure to let us know that we were important. She'd spend every day lying by a pool, eating chips and salsa, if she could.

CHRISTINE PAOLILLA WENT the appeal route. In the Fourteenth Court of Appeals, on November 29, 2008, she filed an appeal based on the argument that the "trial court abused its discretion in setting the amount of bail at $500,000. . . ."

It did not take long for a decision: *In light of [the filing] we [the court of appeals] do not find the trial court abused its discretion in setting the amount of bail at $500,000. Accordingly, the judgment of the trial court is affirmed.*

I have been told that she has filed additional appeals, as any defendant has the right to do. On May 26, 2011, the panel of justices affirmed the court's previous judgment.

I wrote to Christine (twice) and her mother, Lori Paolilla, but never heard back from either one of them. There were others, too, I requested interviews with—lawyers, family members of victims, friends of Christine and Chris Snider—but who never responded to my inquiries. Fortunately, there were scores of other sources that did talk to me.

I searched for Justin Rott for months: calls, letters, Facebook and Myspace messages. I finally heard from him long after I had turned in my manuscript. "I was in rehab," he said. Justin and I had a few long talks and he backed up most of what I had written about him and Christine from the record and additional interviews with other sources. I found him to be sincere and truthful. Definitely honest about his life and the mistakes he's made. His main worry was that I would paint him as some sort of dope addict who lured women into his embraces so he could turn them into drug-buddy addicts. This is simply not true. Justin Rott told me how much he loved Christine— and still does—and how hard it was for him to speak the truth about what she had told him. I give him a lot of credit for what he did.

George Koloroutis and his daughter Lelah are involved in a Missouri chapter of Parents of Murdered Children. "My hope and prayer is that it can help parents or loved ones that find themselves in a similar situation," George said of his involvement. "My daughter and I now sit on the board of [it] . . . [and] we have found this to be quite therapeutic for us (just being around people that 'get it'), while offering help to those parents and siblings that are new to losing a loved one due to violence and that are going through what we did. Trying to help these people feels like something Rachael would do. It feels like if some good comes out of all this, it is a way of honoring my little girl."

If you, or someone you know, wants to reach out to this group for help, or donate some much-needed money, please visit the website: *www.kcpomc.org*

In closing this book, I could think of no better way than to allow Lelah to share a poem she wrote after her sister's murder:

In the Living Room
by T. Lelah Koloroutis

Is there memory in the ghostly realm that you inhabit?

*What I mean is: Do you remember the late evening in
Grandma Fern's living room where I haphazardly held
the bowl of three-scoop ice cream that you had just
handed me out to the side in a tilt?*

*Remember how we never could tell the story of the ice
cream hitting the ground without laughing?*

*Or do you remember Mama bouncing around the
kitchen with her 80's curls, bobbing as she shook the
milk carton up and down and sang The Cars [song]
"Shake it up" to our little girl giggly faces?*

*Or do you remember the way Dad's face beamed when
he bought us too many presents again? Remember the
one year that he led us to the garage to "get something
for Mom" and the excitement on his cheeks and lips
when we sped our matching bicycles around the block?*

*Or do you remember picking our little sister's name out
of the name book while Mama's stomach was fat and
round? We decided she had to be "S" so she fit between
"R" and my "T." Remember the day [she] was born and
all the little milk duds on her nose and her wrinkly little
fingers that latched around one of yours?*

*Does memory exist in the same sense of urgency on that
side of the universe, or is it lost between the shift of fleshi-
ness and your present state?*

And can you see us now?

Can you see how my heart beats dangerously fast every time I pass a Denny's because the last time I saw you, you were rolling silverware in your red shirt before our shift ended?

Or can you see Mama in the kitchen looking for a cigarette to drag on?

Or can you see Daddy driving away from work with tears welling in the upside down moons of his eyes?

Or can you see [our baby sister] hiding in the dark of her bedroom, whispering, "I don't want to cry anymore"? Or the way she associates the color red with your death?

And can you see us when we all sit alive in the living room telling stories about memories?

Acknowledgments

THESE BOOKS I write are not possible without the help of my sources and the people around me who help in ways they do not even realize. It feels redundant to keep thanking the same people, over and over, but they are, truly, the backbone of what I do.

First and foremost, I am entirely grateful and honored to have so many readers. It is because of so many of you fine people, who keep coming back, book after book, that I am allowed to live my dream every day. I never take any of this for granted; I need you all to know that I am grateful every minute of every day for the opportunity to write books.

Thank you from the bottom of my soul.

Of course, I would not have written this book without the support and help of George Koloroutis and Nichole Sánchez. I appreciate the trust these two wonderful people put in me, and my hope is that nothing I wrote upset either one of them. If so, it was unintentional.

I also need to thank Tom Ladd, Brian Harris, and everyone at HPD who helped.

My family: Matty, Jordon, April, and Regina. My friends, too; everyone at St. Luke's Church; those great people at Hall Memorial Library in Ellington, who continue to support my career; and those of you who surround my life. I appreciate all of you for allowing me to talk so much about what I do.

I also want to thank Elena Siviero, who runs the M. William Phelps Fan Club on Facebook. I know it takes time to do those things and I greatly appreciate Elena volunteering. Please sign up on the fan club page: *http://www.facebook.com/#!/group.php?gid=52752001614.* And also Sandy Sibert who maintains my website, www.mwilliamphelps.com.

Kensington Publishing Corp.—Laurie Parkin, the Zacharius family, in particular, and my editors, Michaela Hamilton and Richard Ember, along with Doug Mendini and copy editor Stephanie Finnegan, and every other employee who works on my books—has been there with me for over ten years and sixteen books now, supporting me, and always trying to figure out ways to reach more readers. I am both indebted and grateful for having such a great publishing team behind me.

Peter Miller, my former business manager and literary agent was a very important part of my career for many years and I appreciate and am grateful for everything Peter has ever done for me. PMA Literary and Film Management, Inc., anchors Adrienne Rosado and Natalie Horbachevsky have been equally important and helpful to me.

I want to extend immense thanks to Andrew "Fazz" Farrell, Anita Bezjak, Therese Hegarty, Geoff Fitzpatrick, Michael Dawes, James Knox, and everyone else at Beyond Productions who have believed in me all these years, along with my "Dark Minds" road crew: Colette "Coco" Sandstedt, Geoff Thomas, Jared Transfield, Julie Haire, Elizabeth Daley, Jeremy Adair, and Peter Heap; along with my producers at Investigation Discovery: Jeanie Vink, Sara Kozak and Sucheta Sachdev. A special shout out to Henry Schleiff, President and General Manager of ID, who has been behind my series since day one.

I greatly appreciate all of your help. I am grateful for everyone working on the "Dark Minds" series—you are all wonderful people, some of the most gracious and astute professionals I have *ever* worked with, on top of new friends. I look forward to the road ahead and where we're going to take this series!

In addition to being a great friend and the best serial killer profiler on the planet, John Kelly has become a mentor to me in both life and work. I love the guy. Thanks for doing the series, Kelly. You're the best.

I would be negligent not to mention all the wonderful booksellers throughout the country.

Lastly, HPD police officer Philip T. Yochum Jr., who was part of the HPD's investigation, working with Tom Ladd early on, passed away on Sunday, October 17, 2010, after a brief battle with cancer. Officer Yochum joined HPD on July 25, 1994. He was survived by his wife, Melanie Yochum.

Enjoy this exclusive preview of M. William Phelps's next exciting
true-crime release!

KISS OF THE SHE-DEVIL

A Deranged Lover . . .
A Band of Bloodthirsty Killers . . .
A Murder Caught on Tape.

M. William Phelps

Coming in the fall of 2012 from Pinnacle Books

1

IT WAS JUST about 9:00 P.M. Time for the library to close. Barbara Butkis, a fifteen-year librarian supervisor, planned on staying late tonight. She needed to get a few things done with the library's computer system. This type of work needed to be done after hours. Barb had explained to Martha "Gail" Fulton, a library aide, that she didn't need to stick around and help. Gail was always asking how she could do more. Barb explained that she and another employee could take care of the extra work. It was nothing. Gail was having some problems lately within a troubled marriage. It was no secret to most at the library that home was probably the best place for the forty-seven-year-old married mother of three grown children. Gail had recently taken her husband back after he'd had an extended and tumultuous affair with a Florida woman. But that was Gail: the forgiving, devoted Catholic, always willing to pardon and forget for the sake of saving souls.

All the employees generally met near the staff door heading out into the parking lot at the end of the night. Barb and another coworker, librarian Cathy Lichtman, stayed behind.

"Computer backup," Barb said to the others as they gathered, ready to leave.

It sounded boring and tedious. The only plus for Barb was that it would take maybe ten or fifteen minutes, tops.

The Orion Township Library, located on Joslyn Road, just north of Clarkston, was a central point in the quaint Michigan town of Lake Orion, "where living is a vacation," the town's website claims. Lake Orion is forty-five minutes due north of the more well-known and popular home of the Tigers and Pistons, the Motor City, Detroit. By small-town standards, the landmass of Lake Orion is infinitesimal: 1.2 square miles, 440 acres of which is taken up by the lake. On that cool October night, when Barbara Butkis and Gail Fulton's lives changed forever, there were fewer than two thousand residents registered in Lake Orion. So, without having to say it too bluntly, this was a town, literally, where not only did everybody know everyone else's business, but nothing much beyond bake sales, PTA meetings, and bingo games occurred. Lake Orion, you could say, is as charming and dainty as any fabricated plastic town in the middle of a child's train set: perfect and pleasant and quiet. Maybe even boring, too.

Just the way everyone in town liked it.

Her work imitated her life—Gail Fulton was flexible: she worked every Monday night (tonight) from five to nine; but would also come in on several additional, alternate days and nights at different hours. Those Monday nights were Gail's, however, and had been since she'd taken the job eighteen months earlier. The job Gail did, and did very well, was what you'd expect a librarian's assistant to do. We've all come in contact with these unremarkable, normal-looking women and men throughout our days inside libraries. They push carts of books from one aisle to the next, quietly, in solitude, depositing them into their respective, numerically chosen slots, once in a while answering questions from patrons. It is relaxing work, if you love it.

Gail walked out with the others. "Good night," she said. "See you all soon."

Her maroon van was parked in the lot just out the door, about twenty-five yards straight ahead. Gail walked over to the van and, immediately, noticed something different about it. The way the vehicle sat. She couldn't put her finger on what it was, but something didn't look right.

Huh?

Gail shook off what was an odd feeling before placing her pocketbook on the passenger seat and getting in on the driver's side.

Inside, she turned the key, backed out of her parking space, and drove away.

Gail Fulton got about ten yards before she realized one of the tires on her van was flat. So she turned, driving around a small parking lot island of mulch and shrubs, before pulling back into the same parking space she'd just left.

Gail got out and had a look.

She stood staring at her flat tire, looking back toward the library. All of her coworkers, save for Barb and Cathy (who were still inside finishing up that computer work), were gone by now, on their way home to another peaceful night in paradise.

As Gail started to walk toward the employee entrance (not yet out of the immediate area where she had parked), a car, with its lights bright and shining in her face, pulled up. There was a man and a woman in the front seat. A second man, dressed in a black leather jacket, black gloves and a do-rag, was sitting in the back.

Gail didn't like the look of this.

The man dressed in black got out.

No one said anything.

Gail looked concerned; she kept looking back toward the library, no doubt hoping someone would come out.

2

BARB BUTKIS FINISHED the computer backup with Cathy Lichtman and got her things together. It was around 9:10 P.M., October 4, 1999, Barb later recalled, when she and Cathy prepared to leave the building. Outside, it was as dark as a graveyard this time of night. Cooler than normal, too. Leaves just starting to drop off the trees. A slick sheen of drizzle on the ground. All the doors in the library were locked. Nobody could walk in off the street. You'd have to know what Barb later described as "the key code" in order to open the door.

Gail knew this code.

Barb and Cathy stood near the employee exit at approximately nine-fifteen. Barb punched the alarm code number to set it, watched Cathy walk out in front of her, and then followed behind.

Outside the building, Barb made sure the exit door was secure; she pulled on it, hearing that click of the lock, feeling the metal resistance.

They could go home.

"Have a good night, Cathy," Barb said.

"You too. See you tomorrow."

Barb and Cathy walked toward the parking lot. As Barb later explained, "[We] usually kind of look back and forth because it is evening, to see if there is anything in the parking lot before we start approaching our cars. . . ."

After making that routine gaze into the night, looking for anything out of the ordinary, Barb looked straight ahead—and something caught her eye.

It was on the ground. Maybe about twenty feet ahead.

Fabric?

Yes. It looked like a piece of clothing. But neither Cathy nor Barb could tell what it was, because, as Barb later explained, who expects to see clothing on the ground as they leave work?

Barb and Cathy walked toward the fabric.

A pile of clothes?

Strange, a set of clothes spread out on the ground like that. Here. At night. In the parking lot of a library.

Kids? Maybe a pre-Halloween prank?

No. Couldn't be. Barb noticed what she called "breath or steam coming from the object."

Walking up next to the fabric, Barb and Cathy noticed something else.

"It was a person," Barb said.

"Gail . . . !" Barb yelled, recognizing her coworker lying on the tar.

Cathy was just as shocked to see Gail on the ground, barely moving.

Gail was on her back, nearly motionless, moaning softly.

"She was very still," Barb said later. "I could not tell at that moment what had happened to her, if she had fainted or—I couldn't tell because she was lying on the ground."

Barb knelt down beside Gail. "Honey? Gail? Talk to me!"

No response.

Cathy stood beside Barb. Then she knelt down near Gail's head.

Barb reached for Gail's wrist to check for a pulse.

"I'm going to call 911," Cathy said, standing up, turning, taking off for the library.

"Gail?" Barb said with her fingers applied gingerly to the back side of Gail's wrist. (Later recalling the moment, Barb remarked: "Her eyes were just staring. . . .")

Cathy had the phone in her hand, the door to the library open, yelling to Barb, who could not find a pulse. "Is Gail diabetic, Barb?"

Obviously, Cathy was speaking to a 911 operator on the other end of the line, who was instructing her on which questions to ask.

Barb knew this was no diabetic coma or fainting spell; she could see what she thought was blood coming from the top of Gail's head. As Cathy continued to yell questions, Barb then noticed a large pool of "liquid" surrounding the back of Gail's head, tacky to the touch, seemingly growing in size as she focused on it. The fluid was dark, thick, and spreading in a halo pattern around Gail's head.

"Oh my . . . ," Barb said to herself.

"Is she breathing?" Cathy yelled.

Barb thought about it. That growing pool of fluid had to be blood—lots of it, in fact, pouring out from the back of Gail's head.

"She's been hurt bad," Barb yelled back at Cathy. "Someone hurt her *very* bad."

Cathy hung up with 911 and grabbed a blanket. Barb met her at the door, took the blanket, ran back to Gail, and then placed it over Gail's body.

"Gail, honey . . . can you hear me?" Barb asked as she consoled her friend, trying to keep her warm and alert.

Cathy walked up. She had a towel, which she applied with hard pressure to the back of Gail's head, where the injury seemed to be located. The tears came when Barbara Butkis realized Gail Fulton had been shot in the head, maybe in a few other areas of her body, too. There could be no other explanation.

Gail was still alive, though: breathing laboriously, her pulse weakening by the second, but the woman had a heartbeat. She was fighting.

Sirens pierced the night as Barb and Kathy did their best to let Gail know she was not alone. They would not let her die out here by herself in the dark.

This murder of a local housewife and librarian would send the Oakland County Sheriff's Department to call on OakForce, a multiagency crime-fighting organization, a team of lawmen that had been formed, as luck would have it, that very same week. Comprised of local FBI, members of the Michigan State Police and Oakland County Sheriff's Department (who were there at the scene tending to Gail), on top of police officers from the nearby towns of Pontiac, Southfield, and Troy, the agency was put together to investigate major crimes. And it was clear immediately, from the way in which this woman, a harmless librarian's assistant, whose father, Noe Garza, and her uncle, Margarito Garza, were former federal judges, had been found, that she had been targeted. Gail's mother, Dora Garza, was a well-known community and church leader. Gail and her family were people, some might say, whom others had held grudges against.

Had Gail Fulton been the object of a paid hit?

A patrol officer, who happened to be nearby when the call came in, arrived. He walked around the scene, surveying what he had. Barb mentioned something she thought might be of some help.

"Cameras," she told him. "We record what goes on out in the parking lot and around the building."

"You do?"

"Yes," Barb said. Then she pointed to a camera on the building facing Gail as she lay in a pool of her own blood, fighting for her life.

Gail Fulton's murder had no doubt been caught on tape.